T0148153

When Everyone
Wins:
From Inequality to Cooperation

Advanced praise for *When Everyone Wins:*
From Inequality to Cooperation

Drawing from the insights of the behavioral sciences and the moral heritage of the world's religions at their best, David Gray offers a compelling case for mutually beneficial cooperation rather than mindless win/lose competition as the way ahead for groups both small and large. Gray acknowledges there are times and circumstances when one side must win and the other side lose. Due to the failure to recognize the inherent value and potential of all people, there are countless missed opportunities for effective teamwork "when everyone wins." The argument insists that affirmations of freedom and human equality are inseparable. An honest exposure of the dark side of American culture, economy, and foreign policy reveals a disregard for the importance of the common good, and an unacceptable tolerance for the widening gap between the super-wealthy 1% and the remaining 99%. Provocative, passionate, and practical, the book contends that power sharing is not only the right but also the wise thing to do. I strongly recommend it.

Daniel L. Migliore,
Professor of Systematic Theology Emeritus,
Princeton Theological Seminary

When Everyone
Wins:
From Inequality to Cooperation

David Gray

Archway Publishing books may be ordered through booksellers or by contacting:

Archway Publishing
1663 Liberty Drive
Bloomington, IN 47403
www.archwaypublishing.com
1-(888)-242-5904

Scriptures taken from the Holy Bible, New International Version®, NIV®.
Copyright © 1973, 1978, 1984, 1988, 2011 by Biblica, Inc.™ Used by permission
of Zondervan. All rights reserved worldwide. www.zondervan.com The "NIV"
and "New International Version" are trademarks registered in the United
States Patent and Trademark Office by Biblica, Inc.™ All rights reserved.

ISBN: 978-1-4808-1061-7 (sc)
ISBN: 978-1-4808-1062-4 (e)

Library of Congress Control Number: 2014914751

Printed in the United States of America.

Archway Publishing rev. date: 09/05/14

Dedication

To all those who have taught me—
parents, brothers and sisters,
my wife, Phyllis,
my children,
teachers, mentors, colleagues, students, and friends.

CONTENTS

FORWARD

DAVID GRAY HAS produced an amazing synthesis of research from the social sciences, social psychology chief among them, but including political science, sociology, anthropology and economics, with history and religion in this very timely book. It explains how to move from individualistic competition to cooperation. The aim of the book is to explain how social systems, from families to countries, with a chief focus on corporations, are driven by individualistic motives for power, and how people may move from this mentality to a more sustainable and healthy perspective of mutual benefit.

The book is extraordinary for the parallels that it draws from diverse areas such as family dynamics as compared to corporate take-overs and the politics of war. By applying the solid theories of social psychology across so many domains, Gray makes it possible for the reader to recognize the exercise of power within his or her own context. Gray goes on to give examples of alternative strategies where "everybody wins." It should be a thought provoking and useful read for anyone, because all people fall somewhere within the continuum of power. Gray speaks to those without power, urging them to recognize the systemic nature of oppression and to seek allies in fighting it. He also speaks to the somewhat empowered middle class, urging them to recognize the power tactics in play and to resist such tactics rather than perpetuate the status quo.

I have known David Gray for over 30 years. This book is a natural outpouring of his professional and personal activities. David served 17 years as psychology department chair. During that time he creatively developed the psychology faculty, facilities and curriculum. Many years later he hired me into that department. I found a democratically run department that was based on the very principles of cooperation and democratic leadership that are presented in this book. It is characteristic of David's leadership style that he included students and support staff in the planning. He successfully argued for an architectural style for offices and labs that promotes a positive working environment for students, faculty, and staff. Dave truly practices what he preaches. When I followed him as department chair my job was made easier by the firm foundation of democratic, flat organizational style that he had implemented.

Dave's earlier scholarship informs this work. He was among the first to study attitudes toward the environment. He published *Ecological Beliefs and Behaviors: Assessment and Change* in 1985, before the field of environmental psychology was fully developed. He then led undergraduates in the study of implicit stereotyping, focusing mainly on race. His later research was on the belief in equality, which he studied in the U.S., Germany, Russia, and Poland shortly after the collapse of the Soviet Union.

David Gray extended his scholarship in his study of archery. It may seem a sharp change of direction, but in his book, *Bows of the World*, Gray makes a strong argument for the remarkable intelligence of very early people about bow and arrow production and use. His own personal training for horseback archery takes him to another level into inter-species cooperation. Gray co-edited a volume, *Mounted Archery in the Americas* in 2007.

This book resonates with the character of the author in other ways as well. David Gray is a forthright plain speaker and his tone in this book is provocative. He desires to provoke the reader to think more deeply about the present conflicts and where unthinking acceptance of the status quo will lead. Gray aims to provoke people not only to understand the social psychology of individualism, bullying, and power motivation but to understand the alternative, cooperation for mutual benefit.

In the first section of the book Gray recounts some of the classic works on cooperation and delves into the conditions that enhance cooperation. His description of the now famous Robber's Cave research on cooperation and competition is shored up by a fairly comprehensive survey of the evidence. The general model moves from competition to cooperation by placing functionally equivalent groups under mutual threat resulting in increased motivation to cooperate. This section includes an intriguing chapter that describes why twisted fears and contrived threats are unlikely to sustain successful cooperation. Superordinate goals can be used effectively to foster cooperation and mutual benefit.

The importance of norms and the social constraints on cooperation are described in the second section. Norms can have both beneficial and harmful effects on cooperation. Gray's analysis of great leaders' resistance to conformity includes such historical figures as Moses, Martin Luther King, Rachel Robinson, and Daniel Ellsberg. This section is likely to be most useful to leaders who need to understand how norms affect them and those that they lead, as well as how to shape cooperative norms. This section also shows how social and physical structures can perpetuate inequality with many concrete examples.

The meaning of equality is the focus of Part III. Gray starts with the research on equality as an attitude, how it is formed and what it can affect. He contrasts Belief in Equality with Machiavellianism, Social Dominance Orientation, and the Authoritarian Personality. Gray's historical analysis is both provocative and compelling as he gives examples at all levels of society to show that actual equality has been declining in recent decades. This section may be uncomfortable for some readers because Gray provides examples of inequality that many may take as appropriate status quo. As is his nature, Gray does not pull his punches but asks the reader to thoughtfully consider the wide range of contexts that produce inequality and the need to overcome them in order to reach mutually beneficial cooperation.

Power and friendship are seldom considered together, but Gray shows that friendship is an important human dynamic that can reduce power differentials and move social systems forward in terms of problem solving and cooperation. He begins this section with an analysis of power and why some people hoard it. This chapter gives a deep analysis of the widening income gap, which also means a widening power gap. Gray emphasizes that power hoarding is not an issue caused by moderately wealthy individuals, but rather by the extremely wealthy, whom he refers to as wealth supremacists. He moves on to examine shared power, including the effects of powerlessness. The next chapter focuses on democratic leadership based on shared power. Friendship can strengthen shared power by highlighting mutual goals as well as individual strengths. Gray argues that friendship can break the stereotypes that blind leaders from being able to tap the true potential of those they lead.

Gray concludes the book with a very practical chapter on how to apply the principles of cooperation so that everybody wins. His ten-point problem solving checklist should be used by every leader who strives to improve cooperation in the home, workplace or at the national and international level. The checklist starts with determining if there is a problem and moves through a series of steps to solve that problem. Some may argue that these steps are obvious and simplistic, but they are firmly based on the analyses presented in the previous portions of the book. Gray goes on to describe training and development of cooperative problem solving techniques. He provides suggestions for making small but meaningful changes for leaders and for those who are not in leadership positions.

I found this book to be a provocative read although I was already familiar with the social science research that it summarizes. What makes it especially worthwhile is the comprehensive nature of the examples and illustrations. David Gray does not expect his reader to agree with all of his arguments. He even includes examples that he knows will offend some of them. His objective is not to win you over to his side on each controversy he highlights. Rather, David Gray wants the reader to be able to understand how attitudes, norms, and social contexts influence behavior and to be in a position to use that understanding to do positive action. Unlike Machiavelli who counselled the Prince so many years ago for personal gain and individual power, Gray is urging his readers to strive for mutual gain so that everyone can win. Having read the book, I am convinced again that mutual cooperation is a sustainable practice for a positive future. Even with the bleak picture that Gray paints of widening income disparity and environmental decay, his clear directions for cooperation provide hope for positive change driven by individuals and small groups of committed people.

Sandra K. Webster
Professor of Psychology
Westminster College, New Wilmington, PA

PREFACE

THIS WORK IS for any thoughtful reader. More specifically, it should interest readers with concerns about fundamental concepts such as equality and inequality, power and powerlessness, and wealth and poverty. How one construes these concepts either facilitates or inhibits constructive practices of cooperation. *When Everyone Wins* is an essay on the nature and possibility of human cooperation rather than competition. It does not assume that there is no place for competition. A concern for a better discernment of when each is appropriate is examined. A much greater understanding of and use of cooperation between persons and groups in conflict is promoted.

Anyone interested in or curious about some of the contributions of the behavioral sciences to current affaires may find the book helpful. This work attempts to popularize one of the practical behavioral science models that has received international study and application for well over half a century. The model applies to groups of all sizes and types. Its promise is most qualified when applied to macro political groups that have become extremely polarized, but even there it has something to offer.

Illustrations of the principles of conflict reduction range from the micro level (families, small groups, and small communities) to the macro level (nations, and international relations). The author's main professional group during the latter part of his career was the Society of Political Psychology; this may help the reader to see why the illustrations tend to be heavy on the macro level.

I have tried to present a continuous flowing read without detailed documentation. At the end of most all the chapters select sources are given. If a direct quotation is given in the text, then the explicit source will be documented, but generally the sources are more a sampling of what has informed my writing. It will become clear to the reader that opinion and commentary are mixed into the more objective portions of the narrative.

The author is not anti-business or anti-government in spite of the critiques in the text. I am for good business and good government and cooperation among them. The reference to "good" means to have some measure of caring, fairness, and integrity.

There are brief forays into history, philosophy, and religion because nothing happens in a vacuum devoid of context. We are all products of the larger forces around us. References to political and religious fundamentalism are meant to be descriptive and not judgmental. There may be as much or more solid love and compassion among religious fundamentalists as in any other group.

David Gray, New Wilmington, Pennsylvania 2014

ACKNOWLEDGEMENTS

PRIMARY THANKS GOES to my family. My wife Phyllis has supported, critiqued, and improved the text greatly. Our four mature children, Amy, Lisa, Gwen and Josh have enriched their father by travel, reading, discussion, and sharing sources. I would not have known that the *New York Times* could be delivered to my mailbox early in the morning in our relatively remote village here in western Pennsylvania if it had not been for my son Josh.

I am indebted to Westminster College and particularly the Department of Psychology. The College afforded a long career in an atmosphere of creativity and growth. Shared governance between faculty and administration was practiced seriously and illustrates the major model of cooperation presented in this book. My faculty colleagues, and the undergraduate students joined in stimulating learning and a structure for invigorating research at the undergraduate level. I extend a profound thanks to them all. Of course the opinions expressed are entirely my own.

Wikipedia, and other sources of big data, have been very helpful in fact checking and in reviewing historical background. The two columnists found most helpful have been David Brooks toward the right, and Paul Krugman toward the left. Other influences as disparate as my connection with the Presbyterian Church, and my avocation of ground and horseback archery have made their mark on me. A plethora of people and experiences have contributed to my positive bias for the poor and the under-represented.

The personnel at Archway/Simon and Schuster have been gracious and very helpful. Frederick Horn has contributed invaluable proofreading and formatting assistance.

When Everyone
Wins:
From Inequality to Cooperation

INTRODUCTION

WE ALL WANT to win. If we identify with our favorite sports teams, we want them to win. We feel bigger, better, more pumped up when they win. Their winning enhances our temporary sense of status. Winning competitive performances, whether personal or vicarious, makes us feel superior, gives a high, and replaces the humdrum of daily routine with euphoria.

When our teams lose, we feel down, diminished, of lowered stature, and defeated. Even when highly skilled players or teams sink into a slump, they tend to feel inferior, and it seems like they will never do well again; confidence eludes them. The fans cool off, and attendance in the stadium decreases. Everyone loves a winner, and no one loves a loser.

When competitors are consumed with the burning desire to become #1, the goal can have a powerful magnetic-like dynamic that impels a team toward excellence. The value of excellence, do-ing one's best, even being #1 is a widely accepted value in Western culture, and in Eastern cultures as well. Striving toward perfection is shared by many in the United States as well as in Japan and other nations. A "lifelong striving toward perfection" is a Shinto value, and a Christian version is expressed in the words, "Be ye perfect as your Father in heaven is perfect." There is no expectation of reaching per-fection, but traveling in that direction, if at a realistic rate, has great potential to add verve, wellness, integration, and harmony within the individual and group. Hopefully, we want to foster the striving toward excellence.

But there is a rub. In the game of life, we often win at the expense of others. If the rules are unfair, if the "playing field" is uneven and the advantages are very skewed, suffering ensues for the underdog and disharmony runs through the veins of the whole society. This is not necessarily true in competitive sports. If all things were equal, like market sizes and national sports teams' budgets, the loser this year may be the winner next year. Thus, challenge and hope are always alive. But market sizes and franchise budgets are not equal, and some teams are not likely to win. Beyond the world of sports, when an individual, company, or nation is a loser the structure may be such that they will nearly always be losers. When women were denied education and its related power and males were dominant, women were the losers. When agencies, companies, or nations are small, large entities can set the rules and the small fry will usually be the loser. "Free trade" sounds very liberating, but in reality the behemoth corporations set the rules that favor them (example, closed meetings of the World Trade Organization). The little organization is left on an uneven playing field or shut out entirely.

Responses to dominance

There are three basic reactions to dominance by those who are the losers. The reactions range from apathy, to compliance, to aggression. When we suffer physically or psychologically, a common reaction is to try to numb the pain by taking an Ibuprofen, using alcohol, or some other drug. Or, perhaps, we just learn to try not to feel, that is, to become apathetic about not being able to give our child the opportunities we had originally desired. And if it is bad enough, we may escape into a psychotic fugue. All these adjustments kill feeling. I hope we do not want to foster these reactions.

On the other hand, most people who have the deck stacked against them respond by some degree of compliance. They follow the rules, at least when they have no choice, but they do not believe in them, and their heart is certainly not in them. In communism, the comrades muttered, "We pretend to work and pretend to get paid." In capitalism, the bigger the gap between the rich and the poor, the more the poor tend to disengage from the system.

Aggression is a third response to oppression. We may engage in indirect aggression by identifying with the dominant figure or aggressor and thus vicariously gain power, stature, and favors. It was not uncommon in the world's worst prisons and concentration camps for a few of the prisoners to become champions of a brutal system. Soldiers fighting dirty wars would go crazy unless they identified with aggressor nations and thus develop a strong sense of nationalism often in the guise of patriotism. In a dirty war, the inner person is seared, torn, and shredded by the dissonance of senseless killing of thousands on women and children civilians and demolition of a nation on the one hand, and the inadequate payoff, support, and high personal risk on the other hand. The resolution is that the combatant becomes a total believer in the justice of the cause and dismisses the dark side as unfortunate, but necessary "collateral damage."

In a somewhat different vein, we may project our faults and failings onto others. When we are angry and in the frustrating state of failing to meet our goals, we often blame others. Disregard and abuse of these around us may follow.

A behavioral science model of cooperation

There are better ways than win/lose, one up and one down, and dominance/submission. Yes, there will always be wars and rumors of wars, and the poor will always be with us, and some husbands will go on beating their wives and abusing their children. And there will always be some crooked CEOs who will commit colossal frauds and obliterate the pensions of thousands of their workers. It is my belief that modern humans know some creative ways of doing better, garnered from the wisdom of the ages—from the great poets, science, behavioral science, and the more redemptive portions of the world's great religions, and history. We have relatively recent and fresh insights about the powers and principles of cooperation as opposed to the pervasive competitive patterns of behavior.

This book champions cooperation and its advantages we have come to know over the ages, but, especially, in the last half century.

David Gray

The behavioral sciences have significant contributions to make about reducing conflict and aggression. We know that greed and other dysfunctional behaviors are not all genetic, and we know a lot about what the conditions that increase or decrease these behaviors. We know a fair amount about how to change the values, beliefs, attitudes, and motivations that undergird aggression, and how to nurture beliefs conducive to cooperation.

Field and laboratory studies on cooperation as conceptualized in this book began in earnest largely in the United States, and in England around the 1950s. Scientific, juried reports of these studies number somewhere in the hundreds and now originate from virtually every part of the academic world. A streamlined survey of the findings will be presented in the first main chapter and will feature preconditions of cooperation, such as the need for finding common goals, the conceptualizing of all sides as equals, liberal direct and positive experience between opponents. These preconditions can be made or trashed at will. We can either hang on to the old tired adrenaline-driven patterns of belligerence, separatism, superiority, nationalism, greed, and dominance, or we can do the other. It is a matter of both knowledge and will, both of which are difficult to disseminate to be sure. Just in passing, we should note that there are other models of cooperation, such as the prisoner's dilemma, and other forms of gaming approaches. Other disciplines besides social psychology are active in studying cooperation and competition.

When I began teaching organizational, political, and social psychology in the 1960s, students were responsive to the fact that the behavioral sciences had something valuable to say to the civil rights struggles. In my judgment, our research and knowledge about the basic dynamics of society has quadrupled since the civil rights days. And much of this knowledge is practical and directly usable by the problem solver. We will look seriously at some the highlights of this knowledge. I feel they are not well known or understood by the general population. The major mission of this book is to convey well-tested behavioral science principals for positive human relations and explicitly indicate practical implications and applications. The applications will feature small family structures and on up to international relations. The principles are applicable to most organizations regardless of size, scope, or nature.

The first chapter of the book will describe a total integrated model showing how people get into conflict but, more importantly, how they get out of it to the benefit of all. Part of the model includes initial motivation to commence reconciliation, namely the recognition of a mutual threat that poses a real danger to the well-being of both sides. This kind of threat can only be ameliorated by a cooperative effort from both sides of a conflict. Other critical parts of the model are the establishment of equal functional status in negotiating, nurturing norms of cooperation, and ample opportunity for the two sides to get to know each other as fully human beings. Even friendship is an important part of the model in spite of how naïve this may sound. Once the total model is set out in Chapter 1, each of the major parts will be treated in more detail in subsequent chapters.

Perspectives from philosophy and religion

A minor, but important, part of the book will draw on insights from philosophy and religion. These insights have affinity for the major behavioral model of the book. Whether we are aware of these influences or not, it does not negate their flowing through our stream of consciousness. The impact of the Golden Age of Greece has left us with the belief that spirit and matter, body and soul can be easily separated, and that the non-material is more valued than the material, i.e., Platonic idealism. The ancient world was then prepared mentally to separate the religious and the secular, the monastery from the mundane working world, the handling of money from "noble" activities. Modern secular humans do not elevate the spirit over the body; they just tend to delete the spirit entirely. Thus, the poet, teacher, parent, priest, and peacemaker all address the spirit, but they do not make anything; they contribute no material things of value. The Wall Street mentality sees no value in these professions

These subconscious but primary assumptions and beliefs of the ancient Greeks replaced the older Hebrew idea of the human as a unity, a living entity (a *nephesh* in Hebrew). The body and the soul are one, a unity, and both are good and from God. The body was not "the prison house of the soul" as the medieval mystics and later prot-estant Puritans were wont to say. A portion of the older Hebrew idea of unity has reemerged in endeavors such as psychosomatic medicine and the role of the inner game in sports. Also, in business and indus-try, we have seen the emergence of the importance of motivation, satisfaction, attitudes, and expectation. In other words, production cannot be separated from producers and human factors. Abstractions like dignity and worker satisfaction are very real. Abusing the spirit of people for the sake of maximizing profit eventually detracts from corporate profit, stability and vitality in the larger society. Sub-prime mortgages targeted large unregulated profits alone, only to hurt many citizens and our total economy.

There are some assumptions behind the behavioral model that are supported by portions of the best religious, philosophical, and historical perspectives. A very basic assumption of the author is that human abilities are widely shared among all the peoples of the world. If one believes this, one is much more likely to join constructively with those considered to be our subordinates and persons further down the economic ladder. The belief in widespread potential helps support the values of human respect and dignity, which are held in high regard by the great religions of the world.

The opposite view is that of aristocracy where there are only a very few bright people at the top of an organization and all the rest are categorically lower and of less value generally. A great leader can make a great difference, but great leaders in the modern age must know how to use the intelligence of a wide variety of people and believe in those people enough to use them well. The MacArthurs, Bremmers, Rumsfields, Cheneys all saw themselves as infallibles who did not need the wisdom of many others. They saw others as hindrances. Vice President Cheney considered the views of the populace about the Iraq

War with absolute disdain. Admittedly there are many people who are lazy, distrustful, and hostile. And some of them will likely never change. But people get that way by experiences that are destructive. For the most part, the egalitarian assumption, as opposed to the aristocratic one, indicates that we should approach any new individual or group with the expectation that they have potential to be creative and constructive under conditions that are conducive.

The world religions have potential to support us in creative social endeavors. Even though religion is like atomic power, it can be harnessed for either the greatest good or the greatest ill. Each world religion has a body of literature and teachings with considerable variety and sometimes paradoxical or contradictory principles. A sect or denomination within a religion may either build up its belief system by choosing the most nurturing, cooperative elements, or the most divisive and corrosive parts. There is no such thing as one Christianity (rather several hundred Protestant denominations and dozens of Catholic Orders); there is no such thing as one Islam, or Buddhism, or any other religion.

Within Christianity, if one chooses to emphasize the Christ figure as the suffering servant, the person who makes his main public appearance on a donkey, who washes his followers feet as a sign of mature leadership, and as someone who blesses peacemakers and makes the love of neighbor as binding as the love of God, then striving to dominate will diminish. The entire definition of strength and weakness is set on edge. These images create a rich conceptual basis to support behaviors, which are caring and cooperative. If all Christians, and, especially the leadership of so-called Christian nations, would give up the worship of the golden calf, greed, arrogance, aggression, maximizing profits and ignoring human suffering, they would turn to practice the dignity and equality of humankind with an overriding sense of service. They would bring about a peaceful revolution. The best of the world's great religions have much to offer.

On the opposite end of the spectrum, one may select the more militant, intolerant, exclusive aspects of the Judeo-Christian scriptures and writings. Such selections may lead to behaviors that are discriminatory and neglect giving loving attention to the plight of the physical world here and now. Even though Communism had almost everything wrong, it was right when charging that much of Christianity was a "pie-in-the-sky-by-and-by" belief and an escape from the hope or possibility of improving life in the here and now. Other religious selections may draw on the more militant portions of the Old Testament and rigid dogmatic interpretations of the uncompromising "only-one-way" aspect of the New Testament writings. Needless to say, Christianity has been used to justify a catalogue of ugly epics: holy wars and Crusades, coercion of others' beliefs and practices, slavery, colonialism, unfounded and oppressive practices of superiority, and stealing land from supposedly "heathen savages."

Dominance in history

Recorded history tells its own story of the long-range inferiority of winning at others' expense—i.e., domination. Older and current forms of Imperialism and Communism share a common belief that a few know what is good for the many and, therefore, have a right, and even a duty, to impose their will. The English naval supremacy of the seas hardly guaranteed the longevity of the British Empire. What was left in the wake of the breakup of the Empire? What remained when colonialism came apart in the 1950s were regions drawn with artificial borders, untrained and inexperienced leadership, and a lack of sound, independent, indigenous institutions. The void was filled with the worst kinds of dictators, corruption, and conflict. The empire generally did not build things that would last, that would be self-sustaining. If there had to be an empire, it should have built local strength so as to put itself out of existence, which, of course, would be an essential contradiction of empire. The attitude of empire reeks with a very bad odor. "We are superior in every way to you. You are generally naïve and ignorant; therefore, we have every reason to govern you." Domination is not lasting and leaves generations of human degradation, poverty, and suffering in its wake. Admittedly, some solid and lasting educational, medical, and spiritual enrichment resulted is spite of empire.

The supposed superiority of overarching centralized planning in Communism with its domineering governance was inherently doomed from the start. As a world power gains far-reaching strength, it must be a great temptation to leaders to say and think, "We will bury you" as Nikita Khrushchev did. The U.S.S.R. was buried and its legacy is hardly admirable. Countries freed from a false peace of forced compliance reverted to animosities and violence of decades and centuries gone by. A constructive legacy would have been to help the regions address their own hostilities and conflicts in a more modern problem-solving manner devoid of reversion to force.

Likewise, the United States cannot seem to avoid the dominance trap. On the one hand, we have our shining periods of humane building of democratic institutions, addressing human need, and working toward freedom and equality for all, inside and outside our own country. But we have our share of dark times. Real social repercussions and vestiges of slavery are still with us and will go on into the future, at least as a matter of history. For a nation of honor to break almost every treaty it ever made with the American Indian endures as a legacy of shame. The 1830 Indian Removal Bill designed to force the Cherokees and neighboring tribes off their land was an American genocide. Four thousand weak, sick and old Cherokees died along the way on the "trail of tears." Over 40,000 of the southeastern tribes were removed during the 1830s. Gold had been discovered in the Cherokee lands, and the charge against the Cherokees was that they were not using the land efficiently. In fact, they were highly integrated into American society, committed their language into writing, were industrious in agriculture, and published their own newspaper. What America did to the Cherokees is deeply shameful forever. Our acquisition of the Southwest and many of our enterprises in Central America and the Philippines hardly qualify us as a civilized, let alone Godly, nation. Why is it that we can only recognize rogue-like qualities in other nations?

The United States is number one in the air and will use air power to force democracy on other nations, while supporting dictators who are friendly to our businesses or military colonies. We castigate other dictators who threaten our access to their oil supplies and think we can win a war against all terrorists in the world. How silly it is to pit our modern technology of the skies against nineteen box cutters. When Saddam, the Iraqi Dictator, was our ally in the Iran War, he was tolerable and useful. Honesty and better information about other nations would help restore a more genuine power to the United States. Will our supremacy of the skies leave an enduring positive legacy fifty or a hundred years from now? Has our contribution of supreme air power to Israel over Palestine brought peace and human growth to all in that region? If we do not shift gears and radically change the meaning of "national interest" from greed, arrogance, and lop-sidedness to genuine concern for all peoples, our air superiority will sputter out as the navy of the British Empire and the armies and missiles of the Soviet Union did.

The current dabbling in empire by the United States has hardly helped us. Our disregard for international law, loss of good will and weakened cooperative alliances, the use of torture and violation of the Geneva Accords, massive loss of life on both sides of the Iraq and Afghanistan Wars, thousands of our young men and women maimed for life, a country in material and civic disrepair, domestic neglect at home and a sea of long-lasting deep new hatred and hostility toward our country are all the fruits of lording it over others. Hopefully this is just one of those temporary declines of a nation that has so much good and such great potential. Domination should be passé.

Redefining strength and weakness

When Hitler landed in his biplane on the fields of massive and dramatic nighttime Nazi rallies, he was hailed as "the strong arm from on high." Lennie Riefenstal, his cinematographer, took Hitler's photos from a pit in the platform so as to make him look tall and strong. Hitler was supposedly launching a 1000-year reign to be presided over by a super-race. It is true that he temporarily harnessed a great and awful military might. But it sprang forth from the wells of weakness, fear, failure, and falsehood. As a lost youth, he wandered the streets of Vienna and was rejected by an art school twice. He gained some basic success as a soldier in World War I, and he used his own youthful knowledge of failure and rejection to skillfully play upon the minds of his downtrodden countrymen in the aftermath of the World War I. He apparently sensed his own failures, but he came to know how to cloak himself in pure macho—the lightening power of the swastika and great banners blowing in the wind, the torches and dramatic choreography of hundreds of goose-stepping soldiers in the night-time rallies, and the crowd roaring "*Heil* Hitler." His impassioned speeches proclaimed the superiority of the Aryan peoples and the coming triumph their Fatherland. The show of militant force, massing of weapons, and reliance on violence should be viewed as profound weakness. Macho is weakness because it is inept and does not last; it ignorantly rejects other more powerful and lasting ways.

The United States needs to be guided by a sound historic and cultural understanding of disorder in the world of Islam. Admittedly sound understanding of our adversaries is not enough. I am not a pacifist. There is a time to fight. The Nazi machine in Europe and the attack on Pearl Harbor gave us little choice. Attacking the terrorist's training camps in Afghanistan immediately after 9/11 made sense. But our attacks on those training camps only focused on the symptom and not the cause. What is the driving cause of the fanatical Islamists terrorist attacks? Our ignorance of the many features and factions of Islam should be the first signal to us that there is something wrong on our side. Are they jealous of what we have? Are they repulsed at our materialism, lack of modesty, and obsession with sex and alcohol? Do they resent our military bases in their holy lands? Is our lopsided role in the Israeli/Palestinian strife a major burr under their saddles? Are the extremists simply after brute male domination and total religious and political dictatorship? What impact are the extremists having on mainline Muslims? Are they smarting under the very long demise of the great days of the Persian Empire and other by-gone world-class Islamic achievements? What is the nature of the age-old animosity between the Shiites, the Sunnis, the Wahhabi, and, newer antagonists such as ISIS?

What cultural impact did the war with the U.S.S.R. have on the factions in Afghanistan, and what role did the U.S. have in that same war? Yes, the terrorist training camps in Afghanistan had to be attacked and terminated. But for the neocons to say, "There is nothing to understand about them, except to kill them." is surely ignorant and uninformed. A widespread insight of the behavioral sciences is that any social movement, such as Islamism, not Islam, exists because of some basic unmet human need. A given movement may be wrong headed and destructive, but understanding its roots and addressing them is essential to genuine problem solving.

A thoughtful and open analysis of conflict reveals the flaws and strengths of both sides of a conflict. If open analysis prevailed in families, corporations, and international relations, we might have to admit that we are part of the problem. It is too easy to dismiss the other side by saying they are unreasonable and fanatical. Maybe they are, but maybe we are as well. Until we get over that assumption "Our side is always right," we cannot start to proceed toward truth. Surely in real life the "pot often calls the kettle black," and that assumption blocks the first steps toward reconciliation.

A clear distinction between aggression and assertiveness is critical when striving for the kind of cooperation where everybody wins. The social psychological definition of aggression is any act intended to injure or harm another person or object. Assertiveness, on the other hand, is speaking and acting in support of our perceived rights without personally attacking or diminishing the opposition. The research literature shows that aggression instigates and provokes more aggression. If we personally insult people, regardless of the circumstances, they are likely to act defensively with a counter-attack. Assertiveness, on the other hand, vigorously struggles for the objective facts and avoids personal attacks. Tensions are diffused by depersonalizing the issues. Assertiveness demands strength of character and helps assure fairness and high quality decisions.

Thus, cooperating never means "giving in," weakly acquiescing, or capitulation just to get along. In fact, passivity or lack of assertiveness may invite aggression just as aggression does. The predator usually looks for a weak, injured, or non-confident victim. So when this book champions its model of cooperation, it is anticipating very lucid negotiating, incisive thinking, and data-based, tough-minded problem solving.

We often learn as much when we examine the opposite and opposing side of a model as when examining the model itself. I hope that the reader will find it helpful to be introduced to the substantial research legacy on social dominance. It is historically and academically nearly a mirror image of cooperation research and will help inform the presentation of the cooperation model in this book.

Toward the end of the book, there will be a chapter to examine some forerunners of equality and cooperation in antiquity and in the animal kingdom. Hierarchies appear to be the natural and necessary pattern for organization because they are so ubiquitous. There are some relevant and significant exceptions. Probably the most prevalent conceptual picture of the animal kingdom is one of predators living off prey in nature generally "red in tooth and claw." Most of this picture is, of course, absolutely true. Nevertheless, when conditions are favorable and food and water are not scarce, there are very nurturing and caring behaviors within and across some species. Competition and aggression may not be as hard wired even in infrahuman animals as we are led to believe.

It is generally true that organizations from the long past have predominately been structured hierarchically rather that cooperatively. As a culture, we are slowly learning to change our ways. When husbands try to dominate wives, when managers and CEOs try to dominate their workers, and when national leaders try to dominate their constituencies or other countries, there is trouble. People are insulted, dignity is lost, and talent and skills are squelched and wasted, and hostility ensues. The result is that families, organizations, and nations are far less than they might be and are often thrown into protracted conflict. Cooperation, on the other hand, can lead to group vitality, creativity, and productivity for all. That is when everyone wins. However, cooperation is not easy. In the first chapter we will look at the conditions, which must be met in order to make successful cooperation more likely.

PART I

A Model of Cooperation, and Goal Setting

THE SPINE OF the book is a behavioral science model, with applications and commentary. Chapter 1 presents the main points of the model in abbreviated form. In the remainder of Part I, various parts of the model are developed in more detail. Genuine threats have the potential to motivate antagonists to come together to solve overarching problems. When neither side in a dispute can solve a problem by itself, a master goal is required, a superordinate goal. On the contrary, threats that are fabricated and false deflect cooperative and productive problem solving and often lead to increased antagonism and even aggression.

Chapter 1 A Behavioral Science Model

Chapter 2 Mutual Threats, Bone Fide Fears, and Motivation

Chapter 3 Twisted Fears and Contrived Threats

Chapter 4 Superordinate Goals

Chapter 1: A Behavioral Science Model

Cognitive science and social psychology have given us some tools and perspectives that are new and powerful. This thrust began to emerge as early as 1954 in a book by Gordon Allport, the dean of American social psychology, entitled *The Nature of Prejudice*. The book stimulated a modest amount of field and laboratory research in the '50s and '60s, followed by an upsurge in the '70s, which has developed into an international effort of advanced research. Currently, at least a dozen highly competitive and juried research reports are appearing each year internationally. There are several terms under which the interested reader may find these research papers—social categorization theory, identity theory, direct contact hypothesis, and shared coping-friendship approach.

Laying the foundation: The Robber's Cave

We can begin this story in the so-called "Robber's Cave" area of Oklahoma where the legendary Jesse James and his gang gathered. In the late 1950s, a two-week camp for young boys was conducted to demonstrate how hostility could be escalated experimentally during the first week and then deliberately lowered by cooperative payoff structures in the second week. Muzafer Sherif (1961), a major social psychologist from the University of Oklahoma at Norman, designed the experiment. He assumed that hostility could be created by creating two highly categorized, segregated, and competitive groups. Thus two busses brought two separate groups to the camp. The groups were assigned to separate cabins and encouraged by counselors to name themselves. One group became the Rattlers and the other the

Eagles. The counselors encouraged strong in-group identity in every way possible. The groups sat on opposite sides of the cafeteria, and sports groups in the afternoon were always formed on the strict lines of Rattlers and Eagles. All activities were selected to be competitive where only one group could win and the other loose; no activities were designed to be cooperative where winning could only occur by both sides cooperating. The experiment worked. At the end of the first week, there were no friendships across groups, but rather, many verbal taunts were shouted back and forth across the two groups about the inferiority and stupidity of the other group. There were generous expressions of disdain if not hatred for each other.

Jerome Robbins used a somewhat similar process of separation when he directed the well-known musical *West Side Story*. He essentially had two castes, one to enact the Sharks and another to portray the Jets. Robbins supposedly deliberately kept them segregated as much as possible and let the feelings of rivalry emerge to feed the drama of genuine conflict on stage.

At the beginning of the second week at The Robber's Cave, the counselors took an entirely different tack. All encouragement toward separation and competition was dropped and replaced with activities that integrated the two groups. The sports program needed some variety, so during that week teams were formed at random, which fractured the boundaries between Rattler and Eagles. But even more importantly, strongly cooperative events were introduced. After a long hot afternoon of playing softball the kids ran to the water truck for drinks, but the tank was empty and the truck would not start. The Rattlers, still having some group cohesion, got behind the truck to push. It would not go; the Eagles said, "Get out of here, you bunch of sissies. We'll move it." It still would not budge because the driver had the emergency brake on. Then, it dawned on the boys that if they multiplied by two, the truck might start and get into town for a new tank of water. They started to find out that rubbing elbows with the other group would not hurt them, and it was the only way to get an important thing done. If you have ever been parched by the relentless Oklahoma wind that they call "Mariah," you will appreciate the depth of the need to cooperate in this dilemma. The scenario was contrived, but the overarching goal of water was very real. Neither side could solve the problem or win alone. It could only be solved by a cooperative effort.

Other cooperative opportunities were presented. Both groups wanted to rent a movie from the store in town, but neither side had enough money. Again a realization dawned. If they combined their funds, they could get the movie and watch it together. At the end of the second week, profound changes were occurring. Friendships were formed across group lines that actually lasted beyond the summer. Boys were writing to each other after camp was over. They still kept their two separate group's names, but the vitriol that passed across the group lines had disappeared. The experiment was designed to show that conflict may not only issue out of the heads and hearts of people, but it may come out of specific physical conditions and structures. These conditions are sometimes easier to change than beliefs and attitudes.

The '50s were known as the Age of Togetherness. The colossal Second World War was over, times were prosperous, and the zeitgeist was upbeat. If people would just get together, they would be happy and solve their problems. Well-intentioned groups were attracted to the Robber's Cave story and launched many attempts to bring traditional antagonists together and try to create harmony. The results were totally mixed. Sometimes it worked, other times no change occurred, and, worse yet, on other attempts even greater hostility was generated. Sherif's principles may not have been fully understood or well followed, but the behavioral scientists also realized that the surface has only been scratched and they had a huge job ahead of them to more rigorously isolate the complex conditions that deflect people toward good or for ill. What have we learned?

David Gray

Categorization:
Conditions that escalate conflict

In-group bias

A generic set of dynamics of prejudice, hostility, hatred, rejection, and disrespect have been well delineated by behavioral research. These dynamics are different from the dimensions of a given concrete physical conflict such as two nations wanting the same oil or piece of land or the same fishing rites. The dynamics here are those that are likely to endure even after the physical conflict has been resolved. For a long time, we talked about ethnocentrism—our own group is seen as the measure of normalcy and goodness. The more another group deviates from our standards, the more offensive it is to us and we perceive it to be inferior or even pernicious. Because ethnocentrism suggested ethnic relations, a more generic term came into use, namely "in-group bias." It basically says that our group is generally better than other groups on just about any dimension you want to name. In-group bias connotes the unfounded belief in global superiority, not just the belief or objective reality that one's group may indeed the leader on one or more specific dimensions

Two of the dimensions that are most salient in this area of research are trustworthiness and morality. In the cold war, the United States citizens tended to feel that they could trust their own government but certainly not the USSR. Soviet citizens thought they could trust their government but certainly not that of the United States. The same held for general perceptions of morality. When persons are assigned purely randomly to meaningless nominal groups in the laboratory, they come to trust their own group over the other group even when there is no reason or history to have this in-group bias. Surprisingly the feelings form very quickly and without provocation or insult from the other group. Imagine how these feelings are magnified following the invasion of rape, mass murder, and indiscriminate bombing of helpless civilians.

We grossly underestimate the power of group membership on our thoughts and feelings. In driving through a respected Jewish section of Pittsburgh in 2006, we saw large banners reading, "We Stand with Israel." These banners were on synagogues ranging from Orthodox to Reformed. The common membership was Jewishness. That membership is marked with the suffering and the pogroms of the diaspora down through the centuries, the holocaust, and the prejudice and discrimination and suffering which endures today and will continue into tomorrow. It would be very difficult for to a synagogue to fly a banner saying, "We stand with Israel and Palestine."

We get a lot of our personal identity from our basic groups, so we want them to be good. Strip away all of our basic groups, and our personal identity would be tattered and eroded. Many persons facing retirement anticipate the loss of their professional or vocational identity and feel threatened as a result. We rather easily succumb to think of our own fundamental groups as being generally good and most all its members as possessing that goodness. Extreme forms of this feeling may be seen in white supremacy, male chauvinism, nationalism with its irrational patriotism and national self-righteousness. I am amazed at how people fail to differentiate between what is good in a nation and what is bad, what is constructive and what is destructive. All human institutions and nations will in reality have a mix.

We commonly cope with the negative patterns in our families and nation with denial. And, of course, denial proceeds at the subconscious level; we do not even know we are distorting reality. With the child, even if the family is physically or psychologically abusive, it is the only support base the child has. It is very difficult for the child to admit to the abuse, which is often mixed with some hugs and goodies as well. The child surmises, "My Daddy hurts me, but he is a wonderful Daddy." Where will the child go to escape the abuse or how would the child replace Daddy? The same mechanism works at all levels of organizations. If one knows there is rotten corruption, greed, and abuse of the less powerful citizens in one's nation, it is easy to let those facts slip into the lower basement of the mind and celebrate even more intensely the uplifting things in one's great nation. Denial delivers us from a lot of pain and dissatisfaction. Deficient leaders must surely know the propensity and power of denial and the desire to fasten on the good and the pleasant. Consequently, the leader can continue to enjoy his or her unjust power and glory.

When someone asks you a question such as, "What do you think of our President?" and if you know that the person can only tolerate a thumbs up or a thumbs down unqualified response, you know that you have met an impoverished, deficient, and thoughtless question. But even worse, think how often you hear these kinds of categorical questions or even how often we may ask them ourselves. The questions go on. "Do you believe this is a great country or not?" "How could you possibly be a Democrat, or a Republican?" "Can any good come out of Nazareth?" "Are you with us or against us in the war on terrorism?" When there is no room for differentiation, for analyzing the pluses and minuses of an issue, you know you are staring at an impoverished question. It should be thrown back to the source as deficient. It certainly is not worth answering in that form.

There may never be room for the "pot to call the kettle black" but we fall into that trap all the time. We desperately want our group, our family, our town, our sports team, and our nation to be good and to be entirely good. When a leader says you are either for us or against us, he is asking you to turn off your brain, stop thinking, and jump on the bandwagon of the extremist and fanatic whose mind is closed because it assumes in has all the truth and all the righteousness.

Seeing the other group as all the same

After seeing our own groups as totally good or nearly so, we look at a significant antagonistic group and tend to see all, or nearly all, of its members as bad or inferior. When we meet a member of that group, we do not need to evaluate that particular person. We already know that he or she is inferior or untrustworthy because of the power of group membership. We even do this perceptually as well. Take a facial memory experiment where a white person memorizes ten facial photographs of black persons. Then, add ten additional black photos and ask the participant to pick out the original ten faces. Whites do much more poorly at this task than blacks, and visa versa when all the conditions of the experiment are totally reversed. The interpretation is that all blacks tend to look alike to whites. When westerners view Asian faces, it is hard to discriminate or remember one Asian face from another. Whites tend to perceive Asians as all looking alike. If whites value the other group less, they pay leas attention and miss much of the rich data of facial physiognomy. Our group membership causes us to ignore the great variety in the other group.

Social distance or segregation

Finally, seeing our own as good and the others as all bad, we have a strong tendency to separate ourselves from them as much as possible socially and physically. Rejection, avoidance, isolation all protect us from rubbing shoulders with the lesser ones who may pull us down, may be ignorant and dangerous, and, at the least, be unpleasant and uninteresting. Kublai Khan, the grandson of Genghis, ruled over a large part of China and was impressed with the presence and behavior of the Christians in his realm. He invited the Christian Pope to send one hundred scholars to his realm to teach his people the heart of Christianity. The Pope refused to throw his pearls before the swine. The Mongols were thought to be all savage barbarians who could not possibly be serious about such a request and could not profit from such teaching anyway. The Mongols were too worthless and treacherous and so distant from Christianity to warrant open communication. Does this sound like the relations between labor and management and heads of state down through the decades and in the present? We know now that even Genghis, and certainly his sons and grandsons, had many advanced ideas about planning, organization, communication, and meritorious and egalitarian advancement.

Social categorization is strong when one or more groups live, move, and have their being in their own little bubble of the world. Each group gets convinced of its own goodness and righteousness, and is just as convinced of the other group's evil or inferiority, and as a result of these two premises, cuts itself off from the other group as entirely as possible. The end result may either be total isolation and denial of the other's existence, or if the other group must be recognized perhaps as a threat, then the conflict either takes on the form of nasty competition as in a "cold war" or at the very worst the hostilities of a hot war. So how do we interrupt categorization before it reaches destructive proportions? How do we break down the walls and boundaries that dishonestly and unnecessarily separate us?

De-categorization: conditions that reduce conflict

A mutually perceived shared threat

Crossing over antagonists' boundaries may actually provide an opportunity for cooperation. Modern terrorists seem to target nations in both the West and the East. An individual nation in isolation is limited in gathering intelligence on terroristic plots. By uniting and sharing international data, the chances of thwarting attacks are enhanced. The threat of terrorism is not falsely constructed by one side for the sole advantage of one side. It is mutually perceived and agreed upon as a significant international problem between several countries. The threat must be real and mutually perceived by the various sides. It will not work for a heavy-handed boss or a superpower to bully subordinates into subscribing to a phony problem or threat.

The general motivational effect of threat needs to be underlined here. Human beings are often lackadaisical about important matters. In the area of behavioral medicine, it is often noted that people only change lifestyles after they have been seriously threatened by health crises such as stroke or heart attack. When the U.S. steel industries were booming just after the Second World War, they had no motivation to change and up-date their technology. U. S. Steel was king. There was no perception that Japan and Germany were rebuilding their mills from scratch with the very newest innovations that were going to overshadow the U.S. Organizational experts such as W. E. Deming and J. Scanlon tried to warn the management of U. S. Steel. The unions were equally unreceptive and self-satisfied. Then there was also the hidden threat of developing countries moving into the production of raw steel. So the genius of leadership is often to uncover a sea of evidence to convince antagonists of a real mutually impending, but not yet clearly visible, threat.

A superordinate goal

This is the type of goal that neither side can reach alone but can only be achieved by cooperation (the water truck example cited above). If Canada stops dumping mercury waste into Lake Superior, but the United States continues to do so, the problem will not be solved. Because both countries contribute to the problem, both must work on its solution if it is to be resolved. Even token efforts may be meaningful if both sides intend something more substantial beyond the token effort. Republicans and Democrats may make token compromises on either the deficit or investment issue (although that would be a miracle). If the tokens are intended simply as a stalling tactic, then no progress is made. But very small starts may be used to help clear the air and initiate a change of direction, be it ever so small at the beginning.

We are often so busy in discrediting or destroying the other side that we cannot see any common ground or possibility for cooperation on a common goal. Many pro- and anti-abortion people have an equal and very strong respect for human life, but each side may be so bent on winning and putting down the other side that finding common goals is out of the question. The anti-abortionist may be intensely concerned with the life of the fetus. The pro-abortionist may be intensely concerned with what often happens to the child who is unwanted. If both sides worked on more general child health problems, both sides would have a chance of seeing their mutual compassion for child welfare. There is a real chance here that mutual

27

demonization could be replaced by mutual trust, respect, and an in-creased probability of finding common goals. This is an extremely emotional issue and the direct contact model will be strained to the limits, as well as any other approach.

Some categories and boundaries are so indelible and deeply rooted that they may resist the best efforts. But we surely have not made the attempt to try the model very widely. The Oslo Accords may not have been perfectly fair to the Israelis and the Palestinians, but they provided a real opportunity at harmony. These accords were informed by the de-categorization model. Some behavioral scientists worked with the negotiators, but, unfortunately, they were hijacked later by uncontrollable events.

The superordinate goal must be realistic

This is an imperfect world full of imperfect people, deeply broken relationships and antagonistic groups. Separation, divorce, dividing of nations, and war may be the only answer in some cases. But the passion of this book is that we have some tools and insights that we did not have thirty years ago, and if we use them more creatively, we can resolve some of our conflicts constructively. Another aspect of realism is that the superordinate goals that we tackle must have a very high chance for success. If we fail in cooperative efforts because they were unrealistic in the first place, there is an overwhelming dynamic to blame the other side and, thus, come to hate the other side even more. Even among friends, when failure occurs, if we are so prone to blame the friend, how much more so the antagonist.

Conflict between nations may reach a point of heated rhetoric and nasty name calling which would seem to preclude any common goals for cooperation. Why not creatively search for a way to foster mutual respect rather than insulting a given nation. When we refuse to talk to another nation and reject it, we deliver a major blow of disrespect that drives it further into the arms and associations of other nations we consider to be our enemies. It has no choice but to find friends elsewhere.

Equal functional status

Another essential condition for conflict reduction and de-categorization is to establish equality of all the parties. Functional and formal status must be clearly differentiated here. Formal and achieved status is not the focus here at all. Educational and monetary achievements and privileges cannot be made equal and are not necessary to make the model work. To demand of a model equal material resources for all would indicate theoretical communism. What is demanded in the model is equal opportunity rather than equal outcome. However, functional status must be equal in a negotiating setting. Each side must have an equal chance to speak to influence the outcome of a discussion. If a person or group with greater formal status and resources pulls rank, communications become flawed. The person with lower formal status will either kiss-up to the superior, say what is expected, or express passive hostility by not talking or being vocally hostile. None of these responses will facilitate sound data-based problem solving.

To assure success, behavioral research dramatically shows that the framing of the problem must be mutually constructed before any attempt is made to start solving the problem. Defining the problem unilaterally gives one side the advantage and the other side a profound handicap that will undermine cooperation between the two sides. Framing also causes the participants to process the same information very differently. If a new experimental drug is "sure to save 200 people out of a total of 600," more than twice as many participants will vote to use it than if the framing is such that "the new drug will lead to the loss of 400 out of 600 people" (Kahneman and Tversky, 1984).

Other illustrations of the effect of framing are the following: if water becomes a contentious issue, defining the problem as one of 1) scarcity or 2) waste will make a radical difference of how the discussions emerge and unfold. In the war on terrorism, if one defines the problem as one of 1) killing them versus 2) deflating the motivation and causes of terrorism, the war on terrorism would be radical different. In this case, the definition and framing was dogmatically to kill them over there before they kill us over here.

Once the problem is mutually defined, the social and communication rules must guarantee equal time for all sides to gather their data and convey their position. The order of presentations and selection of topics must be mutually constructed. The physical setting must also express all the marks of equality, for example, a round table with no head position. The attitude of superiority on either or both sides of a dispute must be jettisoned. Even if one side is objectively superior on many dimensions, it does not matter; the other side must be treated as functional equals in making a contribution to resolve the dispute.

It is a common assumption that the private has nothing to offer the general, the laborer has nothing to offer the supervisor, or the student has nothing to advance the knowledge of the teacher. This is false. The general has a mass of formal knowledge, but there are some things only the infantry person knows about the conditions in the combat trench and the tactics of the enemy in the opposing trenches. The supervisor has much privileged information, but the laborer knows some things about the machines and the nuances of the flow of materials that the super does not. Likewise, the student knows about student culture, mores, electronic games, etc., that may be valuable to a given lesson. It is when all the information can be put together that it will be more accurate and complete, leading to a better solution.

One Secretary of Defense of the United States once told the citizens just to relax about a certain war. "Just leave it to us. It is complicated." The inference is that the citizens could not comprehend such complexity, essentially that they were stupid in so many euphemistic words. I have frequently heard the same from college presidents. "Faculty members do not understand the many facets and constituencies of a college." If one wants to discourage shared governance (i.e., shared power and democracy) in the university setting, it is to the advantage of the autocratic leader to keep the faculty as ignorant as possible. The truth is that the faculty is capable of understanding and, in many cases, is already painfully aware of the multiple and conflicting pressures of a president's job. To cut the faculty off is to throw valuable resources away, to be a wasteful manager, and, in the end, a more impoverished problem solver.

A leader either assumes that every member of a group has something valuable to contribute, or he or she tends to assume the members are not very promising and must be controlled or humored instead. It is condescending and insulting to be treated unequally. It does not mean we are the same and have the same information or abilities. We have very different kinds of information, but it is all valuable, and we have very different kinds of abilities and they can be very powerful when aggregated. There are people at all educational levels who are rather deficient of wisdom and judgment, and there are people at all educational levels who are wise and of good judgment. Stupidity and closed mindedness is easy to find anywhere, but consistent failure to use the person with lower formal status is a putdown and a power play. It is also immensely wasteful of human resources in any organization and destroys productivity.

The early putdown of the Palestinians by the westerners has assured a hostile environment and long-term suffering of both Palestinians and Jews in the Middle East. In 1919 Lord Arthur James Balfour said that "we do not even propose to go through the form of consulting the wishes of the present inhabitants of the country." He was referring to the Palestinians. He went on to speak of the one side as "of far profounder import than the desires and prejudices of the 700,000 Arabs who now inhabit that ancient land" (quoted in Chomsky, 2000). How ignorant can educated people be! In 1937 Theodore Roosevelt spoke of American Indians, Australian aborigines, and Palestinians and said that we had done them no wrong because "a stronger race, a higher grade race, a more worldly-wise race, to put it this way, has come in and taken their place." I discovered both of these quotes originally in the seminal essays by Arundhati Roy, 2003.

A devastating flaw of imperialist minded leaders who believe that they are categorically superior to others is that they cheat themselves of the valuable abilities of subordinate persons or nations. In the great Galveston hurricane and tidal wave of September 8, 1900, 6000 men, women, and children died. The arrogant weather officials from the mainland USA thought their abilities to predict hurricanes was far superior to anything the "inferior" indigenous Caribbean people might generate. The truth of the matter was that the Cuban professionals lived with Gulf-based hurricanes all their lives and had amassed critical knowledge of the particular patterns and behaviors of storms in that area. The Cuban's predictions were correct but were ignored by the higher status USA experts. The result was that Galveston was devastated. Loss of life and property was immense. Much of the loss could have been avoided by listening to the Cuban forecasters.

Negative prejudging and stereotyping often form a basis for discriminating against people and treating them unequally and inequitably. Some argue that prejudice is a fairly modern phenomenon. The argument contends that in pre-modern times strong groups or nations simply took from others by force whatever they wanted without giving any excuse. But in modern times when we are supposed to be more civilized, we need a justification when we loot other peoples' lands or coffers. Typical rationales were "We took the land form the Cherokees because they did not know how to farm efficiently and we had to show them," or "Workers are not very bright and are lazy, so management needs to keep tight control." The British Empire colonized India because "Indians did not have the intelligence or skill to govern themselves, and they had to be taught." These fatuous and bogus reasons or prejudices were supposed to justify trampling on and lording it over others.

In fact, prejudice seems to be as common in antiquity as it is today. In the mid 600s BC the Chinese Tang code called for the segregation of foreigners in such a way as to reveal ubiquitous hatred and suspicion. The same prejudices were common also in Japan, Korea, and Vietnam (Chua, 2007, page 69-71). As late as the 20th century, the Japanese held the Koreans in disdain and saw them as consistently filthy, disorderly, and severely lacking in mental abilities; whereas, the Japanese were clean, orderly, and of superior intelligence actually rooted in divinity (Duus, 1955, pages 397-398).

Perhaps nowhere or at no time was prejudice more virulent and destructive than in the Western world in the early decades of the 1900s. The false science called eugenics had determined which people were genetically superior and which were genetically inferior. Major national policies were constructed accordingly. The toll taken on the populations on the continent by the Nazis may have been the most pernicious, but England and the United States ingested these mistaken ideas and practices as well. We all know of the six million Jews brutally abused and then gassed and cremated at Auschwitz, Dachau, and the other death factories. We may tend to forget that homosexuals, mentally retarded, and Gypsies were also annihilated. Poland suffered greatly because the Slavs were also supposedly inferior, and Hitler coveted their fertile plains. Under Hitler' plan to acquire the agricultural plains of Poland, millions of gentile Poles were crowded into warehouses and burned or exterminated by many other means.

In England, Eugenics received the blessings of the highly educated as seen in the volume entitled, *Foundations of the Nineteenth Century* by the respected historian Houston Stewart Chamberlin. Based on pseudo-science, all non-whites were thought to be genetically inferior intellectually. The belief in the superiority of the privileged and so-called blueblood lines were victims of the haughty attitude of the Caucasian aristocracy as well as from their condescension toward commoners, colonists, and foreigners. This air of absolute superiority mislead them to believe that they could continue to rule their colonies as lords even as the world was drastically changing and universal education was expanding. Being forced to extricate themselves from running a world-wide empire, western powers left in their wake peoples who were never given the opportunity of practicing the arts of self-governance. In addition, arbitrary national lines were drawn in such a way as to create ongoing animosity.

United States was not at all exempt from the mistaken racist and ethnic ideas of the eugenics movement. Public policy was strikingly dictated by eugenics in the early part of the 20th century. Immigration was curtailed, especially from the eastern European countries because invalid intelligence tests showed retardation as high as 60% of the cases coming into Ellis Island around 1920. Many were returned home; in fact, whole boatloads were returned. Sterilization of those presumed as retarded was conducted in some states. We know now that these same Hungarians, Romanians, Czechs, Poles have risen to high ranks in our government and corporate world with great success. Andy Grove and his family, had they been denied entrance, the famous Intel chip company may never have flourished.

Anybody who has extensive and varied experience working with people may view this condition of functional equality as naïve. In my experience, it does seem clearly true that some individuals are so lazy, unmotivated, or closed minded that fruitful cooperation with them may be essentially futile. But for most people, we need to think about how we have treated them and examine conditions that make people lazy and uncooperative by disempowering them and providing disincentives rather than incentives. So, in the main, when we face working with a new group of people, we should start with the assumption they have something to contribute, and we should evaluate the conditions of their participation.

Group norms

Groups need to be led to replace old rules of competition with new rules of cooperation. The norms, often unwritten laws of the group, must be for cooperative rather than competitive or antagonistic behavior in order to reduce hostility between groups. A group must build up an expectation or a climate for cooperation. Members of a group must be led to want to give help to others as well as accepting and soliciting help from others. Knowledge, skills, and insights should be shared rather than hoarded.

There will always be a time and place for individualistic and competitive American-like culture. Research literature indicates that individuals tend to be more productive than groups if the task at hand is rather simple, the parts of the larger organizational enterprise are rather independent of each other, and the procedures are well defined and structured. On the other hand, if the task is complex, the parts of the larger enterprise highly interrelated, and if the task is not well prescribed and is unstructured, then the group tends to be more productive. Constructing concrete proposals tend to be best left to individuals, whereas critiquing those proposals clearly requires a group effort. Great scientific or medical breakthroughs are often attributed to an individual, but in most cases rest upon massive collaborate efforts. So we are not denying the importance of individual effort or even healthy competition. We are just trying to put it into perspective here.

Traditional wisdom often has it that individuals must be changed one at a time as a precondition for a group to change. While the primacy of individual beliefs and attitudes are relied upon in education, religion, and in the behavioral sciences as well, a more behavior-oriented and group approach is critical in changing a whole group. Changing groups' norms start with changing behavior and that starts from the top down. It is generally not effective trying to force the group to accept a new norm. There must be a general readiness, at which time the leader must start to articulate the new norm, lead the group to see a clear rationale for the new norm, and find ways to see its effectiveness in other organizations which have tried it successfully. The leader must model the norm. The focus of change will be the group as a whole, not the individual. If the group is not convinced, then, probably they are not ready, need more evidence, or need to delay any action.

On the other hand, there may be some norms that a leader must impose. If you are the leader of a group and you highly value honesty with all your constituents, and you know that more than an occasional dishonest transaction has occurred, then it is your place to declare, "This Company deals honestly with all its constituents. That is who we are. Dishonest acts will not be tolerated. I personally mean that this is a zero toleration policy. Furthermore, I appeal to you all to reinforce this sentiment throughout the company." Parents of school children who do not tolerate fighting in the family might make the following declaration: "We do not fight in this family. Hitting out of deep anger is not the way we settle problems. We talk them out. Hitting is not the way your parents settle problems. You can rough-house and wrestle hard in good fun, but that is entirely different." Brief concise declarations of a norm are effective but must not be very frequent as to become trivial.

The whole point of this section is that group norms have a powerful effect on behavior. The leader must wholeheartedly believe in the norms he or she espouses, model them consistently, and must be their chief spokesperson without haranguing or preaching, while urging all members to embrace and live the norms. If the leaders are not completely sold on the norm, the members will realize that and will not internalize the norm.

Friendship

Close personal contact with members of the other side raises the probability for two sides to reconcile. There must be ample opportunity for liberal, repeated, and genuine personal interactions. This point will be amplified in some of the discussion directly below, but it must be presented now.

Friendships are very real and highly valued by most of us. We are not likely to throw them aside. In contrast, our prejudices about groups that our new friend belongs to often tend to be abstract and gained indirectly. Even though the prejudice may be intense and persistent, the assumption here, which is well supported, is that the concrete friendships will overpower old group abstract prejudices. Any extensive intergroup experience where people live together, work, play, or travel is likely to engender friendships. Friendships work to break down warped and destructive ideas and feelings about other people and their respective groups.

Research has shown us what conditions must be met to significantly raise the probability of reducing hostility and segregation. But we also need to look at the psychological processes unfolding within the individual who is going through the de-categorization experience.

Psychological processes in de-categorization

The origin point for de-categorization is pursuing a superordinate goal and the anchor experience is friendship formation. Of the five conditions developed above for successfully reaching harmony, friendship may not be any more important than any of the others, but it seems to be the pivotal channel through which change occurs. It is significant that Ashmore (1970) refers to his version of the direct contact model as the "shared coping-friendship" paradigm.

Role interpretation

As one makes friends from an antagonistic group, one begins to see those friends in much broader roles. The new friend is not just the Arab I am forced to work with in my employment but is now a father, a son, a mountain biker, or a musician, someone who cooks Cajun food, and is a very warm and compassionate person. So one's new information about these multiple roles opens a floodgate of new positive knowledge about a complex, rich, multidimensional and attractive person.

Brief congruence

As a result of sharing personal experiences and values, one comes to realize that the two people have much more in common than originally assumed. And what they have in common is very basic and possibly universal. In fact, everyone shares universal and common needs. We all want to touch nice things, nice clothes, fabrics, soft smooth skin, an exceptionally well-finished table top. Differences in clothing are superficial. The Indian sari is very different than a western dress, but beautiful Indian silks and soft Irish wools are equally attractive to those two respective cultures. We all like to taste good food and have our taste buds stimulated. The fact that some have been conditioned to love heavy curry powder while others crave chili powder is superficial. We could list all the exchanges here: we all like to hear nice music but differ on the definition; we all want a sense of safety, a sense of dignity and respect. At the very most basic level, we all want and need basic food and shelter, a provision for health, and a chance to work and provide. And we find that we agree with our new friend on many of the basic things of life. This is not to deny that there may also be irreconcilable and critical differences in beliefs.

The consistency game

The concept of cognitive dissonance has moved into our daily language, at least the dissonance reference. This concept holds that when two elements, two beliefs, two behaviors, or a belief and a behavior are in sharp disagreement with each other, a jarring and uncomfortable mental state occurs called cognitive dissonance. Because that state is uncomfortable, we try to reduce the dissonance. The dissonance is reduced by changing our thoughts and feelings about one of the two elements in order that they become harmonious or congruent. If a person says he or she cares about the poor, but never gives to charity and feels those two elements clashing in dissonance, the person may either give to charity or start to believe that the poor bring it on themselves. This variable is widely researched in social psychology. It is easy to replicate experiments whereby participants are asked to write a short essay (expressing ideas) contrary to their true beliefs. This produces dissonance. We can measure that and not just assume it. The participant invariably reduces his or her dissonance by changing, slightly but measurably, their beliefs. It may be surprising that they tend not to discount the writing of the essay; it is apparently too present, current, and real behavior.

Inconsistency and dissonance are to be expected between prior negative feelings about the negative group and the very strong and concrete feelings one has about the new friend from that same negative group. The friend will be the anchor element and will not change. The dissonance will be reduced by changing one's opinion of the supposed negative group, and consistency will be restored.

Stimulus generalization

Finally for this model to work successfully, a new friend must maintain a significant portion of the appearance, cues, or cultural pattern of the group from which he or she comes. If a successful American Indian looks and acts totally like a white person he is referred to as an apple, red on the outside but white on the inside. Thus we see this new friend as a white person and fail to generalize our good feelings about him to the total group of American Indians. In some way he must continue to identify with his people for us to generalize good feelings from him to his total group.

Everyone wins when artificial and unnecessary walls are torn down. Gentiles who helped Jews by hiding them during the holocaust said, "They are just like us. We are all human beings." The feeling was that the "righteous," as the Jews called the Gentiles, had no choice. They just naturally had to help. Gentiles who did not help continued to refer to two categories—them and us. Those who helped won by doing the only decent thing they could, and the Jews won their lives.

A wonderful story of de-categorization occurred during the playing of Beethoven's *Ninth Symphony* after the Berlin wall came down. Leonard Bernstein, who had a passion for world peace and equality, was the conductor. Note the norm here of belief in peace, and the other prerequisite condition of hostility reduction, namely functional equality. Half of musicians came from the western side and half from the eastern side. Identical concerts were performed on each side of the wall on successive nights. "Ode to Joy" expressed the breaking down of the two categories of east and west, communism and democracy, and the new single category of one people pursuing peace. Bernstein said that he would never forget that concert because it was so full of hope and joy.

Admittedly, some relationships are so broken and of such long-standing depth that restoration may be impossible in a given lifetime.

But in the United States we scarcely begin to use the model set forth in this chapter. Men will be happy to lord it over women if women ever let their guard down. Nationally, we push little countries around as though we had a divine right. Diplomacy is short term because the great corporations who pull the international strings must have a favorable bottom line at the end of the month or quarter. Long-term statesmanship is passé. When do you ever even hear the word statesmanship? The Secretary of Defense trumps the Secretary of State. The de-categorization model provides a realistic opportunity for an alternate course.

On balance, there is considerable room for optimism. Family life has changed radically in the States. A good percentage of marriages have moved in the direction of equality, even though the female may still carry more that her share of the load. Even though there is a loss of union membership and strength and even though there are alarming increases of labor grievances before the Labor Boards, some organizations have substantially democratized the workplace. At least some consulting and training firms are solidly rooted in sound behavioral principles; they are using scientific knowledge to raise skills and understanding of consequences of behavior. The result is that greater opportunity is spread around for persons at all levels. The caveat, though, is that the progress that has been made can easily be lost unless the workforce is alert and resistant to the centralization of power.

The research for de-categorization continues

Even though this book popularizes a formal behavioral science model, I do want the curious reader to appreciate the current ongoing nature of the research and to be able to consult some of those sources. The review by Brown and Hewstone, 2004, is quite reader friendly. There are at least three somewhat different theoretical approaches to the research, and many variables still undergoing elaborate field and laboratory testing.

All three contemporary approaches affirm, to some extent, the original conditions for change set forth by Allport in his well-known

The Nature of Prejudice, mentioned at the beginning of this chapter. The three current approaches are summarized in detail in Zana, 2005. The first approach by Brewer and Miller is called "De-categorization Theory." The intent of direct contact experiences in this theory is to overcome social categorical thinking entirely and replace it with differentiation, especially of out-group members. People are not at all the same, they are varied, and as we come to experience that, the out-group category ceases to have usefulness. In a very similar vein, personalization (via contact and friendship) reveals idiosyncratic and highly nuanced information about self, in-group, and out-group members and, thus, decreases the original value of group categories.

The second approach by Gaertner and Davidio does not envision the dissolution of social categories but suggests that direct contact causes participants to redraw boundary lines to include the prior two antagonistic groups into one new super-category. They call it the "In-group identity model." The identity of out-group members is downplayed; whereas, the third approach maintains the importance of continued out-group salience.

The third orientation is called the "Intergroup Contact Model" by Hewstone and Brown. They believe their model is more integrative because it includes the variables of the first two models but also maintains the older view of the importance of ongoing out-group salience, which allows stimulus generalization. If you like your new friend from the out-group, you will tend to like the whole out-group more than previously, provided your new friend is somehow still identified with the out-group. Hewstone and Brown have also looked in detail into the mechanisms of change. Getting more accurate and varied information about the out-group facilitates positive change. But even though cognitive mediators are powerful, emotional factors mediate the change even more. Emotional factors such as the degree to which one is anxious or threatened subjectively by the out-group individuals, or the out-group as a whole has a serious dampening effect on the direct contact experience.

A still different current research reformulation is to combine the conflict reduction efforts with social and group identity more formally. Social identity was always present to some extent in the conflict reduction literature but never this prominently (Ashmore, Jussim, and Wilder, 2001).

In the following several chapters we will elaborate in more detail on some of the critical issues when applying the direct contact model. These issues will include authoritarianism, dominance, cooperation, power, wealth, fear, dissent, status, equality, and regulation. These are all issues that must be faced correctly in order to replace friction and poor performance in small or large groups with group cohesion, satisfaction, and productivity. In the main, the group dynamics principles outlined in this chapter, and examined in more detail in the following chapters, apply from the smallest to the largest groups and all kinds of intergroup relations.

★★

Allport, G. 1954. *The nature of prejudice.* Reading, Massachusetts: Addison-Wesley Publishing Company.

Ashmore, Richard. D. 1970. Solving the problem of prejudice. In B. E. Collins, *Social psychology; social influence, attitude, change, group processes, and prejudice.* Reading, Massachusetts: Addison-Wesley Publishing Company.

Ashmore, Richard. D, Jussim, Lee, and Wilder, David. (Editors) 2001. *Social identity, intergroup conflict, and conflict resolution.* New York: Oxford University Press.

Chamberlain, Huston Stewart. Originally 1911. *Foundations of the Nineteenth Century.* Reprinted in 1968. New York: H. Fertig Co.

Chomsky, N. 2000. *Fateful triangle: The United States, Israel and Palestinians, 2nd edition.* Cambridge, Massachusetts: South End Press. Page 90.

Duus, Peter. 1955. *The Abacus and the Sword: The Japanese Penetration of Korea, 1895-1910.* Berkeley and Los Angeles: University of California Press.

Kahneman, D., & Tversky, A. 1984. Choices, values and frames. *American Psychologist, 39, 341-350*

Roy, Arundhati. 2003. *War Talk*. Cambridge, Massachusetts: South End Press.

Sherif, M., Harvey, O. J., White, B. J., Hood, W. R., & Sherif, C. W. 1961. *Intergroup conflict and cooperation: The Robber's Cave experiment*. Norman: The University of Oklahoma book Exchange.

Zana, M. P. (Editor). 2005. *Advances in experimental social psychology*. New York: Academic Press. See the chapter on "An integrative theory of intergroup contact" by R. Brown and M. Hewstone.

Chapter 2: Mutual Threat and Potential Motivation

MOTIVATION FOR INDIVIDUAL action very frequently requires a bona fide and substantial threat. If we do not act, we may lose a job, miss a promotion, lose the confidence of a child or spouse, become diabetic or a cardiac victim, or be penalized by the IRS. An old Bugs Bunny cartoon treated the topic of motivation. The setting was the turnip patch—the staple food to sustain the bunny species. As long as the patch yielded well it was often neglected and taken for granted. But when drought or disease struck, the very existence of the bunnies was threatened. That is when the bunny population became motivated to take care of the turnip patch.

Beyond the individual level, two parties who are antagonistic are most unlikely to come to some new point of cooperation unless they mutually perceive a common threat that causes an equally great concern to both sides. We frequently start to think about cooperation when there is a shared need or danger that we cannot meet ourselves. A common enemy makes strange bedfellows.

Even though hatred and hostility may fester within extended families for decades, and animosity may linger between nations over centuries, there is always the creative possibility that a mutual threat and a shared realistic goal can move the opponents toward reconciliation. Sometimes it is very difficult to put one's finger on a common threat and a corresponding potentially cooperative goal. But so often we miss opportunities, or our timing is off. Defending one's self against the "enemy" and expending great energies to reveal the enemy's alleged aggressive intents too often slams the door on getting a glimpse of some common interest.

Planned wilderness and survival experiences have great potential to reduce hostility between antagonists. Hostility reduction is accomplished by having the participants work through an experience that is mutually threatening and demands cooperation as the only way out. Their activities may include sailing across a dangerous body of water, crossing a desert, orienteering in difficult terrain, or rappelling a demanding cliff. The mutual threat is in the inherent danger and difficulty of the task, which constitutes the motivation to act in an absolutely cooperative manner or risk loss of life. Uncooperativeness or carelessness could result in a fatal accident. Succeeding, on the other hand, will give the participants a sense of joint achievement and quite possibly some human bonding.

In the days of early arms reduction talks during the JFK era, the U.S. and the old U.S.S.R. agreed to burn several dozen completely outdated and worthless bombers. Each side would do this while the other side directly monitored the destruction. Little was lost on either side; it was token disarmament. But if more tokens could follow, then something more substantial might be possible. Both sides realized that the world might be more dangerous rather than safer by rapid escalation of nuclear arms. And, undoubtedly, another motive was to reduce the terrible cost of escalation. The mutually perceived threat of potential mass destruction was motivation enough to take the first steps in controlling arms, especially nuclear arms.

Periodically Canada and the United States get alarmed about the amount of pollution in the waters they share—the Great Lakes. Lead, mercury and other toxins are elevated from time to time resulting in dead fish, closed beaches, hazards to health, and a threatened tourist industry. At different times in the histories of the two nations, the threat has been egregious enough for the countries to take united action. Being a resident of western Pennsylvania, we sometimes would go the beaches of Presque Isle on Lake Erie. In periods of great pollution, it was not uncommon for the beaches to be covered with dead fish and smell with a foul odor. The beaches would close to fishing and swimming, and picnicking was out of the question. The extensive heavy industry on the northern and southern shores of Lake Erie was the culprit. The toxins came from both countries and got mixed in the ebb and flow of the lake. It was only when it became bad enough that the two countries involved were moved to do something about it.

The case of DDT

Mutual threats are sometimes self-evident and demand attention by two antagonists. But too often, actions are unilateral and the effects may be far off and totally unforeseen. If the chemical companies of U.S. ban DDT but continue to sell it to third world countries, mutual harm is likely to follow. One problem is that the bottom line may not be impacted for a number of years later, so we go on selling it. But anyone with a bit of a long term vision will see that animal and human life will be harmed in a third world country, and they will sell seafood back to us with excessive levels of DDT, causing a destructive impact on our own human health.

A caveat is that most all legislation to solve large social, relational, and physical problems is complex and has unanticipated consequences. While the faithful following of the direct contact model may produce central positive change, there may be negative side effects. All the consequences are difficult to anticipate. In the case of DDT, restricting its use in developing and tropical countries has recently been correlated with a significant increase of mosquito populations resulting in serious increases of malaria. The World Health Organization claims that about one million die each year of malaria, most being children. The faithful use of mosquito netting while sleeping seems to be a very effective substitute weapon to DDT in fighting malaria but many people still fall through the cracks as it were.

Nuclear proliferation

The nuclear threat of the last half-century was finally mutually perceived by the old U.S.S.R., the United States and others as a serious threat to peace and a viable future. When the stockpiling and the capacity for massive overkill became self-revealing to both east and west, the international nuclear anti-proliferation activities became serious and active. This was something that could not have been addressed if only one side had seen the threat. When the profound threat was mutually perceived, a potential for action was created.

As long as the mushroom cloud of nuclear annihilation hovers poignantly in our memories, humanity has a good chance of restraint to insure mutual survival. The Japanese population of Hiroshima and Nagasaki were basically exterminated. It has been reported that Gorbachev was shaken by the suffering of the people of Chernobyl and the threatening clouds of radioactive material drifting across Europe. There are at least two nuclear dangers for the future. The one danger is that future generations may forget the eyewitness reports of terror, incineration, disintegration, and the hideous radiation effects on the survivors on the margins of the two Japanese blasts. If we ever forget Chernobyl, Hiroshima and Nagasaki, or in some warped sense deny their reality, there is great danger. As long as the super powers remember the past nuclear terrors, hopefully they will successfully maintain restraint and safety. Nevertheless, insanity may emerge even for supposedly rational nations such as the United States that has explicitly put the nuclear option on the table in its arsenal against terrorism.

The second danger comes from the fanatical splinter groups bound to strike terror on the major powers. Even though the 19 box-cutter terrorists were educated and had a lot to lose, many of the terrorists feel they have nothing to lose and feel that there is no hope in the future. In nations like Iraq and Afghanistan, which have been torn apart by wars for at least two decades, life, limb, and property have all been shattered repeatedly. Prosperity is not in their dreams and unemployment may reach as high as 60 percent or more. They subjectively have little to lose, and perhaps much to gain, in fanatical religious suicidal service. What an honor to carry a small nuclear device into the den of the infidels. A fanatical group, or even a small county, may work for years to deliver an ingenious nuclear micro-strike.

The nuclear threat can only be a mutual threat for both sides if the stakes are very high for both sides, that is, if both sides truly have much to lose in going to the nuclear option. Therefore, the only lasting prospect for mutual security is to put strategic efforts into seeing that the other side has something to lose, like increased prosperity. Mutual threat unfortunately cannot be a motivational starter at this time for the western countries, vis-à-vis terroristic groups, or terribly underdeveloped countries.

The groundwork suggested here lies outside the direct contact model. Herculean work would have to be done, and our foreign policy regarding terrorism would have to change radically just to prepare the ground to make the cooperative model potentially operative. To be sure, we have to mercilessly obliterate terroristic training camps and planned attempts to deliver a destructive blow. But simultaneously we need to start to treat terrorists as equal human beings and as groups with meaningful missions from their perspective. They seek respect and status in the world, and chafe at our occupying their holy lands and our being so domineering and dominating. The fact that the United States invaded Islamic Iraq against international law and without provocation could easily enrage any rational Iraqi citizen. We slaughtered tens of thousands of their civilians and shredded their infrastructure. Furthermore, to occupy their country for over several years and to frightfully mismanage the occupation would certainly further enrage the rational citizen, let alone the fanatical elements.

Centuries before the United States was conceived, Persia (Iraq) had a learned and highly advanced culture. The Islamic peoples were probably the main source of enlightenment that penetrated the dark ages. A repressive and unlearned Christianity allowed Europe to strangle for nearly a thousand years. Current near eastern Islamic countries in the main tend to be deserting the modern world and the prosperity that the open market system can bring. Retreating into theocracies under Sharia law is ushering in a dark age for these once proud and advanced societies. But we are certainly generously helping their decline. There will be little chance at securing the world from terrorists until we abandon the wrong-headed war on terrorism and replace it with cooperating where we can, and, above all, get out of their face and out of their way. Modern Iran is a highly advanced nation. Fanatics are taking it backwards but it remains hideous and wrong minded not to talk to them.

The mutual threat of AIDS

Odd bedfellows have been brought together by the universal AIDS threat. Clintons, Bushes, Gates, Obamas, and many national governments and organizations have exhibited foresight in recognizing the immediate face as well as the socially devastating side effects of AIDS on the whole world. The suffering of adult victims should be motivation enough for a cooperative response, but the devastation has a longer arm. AIDS correlates with adult incapacity and poverty, orphans, a breakdown of the family, social, and economic structures, adding to the causes of social unrest and international instability. In spite of the wonderful inroads made by world health initiatives, thousands are still dying of AIDS. One estimate of the numbers of children orphaned by AIDS is around 20 million globally. Many of these lives will be ripe for Islamism (as distinguished from mainline Islam) or the next crazy ism that may not even exist at this moment. These consequences of the unchecked disease are not in the interests of any of the parties involved; the consequences are mutually threatening. Thus, there exists a multilateral motivation to act. The George W. Bush administration more than doubled our monetary commitment to address the world-wide AIDS problem and the Obamas administration has followed that commitment.

Marriage

The motivational power of mutual threat prevails at all social levels. Consider a marriage relationship. Meeting the mutual physical, psychological, spiritual, and economic needs of a married couple can motivate a lasting union. These needs can only be satisfied genuinely by both sides recognizing the mutual threat of not contributing liberally to the needs of the other. The mutual threat is deterioration and collapse of the vitality of the relationship, if not the formal marriage itself. The sad fact is that one side, often the husband, fails to see the relational danger *and takes more than he gives.* If a couple both sense that their relationship has become silent, cold, and empty, and if it bothers both of the spouses profoundly, then the motivation may emerge full blown to do something about it. But if the malaise in the marriage disturbs just one side, the likelihood of cooperative rebuilding will be very low. The threat must be mutually perceived.

The threat of globalization

Globalization presents a mixture of economic threats as well as economic opportunities to working class people around the world. When Boeing moved one of its manufacturing plants to Malaysia, workers in Seattle were abandoned, but poor, relatively unskilled youth from Malaysia had opportunities they never dreamed possible. While Malaysia is a prosperous and advanced country generally, some of the new workers came from villages with extremely low economic opportunities. Boeing's arrival was a great blessing for them.

The free movement of capital and business is not always such a blessing. The "spiral downward" phenomenon means that international manufacturing corporations are mobile and will keep moving their labor sites to secure the very lowest wage opportunity. Jack Welch, the former and celebrated President of General Electric, contended that the ideal metaphor for an international business is a great barge. The managers of the barge should be ready to pull out of port on any chance of lower wages or advantages at another place. The barge managers should have the mentality to move quickly, overnight, and as frequently as possible. The complete free trade champions contend that there should be no regulations to moderate such industrial nomadism. Free trade in some cases will mean that if workers in one port hold out for a 10 cent increase in wages, they will likely be abandoned by their employers. The workers are, then, faced with sudden unemployment and, in many cases, a community devastated by environmental pollution as well.

The poignant threat and loss felt by the work force just described has not been felt by the multinational corporations to date. There is no mutual perception of a problem, and thus no likelihood of the corporations sharing their profits more equitably, or acting more responsibly environmentally. The World Trade Organization (WTO) meets in secret with protected agendas and no input from the working class. The WTO resists any regulations from governments that may restrict free trade, but in the meantime, they construct their own rules and regulations to guarantee the advantages of big international business. Workers can demonstrate at the WTO meetings but they are not allowed near the meeting site. Or they can attend the large international Social Economic Forums, which are held periodically. These meetings are about as close as the international labor force has come to international unionization, but the movement is still far from that. Elite international corporate leadership knows that this modern movement has nothing particular to do with communism but the "pinko" label is occasionally waved about to discredit the Forum movement.

Democratic governments concerned with human rights should be a counter-force to the maximizing profit obsession of the corporate world and organizations like the WTO, but that is not generally the case. The relationship between the two is too ingrown. As the world shrinks, the plight of the poor and severely economically challenged may weigh more heavily on the conscience of the citizens of the free world. A more enlightened citizenry, whether from self-concern or altruism, may finally bring enough pressure on their governments to challenge the rogue-like corporate powers. It would seem that until social unrest intensifies or international unionism occurs, there will be no chance that the two sides will see wealth disparity as a mutual threat.

Leaving the wide scope of the WTO and focusing on the more micro level of any one production firm, a threat of poor quality products or inefficient production should be an obvious threat to both labor and management. Consumers will generally bypass the product if quality is shabby and the cost is non-competitive. Companies can often move very quickly or change their product mix, but labor is stuck in one place. A mutual threat is not likely to be a reality in this scenario. Job security and a living wage are both critical for the worker. Substantial profit and a positive corporate image are paramount to the stockholders. Unfortunately labor and management often fail to realize the mutual threat until it is too late.

Local economic decay

Unions were desperately needed in the early decades of the 20th century to counter the irresponsible greed and carelessness of the giants of industry, but in later decades, union demands probably became excessive and were exacerbated by corruption in the leadership. On the management side, generous profits after World War II and a lack of long-sighted vision blinded leadership. In the meantime Germany and Japan were rising from the rubble and building efficient, up-to-date, totally modern plants. Our steel plants were becoming old and outdated. In addition, the production of raw steel was passed on to third world countries with cheap labor in the 1980s. Threats about closing plants were common because the workers' demands were supposedly excessive. The cry of "wolf" stirred little attention. The wolf finally came and both labor and management were losers, especially labor.

U. S. Steel could have profited from the new quality control ideas of William Deming and the profit sharing strategies emerging in the 1960s. Instead Deming took his quality control expertise to Japan, and we were the losers. We were stuck in complacency and short-sightedness. The unions could have moderated their demands, cleaned up corruption, and insisted on the modernization of the steel plants. Low horizons on both sides blocked a clear view of the coming wolf.

Some steel entrepreneurs such a Nucor stepped into this situation by the early 1990s and successfully launched new electric mills, which could appropriately fill the niche of specialty steels and specialty additives. These new ventures tended also to follow more humane working conditions and compensation. Mutual respect and dignity of all persons at all levels fared better and some of the old antagonisms were avoided.

Threat of economic collapse

Reports from the World Economic Forum in Davos, Switzerland in the winter of 2009 revealed the gloomiest mood for many decades. Leaders from around the world clearly sensed that something had gone frightfully wrong with worldwide economic institutions and dynamics. The fundamental deterioration of the major banks and financial organizations and the outright collapse of some was a source of great concern. What apparently started in the United States was felt around the world with no real end in sight. Excessive risk taking born of greed and unfettered by any reasonable regulation finally exposed unviable and decadent corporate behavior. Concrete ways for nations to cooperate were far from clear, but the general motivation for the need to cooperate was salient and ubiquitous.

Decay of institutions is probably endless, but voices raised against greed, inequity, fraud and injustice are laughed at until the wound exudes an ugly discharge. The United States has been lurching toward favoring the rich and powerful for the past several decades. Thirty years ago, it was almost universally accepted in developed nations that a major CEO might be paid twenty times more that the average hourly wage. That expectation held to some extent in advanced countries such as Germany and Japan during the past thirty years but was broken wide open in the United States during the past couple of decades. The 1:20 ratio became a 1:400 ratio. Even worse, Enron-type fraud, Madoff-like Ponzi schemes, a-ethical derivative shuffling, and maximizing profits were all too frequent and common. After the turnip patch was severely threatened, our two political parties cooperated enough to pass the economic recovery bills. The threat of collapse may rear up again; financial abuses have returned, and there are some predictions of another collapse in a few years.

Elusive threats vitiating motivation

In the next chapter, we will deal with threats that are manufactured or twisted considerably from the truth. These kinds of threats may be effective in the short run, but people eventually determine that they have been spun badly, resulting in disillusionment and estrangement from the leadership. For threats to be powerful motivators, they must be seen as genuine and serious. To tell teenagers that their brains will be fried like eggs in a skillet if they infrequently smoke marijuana is false and will not work. To tell heavy smokers that they have a 60% chance of shortening their lives by ten to twenty years, at least, has a chance of working because it is honest and true. Lung cancer tends to be a painful form of death.

The elusiveness of threats is a somewhat different issue. Many genuine, serious threats may simply not be visible or evident to the viewer. Threats are elusive when they project no immediate visible evidence or when they are likely to be remote in time or distant in geography. The task of leadership in these circumstances is to articulate the reality of these invisible threats and to educate and persuade regarding the factual basis of the threat.

Some of our most serious threats are invisible. Rachael Carson entitled her book *Silent Spring* for this very reason. Killers may be silent and the wolf may appear in sheep's clothing. A river or stream may be crystal clear and apparently inviting but may be loaded with mercury or other non-visible toxins. On the other hand, a river may be brown and muddy after a storm but be harmless. The effect of environmental pollution or insect damage upon vegetation may be invisible to the untrained or inattentive eye. How many people travel our interstates at high speeds and never observe what should be obvious damage done by gypsy moths, pine beetles, and ash borers. Man-made atmospheric pollutants have been documented to reduce crop productivity by serious percentages, but are totally invisible, short of measuring the crop yield at the end of the season.

Another aspect of elusiveness is that the threat is remote in time; it is far out in the future. Therefore, the threat may be interpreted as unreal or, at least, not something to worry about. These threats are like worms that may hatch fifty years from now and attack the proverbial turnip patch. The threat of crude oil depletion was ominous until the discovery of new natural resources. Since the shale and tar oils and new gas sources have been discovered and developed, the older threat of depletion is greatly diminished. New threats of safety and pollution related to the shale industry have taken the place of depletion.

Many health threats have a remote nature. If a person has elevated cholesterol at age 20, he or she is not likely to worry about eating greasy hamburgers. That same threat should be much more motivational if the person is 70. The problems of home ownership also often seem remote. If one buys a ten-year-old house, all the utilities may seem to be working fine and the roof may look sound. One may want to concentrate on the niceties of moving in and redecorating, but inevitable major repairs better be in the long-range budget.

Capitalism seems to be the best social/economic system to evolve in the modern world, but its obsession with short-term, bottom-line, end-of-the-month or end-of-the-quarter results is devastating. Any system needs balances. Adam Smith, the father of capitalism, warned against unbridled greed. The challenge to the transformational modern leader is to stir people to think beyond tomorrow, to see that many apparently distant problems need to be addressed today.

Geographic distance is yet another dimension which obscures threat. As long as high crime rates are isolated in the "bad" and removed neighborhoods and as long as prisoners are housed across the tracks or out in hinterlands, the rest of society seems not to be too concerned. Surely, drive-by shootings, drug related violence, gang activity, the outrageous rates of imprisonment in our society of the lower classes should alarm us all. They indicate the body politic is not well. But as long as the problems are physically distant, we are content. Globally, the same dynamic is in play. Rwanda is and was far away, Darfur is distant, and the Timor Islands are not even on our geographic radar. Syria is indeed removed in space. United States citizens who can weather the economic downturn quite well may contribute groceries or money to the food banks, but the food banks are not located in upscale neighborhoods. Thus hunger and economic despair remains academic and removed for many better-heeled persons.

Bringing antagonists together requires a search for common values, common ground, common problems, and common threats. Creative and powerful leadership should have the insight and ingenuity to uncover these common problems and assist society to move toward solutions

★★

Biehl, Joao, and Petyrna, Adriana. 2014. *When People Come First, Critical Studies in Global Health.* Princeton, New Jersey: Princeton University Press.

Chapter 3: Twisted Fears and False Threats

As we saw in the last chapter, rationally based fear from social or natural threats often motivate people to take necessary actions for survival. However, it is an entirely different story when organizations or governments fabricate or greatly exaggerate fears in order to realize a political or monetary gain. The whipping up of false fears too often leads to mass hatred vented in violent riots and even major wars.

Not too long ago in our national history (1942) we sent 120,000 persons of Japanese ancestry, all loyal American citizens, into concentration camps out of irrational fear. Families were mercilessly uprooted and lost everything they had labored for except for what they could carry on their backs. As World War II continued and we desperately needed all the soldiers we could get, we turned around and accepted the young men, whom we earlier regarded as potential traitors, from these camps into the armed services. They fought valiantly for us in spite of the bitterness that we had injected into their souls and into the psyches of their loved ones.

Production workers have often been intimidated by the false threat that the plant will have to close down if production is not increased. Some of the workers may know that, in fact, the profits have been large and that the top executives have been making outrageous millions in salaries and stock options. Twisting the truth in order to control people undermines trust and mutual respect and probably reveals a lack of more positive and competent leadership skills and, at least, reveals a lack of integrity. Additionally, when management really is skating on a thin margin of profit and the appeal for a greater response from the workers is called for, they may wrongly believe they are being lied to again. To be captivated by the devil of twisted fear is to be lost. But we are lost in a sea of phony fear so many times in our national history, and in our personal odysseys as well. The topic of this chapter is irrational fear and why people fall for it.

Leadership by twisted fear

We are told repeatedly that nothing is the same since 9/11. One does not even need to say 2001; the date is internationally salient. In truth, very little has changed since 9/11. Admittedly we have been humiliated as never before in that 19 young volunteers with nothing but box cutters could obliterate our two iconic towers of world commerce, carve a slice out of the Pentagon, and even threaten the Capital itself. And, of course, all of this happened on our own safe and hallowed soil. That our middle- and upper-class citizens could be fatally attacked in our modern cathedrals of power was new.

However, the larger and more pervasive truth is that there is nothing new about terrorism around the world, even on our own soil. Was terror absent from the minds of those 120,000 Japanese-Americans with the first knock on their door? Was terror absent from the minds of many of the raids and slaughters of the American Indians, even after they generally and initially greeted our pilgrims and settlers with friendship and lifesaving food. Was terror absent from the Lakota Sioux mothers and children butchered at Pine Ridge? Was terror absent from the black family whose father was dragged from his bed at midnight and hanged on the limb of a tree? Was terror absent from the children who were firebombed in their church while in Sunday school in the 1960s? Is terror missing in the eyes of the innocent family caught in the cross fire of urban gangs and drug shoot-outs?

We seem to have a case of national Alzheimer's disease. We suffer serious memory loss. Generally, the privileged ruling constituency of the United States has been isolated from these horrors. Our national and state leaders are seldom caught in current urban gang crossfire. And the black lynching and Indian massacres are a thing of the past away back there with the Indian Removal Act of 1930. The attacks upon the lives of President Lincoln, Kennedy, and Reagan are often written off as rare exceptions that leave the mentality of the elite safe, undisturbed and insulated from the frequent terrors liberally scattered through our national history.

It is true that the privileged have shared in the hell of the Civil War and the other big wars, but we cannot confuse war with terrorism. War includes the terror of a surprise attack, but in war the enemy is known, is expected to attack, and can often be defeated with intelligence and force. Terrorism is a different thing almost entirely. Terrorism is often not organized by a great centralized power and, therefore, presents no clearly identified target. The target of terrorism and the timing of the attacks are marked by surprise and randomness. One has absolutely no defense and is almost totally helpless and thus terrified.

No, terrorism in the United States is not new, and neither is the prevalent answer to terrorism new—the use of force. It may be that some enemies understand nothing but force. Thus, a significant part of the answer may need to be force. But there are many other more powerful tools than the use of force in the human arsenal. These are examined in other places in this book.

"Everything has changed since 9/11." No, everything is the same. The age-old use of terrorism to ignite fear and intimidation is exactly the same. The human potential for good and for ill is the same. The political manipulation of stoking artificial fears is always the same. "If we can get the populace to fear the enemy enough they will be willing to fight." Fear and anger were palpable in the attack on Pearl Harbor, and on the World Trade towers as well. Our fear of the Japanese attack was realistic and triggered national motivation to combat a visible enemy. But the realistic fears generated from the World Trade attack were soon directed away from the enemy camps in Afghanistan by the slight-of-hand manufacturing of supposed enemies in other places. The shift should have been transparent to all, a shift to stroke egos and enhance power and control through oil, all cloaked egregiously in the deceitful guise of spreading of democracy.

Rational fear is wonderful. Where would we be without it? Fears alert us to danger and allow us to escape or fight. Fear has allowed the evolution of one of God's most noble and beautiful creatures—the horse. As animals of prey, horses use their primary defense of rapid escape. That rapid escape is facilitated through a great and true capacity for the emotion of fear. Realistic fear, somewhat similar to healthy guilt, is a marvelous protector of the human and infra-human species. But when fear is twisted and used to falsely manipulate people, it is a powerful tool for moral decay, loss, and destruction.

The great isms down through the ages have warranted a portion of realistic and healthy fear. Unfortunately a dose of twisted fear has been mixed into our national responses. Isms such as Communism and Islamism have not only been faced as rational threats to be addressed but as sole or primary national agendas. These agendas become great antis instead of great pros. Mobilizing a nation around an anti agenda is usually expensive, impoverished, eviscerating, and destructive. Take anti-communism as an example.

Anti-communism

When a head of the USSR takes his shoe off and bangs it on the podium at the United Nations and says, "We will bury you," it warrants some attention. It was part rhetoric and part peasant-like bluster but was part realistic threat. In the early years of the USSR, our participation in the arms race and the space race was probably necessary. Restrained force is what was understood on both sides, and so massive national resources were committed. Each side feared the other and totally mistrusted each other. Not only was the megalithic USSR consolidated, but China and Southeast Asia, Africa, and Central and South America were all tilting in the communistic direction. And to rub the salt into the wounds of the United States, Cuba was only 90 miles away flying the hammer and the sickle, and yes, installing Soviet missiles. We seemed to be close to World War III, but thank goodness reasonable heads prevailed.

This is not an argument for Pacifism. When the Japanese mercilessly attacked us in the Pacific and the Nazis were brutally crushing our friends in Europe, I believe we had no choice but throw everything we had at the enemy.

This is not an argument that communism was not dangerous. It is not an argument that the rapid spread of influence was not serious. Armaments were undoubtedly necessary, but as soon as the mission became anti-communism, or even containment, the arms race was on. When one side expanded weaponry, the other side had little choice but to do the same. Fortunately, some longer sighted leaders on both sides saw the necessity of arms control treaties and anti-ballistic missile agreements. This helped to cool the atmosphere and to redirect more resources to constructive domestic needs on both sides.

To make any anti agenda an obsession approaching a near-religious devotion is devoid of wisdom and pervasively destructive. Let's describe how this twisted fear and anti mentality was destructive. We have already touched on the blunder of interring 120,000 loyal Japanese-Americans. The infamy of the Joe McCarthy anti-communist congressional hearings should haunt us forever and prevent us from ever letting anything like that to happen again. Some U.S. leaders started to nudge us in that mindless direction in repeatedly warning that critics of the second U.S. invasion of Iraq (2003) were traitors and disloyal to our Commander-in-Chief and to our troops. Intimidation of independent thought and analysis was clearly intended. Intense pressure was applied to any persons of influence who did not tow the party line. The reader is reminded that the careless bandwagon-type of blind thinking got us into the Bay of Pigs fiasco, but it was open analysis of all possible solutions that got us out of the later Cuban missile crisis. So the first thing that is sacrificed in the dynamic of anti mentality is fundamental open-minded data-based decision making instead of fanatical, closed, rigid, extremist dogma.

The Joe McCarthy hearings of the early 1950s cast a pall on fair and critical thought and ushered in the worst kind on fanaticism. A paranoid mind-set saw communists under every rock and in every corner. Once innocent people were seen talking to a communist on the street corner, they were guilty of being a communist sympathizer. It did not matter if they were just giving street directions to a perfect stranger. Or if one's uncle were a communist, one might, then, be brutally examined and possibly declared guilty. Or if one admitted to some possible good aspects of the early communist movement, one was condemned. Many bright, idealistic youth were attracted to a movement where "workers of the world would unite" and egregious inequality would be addressed. Influential movie stars, academics, and some political leaders in our nation sympathized with the element of truth and wisdom in the early claims of communist rhetoric. This is as far as it went for some, while others became serious sympathizers, and some even card carrying communist members.

Actually, any slightest degree of connection with communism could and did often threaten or result in personal destruction by defamation of character, being black-balled from professional organizations, and loss of employment. People lost jobs, and families were destroyed by the intense shame and suffering. More than one movie star "chose" to drive his car "accidentally" over the cliff. Charley Chaplin, the comedian, fled to England. Many persons in all walks of life drowned themselves in the bottle as an escape. The labor movement was tarred with a broad brush as being pink or communist because they fought against unfettered capitalism and worked for the good of the workers. Rational thinking was smothered and Gestapo-like fanaticism ruled supreme until some very sane Senators reined in the McCarthy abuses and put a stop to them.

Anti-movements are negative and devoid of any positive mission; as a result, they often turn hateful, hostile, oppressive, and destructive. They end up doing far more harm than good. The Viet Nam War was more anti-communist that pro-democracy. We feared that all southeastern Asian countries were drifting toward communism, and if one country went that way, then a domino effect would occur and the whole region would succumb. So the wars were to stop communism not to start democracy. If democracy was strong and such a superior form of government, which I firmly believe it is, why would we fear the take-over of the world by an inherently and fundamentally flawed ideology? Again, I am not saying force does not have a place but not first place and not in the place of helping to positively meet human need and suffering. I am not saying that communism did not need to be taken very seriously, but I am saying that to become *primarily* anti-communist was a weak and destitute approach. The irony is that the staunch anti-communist was often seen as the strongest and most patriotic hero.

The same political and moral bankruptcy has been the norm in U.S. policies toward Central and South American countries. We have supported dictators who were friendly to the business interests of United States corporations, as long as they were not communist dictators. How could anyone say that our policies south of the Rio Grande have been pro-democratic? Our mission has been to squelch any government blocking free enterprise and commerce and to cozy up to the worst dictators friendly to our business interests. Our stance has most frequently been anti-communist, pro-business, and the devil with democracy.

The decline of the Catholic Church in South America is a similar story. One may say with considerable accuracy that Church leadership has been more anti-communist than pro-Christian. Because atheistic communism has struck a deadly blow to the Christian church, it is not surprising that much of the Catholic mission might deteriorate into an impoverished anti mentality. As a result, the Catholic Church has not seriously addressed gross inequalities and oppression. In fact, the Church suppressed their own clergy who have moved to change the plight of the poor masses. This is also clear in their suppression of liberation theology, which to many Christians seems fundamentally Christ-like. The perceived alliance of the Catholic Church with the oppressors may explain some of its decline in South America, while other forms of the Christian faith, which more realistically meet the needs of the people, are flourishing. Witness the great appeal and growth of the Pentecostal groups. The twisted fear of the anti mentality leads to defensive negativity and impoverishment.

Anti-Islamism

With communism stalled and the enemies of the cold war diminished, we needed something else to be against. Anti-Islamism and anti-terrorism gave us a new agenda. One twisted fear has been exchanged for another. We needed to purge the terrorist forces that attacked us. The whole world was with us when the Trade Towers came down. Major terrorist training camps in Afghanistan where targeted by our missiles. These strikes seemed justified to the U.S. and to the larger international community. Our old allies and a large part of the rest of the world supported those moves.

But much of the world was soon against us. To leave before the work in Afghanistan was done and invade a different sovereign nation was where our allies separated from us. At the time of our invasion of Iraq, that country was actually antagonistic to Osama, and Iraq was not a center for training terrorists. The United States broke international law by invading a sovereign nation that was not threatening us in any way. Even little Kuwait, which had been attacked by Iraq in the earlier war, did not feel threatened. Our invasion exacerbated hatred within the Islamists, and Iraq soon became an incubator and magnet for terrorists. That fanatical portion of Islam, which correctly recoils at the arrogance and materialism of our culture, but irrationally believes they can force people to their definition of male-dominated morality are to be sure a very real threat to the free world. The Islamists are correct when they put their finger on our national greed, arrogance, and lack of spirituality, but they are surely no better because they brutalize their women and children and drive their economies back to the Stone Age. They are dangerous, and they will undoubtedly strike our allies and us again in the future.

However, destroying major training centers and thwarting plots, contrasted to making anti-Islamism our all-consuming national mission are two very different things. The twist is in the saying that "nothing is the same since 9/11" because the saying was used as a license for illegal, abusive, and out-of-character behavior, including the killing of tens of thousands of their civilians and unacceptable detentions and abuse of prisoners. Twisted fear poisoned our national character. We will never defeat the terrorists just by killing them because there will be an endless stream constantly replenished by their warped leaders and fanatical ideology.

A tornado may be a meaningful metaphor for the twisted fear of the anti mentality. A tornado sucks up nearly all the resources in its path and chews them up by twisting turbulence. Twisted fear sucks up the resources of a person, group, or nation and leaves little left over for constructive behavior.

The depraved use of warped fear unfolded dramatically in the visit of Mr. Ahmadinejad, the President of Iran, to the United States in 2007. The national propaganda machine had so thoroughly demonized the man over several years and intensely twisted our feelings that mobs shouted, "The evil has landed!" and worse. It is true that he has said frightful and despicable things, but they should be taken seriously and in balance. Much of his rhetoric was simply smoke, intended to rankle the big country he hates and to play to the grandstands of his hawks back home. But Iranians were generally not with him and he had relatively little power. Furthermore, even though it is supposedly arch heresy to say so, he spoke some truth and had some basis for his hatred.

We have twisted the fears of our citizens by not being equally concerned about Palestinian problems as much as our concerns for Israeli. How much have we played favorites to the Israelis by supporting them with funds and armaments many times greater than our largess to the Palestinians? How little have we condemned the occupation of Israel on Palestinian land? How little have we reinforced the thirteen UN resolutions against Israeli abuses? When the Palestinians did conduct a legitimate open democratic-type election, we rejected the result (Hamas) because it did not suit our wishes and biases. We, along with Israel, further crippled the Palestinians by freezing legitimate funds after that election. There is also that thorn in the Islamism skin about our having a huge military base in their Holy Land.

It is time for the world to care for both Israel and Palestine. But in trying to stop playing favorites to Israel over Palestine, we cannot forget the centuries of suffering and pogroms of the Jewish people. Repentance on the part of Christians may never be enough. Perpetuating the myth of the Jews as "Christ killers" fostered much of the hatred and violence. The icons of Anne Frank, Schindler, and Auschwitz should be burned into the minds of every American patriot. We are saying that we will be true friends of the Jews when we are true friends of the Palestinians, supporting justice and refusing to tolerate injustice on either side. Anti-Hamas programs will fail. Equal nurturing of the two peoples is the only chance for success.

The Ahmadinejad visit revealed the degree to which our nation slid into a deep canyon of ignorance and foolishness through a manufactured tornado of twisted fear. I believe our reaction to that visit is a reason for real fear. To try for some perspective and maturity, we should consider how Nikita Khrushchev was treated in his visit to the U.S. in September of 1959. Here was the leader of the worldwide communist movement and the formal head of the rival world power to the United States with demonstrated nuclear muscle and space success. Although he condemned the atrocities of Stalinism, his people were hardly free of significant oppression. Nevertheless, he was recognized with a 21-gun salute at his arrival at Andrews Air Force Base. He was welcomed by a reception line of over 60 top officials ending in President Eisenhower. He rode with Eisenhower in an open limousine to his quarters across from the White House. He was treated to State Dinners, visited Eisenhower's private quarters, the Agriculture Department's 1,200-acre research station, and then on to Manhattan, San Francisco, and Los Angeles. He joked with the CIA chief about pooling their intelligence because "it probably came from the same source."

That was a different America. It will not work to say that the world is different today. The international mistrust and potential for violence is the same except that we do not have the USSR as a control over conflict. There is strong reason to fear the twisted fear and hatred that has been hammered into the American psyche. Hopefully, it is just one of those dark historical valleys from which we will ascend.

The basic and all-consuming question should be "What are we for?" not "What are we against?" How can we make a refreshing breeze to blow instead of releasing a devastating tornado? What were the causes that fanned communism and what are the causes that feed oxygen to the fires of Islamism? The hawks say it is utter stupidity to try to "understand them." The only thing to understand is that "if we do not kill them over there, they will kill us over here."

Nevertheless, when you hear "kill them over there before they kill you over here" and "nothing is the same since 9/11," the intent is to intimidate, engender fear, and make our citizens more willing to blindly follow the juvenile macho lines of invasion, shock and awe, "kick ass," and victory. But it is not healthy honest fear because it has been twisted and spun tight. Fear is extruded out of twisted data—propaganda. Sometimes, a whole lie, other times deceptive half truths. We were told on every opportunity that Al Qaida was in Iraq. It is certainly true that Al Qaida was in Iraq, but it was not there when we invaded. The constant coupling of al Qaida and Iraq eventually warps the mind into believing that al Qaida has always been there and, by implication, that is why we invaded. Democracy feeds on honest, open, data-based communication and policymaking.

Anti-abortion and anti-homosexuality

Anti-abortion and anti-homosexuality are two other antis that generate much heat, hatred, and hostility. It is one thing to be for life, for the dignity and sanctity of all human life, but these two antis carry much too much hatred and repulsion. To be against abortion and to stand for the protection of the unborn fetus is honorable indeed, as it is laudable to stand beside all the weak and vulnerable of the world. However to make these two issues the touchstone of absolute religious and civic truth surely falls far short of a high moral road.

If the religious right would balance their passion against abortion with equal passion for the hungry, the poor and oppressed here at home and around the world, then anti-abortion would make more sense. To be very fair, many on the so-call religious right are not single-issue believers but do practice mercy and generous giving to all those in need.

Where does the twisted hatred come from that leads to terrorizing and hanging a homosexual youth, for bombing a abortion clinic or threatening a physician with his or her life? Rigidly believing that one has a perfect grasp on eternal truth makes it more likely that one will hate those who disagree.

Lack of knowledge does us all in. If we do not know any "out-of-the-closet" homosexuals who are very normal in every way, it makes our insistence on conformity tend to persist. If we refuse to appreciate the overall belief in the sanctity of life by a person who believes abortion has some rightful place, the two sides will never be more connected. Likewise the left-leaning person must appreciate deeply how much the pro-life person feels abortion is an accurate indicator of a general loss of sanctity of life as a whole.

The sexual activity in question in the Sodom and Gomorrah story in the Old Testament was indeed homosexuality, but the much greater issue was rape, and a massive gang rape at that (Genesis Chapter 19). Two men arrive in the city and were guests in one of the houses. "All the men from every part of the city of Sodom, both young and old, surrounded the house." They said, "Bring them out to us so that we can have sex with them." Massive gang rape is what is being condemned most strongly in this story. Jesus never mentions homosexuality or abortion at all, let alone emphasizes a certain position on them as a sign of true faith. Sodomy is condemned nine times in the New Testament, and the word "homosexuality" per se is only mentioned once (I Corinthians 5:9). Saint Paul condemns homosexuality in this passage equally with adultery, theft, drunkenness, greed, and swindling.

The passage in I Corinthians 5:9 suggests we should be equally hateful (if hateful of anybody) of adulterers, and the greedy swindlers on Wall Street? Why don't we have equal hatred for the DUI driver who is often a real killer, the swindling Madoff- and Paulson-type figures who helped generously in the collapse of the world economy in late 2008 and the ubiquitous suffering that behavior showered down on the common person. Our hateful and fearful attitudes seem to say that the Madoff figure is cleaner and less dirty than one homosexual person who is not forcing sex on anybody. There is something incredibly incongruous here. Some hate-mongers and talk show people have helped to make a religion out of these two antis; they have lined their pockets richly and have fanned their egos amply by attracting a vast following.

Through conventional eyes, Romans 1:26-27 seems to be the most unequivocally harsh condemnation of "unnatural relations" of persons with same-sex partners. A careful reading of the passage reveals that relations that are " inflamed with lust" are the targets of condemnation. Heterosexual relations that are inflamed with lust are equally condemned in the Scriptures. Loving, committed, homosexual relations are not condemned in this troubling passage in Romans.

A cautionary note may be appropriate at this point. If you happen to be bound by the Christian faith, there is a commandment to "love your enemies and pray for those who despitefully use you." Even if we thoroughly despise the actions and policies of our leadership, or the leadership of the Islamists, there is no room for hatred, only room for compassion and concern for those individuals. We are just as duty bound to lucidly and forcefully critique and reject negative policies and actions wherever they are found. Unconditional positive regard for our fellows requires that we not only value a person for their inherent worth but at a more demanding level we separate the person from their acts. If we do not follow this stringent standard, we add to the hatred and hostility that is already overflowing.

Rational fear is good and can actually bring antagonists together in a common cause. But twisted fear based on deception can do nothing in the long run but corrupt, corrode, divide, and destroy.

Raison d'etre

An insight of many in the behavioral sciences is that when there is a social movement, it is an indicator that there is a significant unmet human need. This, of course, does not mean that all social movements are good and that their acts are automatically justified. And it does not overlook some movements that are largely the products of fanatical charismatic leaders, or that once a movement gets started, it may come to have a life of its own and, therefore, may be more difficult to address the potential sources of the original unrest. What is the origin and cause of the Isms? Understanding the causes and aggravations will not stop the violence of the Isms, but it will temper our selections of solutions to the problems.

Why did the American northeast become a cauldron of labor unrest and violence in the late 1800s and the early 1900s? Were workers evil insurgents and terrorists? Hardly! Why did the masses in Germany shout their allegiance to Hitler? Why did worldwide communism come into being? Why the Civil Rights marches? Why could Jim Jones and David Koresh lead so many astray? Why feminism and the broader women's movement? Why did worldwide Islamism arise (clearly, no reference to mainline Islam as such here)? Some might say, "There is no end to the string of terrible ungodly isms. Unionism, Nazism, Communism, racism, fanaticism, feminism, and, now, Islamism. What will the next dreadful ism be?"

Social movements such as these arise because there is often some legitimate fundamental need not being met. The movement itself may be inherently constructive or destructive, but it is the catalyst that I am pointing to here. Why did the movement bloom, and were there legitimate causes?

The famous industrialists at the end of the nineteenth century became very rich and powerful through oil, timber, mining, coal, coke, iron and steel, and railroads. To be sure, the Carnegies and the Fricks made a singular contribution to the industrialization of the northeast, but it was at the inexcusable expense of labor. Men worked twelve hour shifts seven days a week with a twenty-four hour shift when they rotated from day-turn to night-turn. They worked in alternately freezing and roasting mills with no safety precautions. They lost arms, legs and eyes, and, at best, were worn out at forty-five years of age. Accidents were supposedly "acts of God" and, of course, there was no money or wherewithal to take the companies to court. The catwalks in the mills were slippery and often had poor or missing guardrails; men fell into molten vats of steel and vaporized.

Apparently the men at the Homestead Mill outside Pittsburgh, Pennsylvania, were paid fairly decently for the standards of that day, but the Carnegie Company was about to cut wages. This threat, on top of all the inhumane working conditions, caused the men to resist. The Company took the initiative and clamped a lockout on the mill, brought in scab workers, and sent two barge loads of Pinkerton Guards to keep control of the Homestead Mill in 1892. The workers in mass, including their wives, violently attacked the Pinkertons and drove them back to their barges with axes, clubs, and guns. The state militia, almost always on the side of the establishment, came in and crushed the united stance of the workers. Unionism in the northeast suffered a near lethal blow and did not re-emerge in strength until two or three decades later. The workers were not evil, although they struck surprising terror in the Pinkerton Guards. There was a legitimate reason for their violence. While violence cannot be condoned, it needs to be understood. The inhumane treatment of the workers could have been addressed and ameliorated. The attack by the militia on the worker terrorists was fundamentally wrongheaded.

Keeping the focus of the book in mind, cooperation and partnering where everyone wins can never occur where fear is spun and twisted and leadership is by deception. Under those conditions trust is impossible and cooperative rational problem solving is extinct.

Understanding why people rebel, revolt, strike, or wage violence is essential if productive solutions are to be found.

What were some of the wellsprings of Nazism? What was the cause of this madness, and could the free world have done something to avert it? The focus here is the suffering of the German people after World War I. Hitler capitalized on it to usher in his depraved Third Reich. The German people were on their knees and rooting in the garbage dumps. Inflation swept the nation like a forest fire, unemployment was widespread, and the heavy reparations demanded by the victorious allies laid the national economy low. The peace Treaty of Versailles stripped Germany of some of its most productive territories as well as profitable colonial holdings. The fear of starvation and hopelessness was thick and ubiquitous. The nation was down and demoralized. Hitler took desperation and turned it into the very opposite—the belief that the fictitious Aryan German people were the superior race of the world and they would rise and rule the world for a thousand years.

People started to have hope again. In the early 1930s, Hitler's National Socialist German Workers' Party ("Nazi," key letters from the first German word of the party, *Nationalsozialistiche*) started programs to lift the spirits of the German people. Hitler developed jobs and actually provided free Mediterranean vacations. Free tickets to operas and concerts were provided on a first come basis. These luxuries were unbelievable in an era of mere subsistence.

It started so deceptively egalitarian—the poorest laborer had as much chance to draw a front seat in the theatre as the upper class person. It was a malignant ruse. By 1939, Hitler's stance had changed radically. He was lumping together socialists along with all the other supposedly less-than-human creatures, such as the retarded, homosexuals, and Jews. Many suffering Germans came to believe that these people were filth, staining the soil of the Fatherland and, therefore, had to be eliminated. Many bought his twisted vision and shared his supposed revulsion and fear of the supposed sub-humans (*untermensch*). In order to make the Fatherland safe and clean, six million Jews, even more millions of gentile Poles, and countless others were annihilated, without counting any of the military casualties. Scapegoating hatred may have been stronger in this case than fear, but when there is hatred there is often fear. Witness homophobia as an example. Racism is similar in its mixture of hatred and fear.

There was a reason that so many German citizens developed a loyalty to Hitler. The Allies, instead of seeking vengeance and reparations, could have helped the nation to rebuild and could have facilitated a new hope. Hitler would have had little chance under those conditions. It is very hard to swallow one's pride and help your former enemy. The story was so delightfully different after the WW II. The Marshall Plan took a totally different strong rebuilding tack. Likewise, our occupation of Japan after the war was more constructive than not.

Then, communism came. It was extremely difficult for hardline capitalists and extreme free market people to see that we had cultivated the soil to be receptive to communism. Rather than correct and modify some of the inequities within Czarist Russia on the one hand and the greedy abuses of capitalism on the other hand, we rather chose to fight the Red Menace with guns, bombs, and sanctions. Communism was born in Czarist Russia in 1917 and spread rather rapidly and successfully from there. It was successful in countries where there was a great disparity between a very small wealthy ruling class and the rest of the people. These countries usually had a non-benevolent dictator at the helm. Communism succeeded where there was little hope of escape from political and economic oppression.

In the case of Cuba, the United States often supported the country from the Spanish American War onward. We wanted to protect our companies' interests in sugar cane, ranching, oil refineries, and other industries, but, unfortunately, we never expressed sufficient concern for the poor masses. The dictators Machado and Batista brought some prosperity and generally favored U.S. interests so were tolerated by the States. The soil was ripe for the budding of Castro's communist revolution. When Castro took over American companies and our relations with Cuba soured, we withdrew support from Cuba. The events drove Castro into the arms of the USSR for help.

Cuba realistically feared an invasion from the United States and asked for Soviet protection, which gave Stalin a great opportunity to install missiles. The communist ideology, which values the state over the individual and replaces a Supreme Being with a Supreme Dictator, was played out fully in the bloody years of Stalin. Thousands of Stalin's opponents were summarily shot, and upwards of thirty million perished in prisons and the slave camps of Siberia.

The realistic fear became twisted when we came to concentrate on stopping communism rather that preventing it, physically fighting it instead of attacking the conditions that fostered it. It really meant that we overvalued the inherent strength of the communist ideology and failed to value the superior democratic beliefs in freedom and equality. So we became anti-communist instead of pro-humanity. We are locked into that counterproductive and totally unnecessary anti mentality with Cuba to this very day.

State communism was and is rotten on the inside. It is rotten in that it kills individual initiative. I have the indelible image in my mind of the façade of a hotel being renovated in Warsaw just as the iron curtain was coming down. The rusting scaffold had obviously been up for years. Construction activity at the site was at a snail's pace. It did not matter what an individual did, he or she could make no difference. The economy was all centrally planned and predetermined. Yes, unemployment was low or non-existent, but nobody cared. In addition to this inherent motivational disorder, there was the great distance between the salient rhetoric celebrating equality, and the excessive lifestyles of the communist elite. So in a double sense our fears were twisted. We failed to see how rotten and weak communism was, and we failed to nurture the incredible strength of true freedom and equality to address human needs.

In both racism and feminism, the suffering of second-class citizenship and the related dis-empowerment involving large portions of our population gave a lie to our claims of democracy. The myths of black inferiority and female fragility seem silly to us now, but they were devastating to blacks and women. These problems are not solved and the battles for equality will go on indefinitely, but a corner has been turned. Instead of accepting and freeing these large pools of talent, we chose for a long time to fear their competition and manufactured fears and prejudices designed to block change.

Islamism certainly has its reasons for being. Some Muslims perceived a very nasty bully nation invading one of their sovereign countries in 2003 with great force and with total disdain for international law. We uttered uncouth and ignorant remarks like "crusade, shock and awe, and kick ass" with disgusting arrogance and swagger. The bully nation shattered homes, schools, offices, industries, roads, bridges, water lines, and electric grids. We, then, boasted about rebuilding some of these things, but billions of dollars were unaccounted for, and Iraqi labor was barred. We annihilated some hundred thousand innocent men, women and children. We did this in the name of cherished family values, freedom, and democracy.

An Iraqi may have put it in these words, given their perspective: "My two sons were on their way home from school and were dreadfully and fatally mangled by a U.S. bomb. My husband's arm is no good since being hit by a random gunshot. Sometimes we have a few hours of electricity, and have to carry water from several blocks away if it is available. We are often hungry and dirty most of the time. There is no work anywhere. The foreign contractors will not even consider our men. There is very little hope. Our daughter talks about making something of herself—becoming a holy bomber. Some of the American soldiers seem to be ok; they play with the children and give them good things. Saddam Hussein was terrible but life under him was good as long as you kept your mouth shut. We had everything. Now we have nothing. My older brother is a lawyer and has fled to Syria with a million others. Our neighbors have both escaped to Jordan. Now it seems like the occupation will last a long time, and if they ever do leave, our best and brightest people have gone. We just hope to make it through today."

These words could very well be those of the moderate rational believer, or even a secular citizen. Imagine how much worse this message would be when magnified and inflamed by the extreme fanaticism of the Islamists.

Twisting the truth at the microcosm

It may be easier to see and accept the twisting of truth at national and international levels. It is not as easy close to home. But twisting also happens destructively at home and at the job. The principles of cooperation apply at both the macrocosmic and the microcosmic level. The smaller level may be the more important level in that we have direct responsibility and some direct degree of control.

Take a child who is having some academic trouble in school and the father is doing some pretty heroic tutoring of the child at home because of having more free time than the mother. The tutoring parent, the father, has a conference with the teacher and is disappointed that things are still not going well. The father then misleads the other marriage partner that Johnny is doing "pretty well." The other partner finds out later that she has been mislead by her husband. Bad feelings emerge. It is not entirely different from the United States government telling the people that we were winning the war in Vietnam, only to find out later that that was not the case. The result of that deception was the demise of President Johnson and disillusionment in the whole nation that we never really got over.

Family finances are common grounds for deception, especially if one spouse is totally in control of the resources and little sharing of information occurs. As a spouse starts to realize something is more and more strained and mysterious about the family's finances, the controller may block information and/or twist what is revealed to make it look more promising than it really is. Whether the controlling member is squandering resources for some clandestine purpose, such as gambling, or is just inept in monetary management and has kept it secret for a long time, it is bound to generate hostility and threaten the marriage when the truth emerges. It is critical for both spouses to know the truth about their accounts so that they can constantly live within their means or go into debt wide-eyed with both members understanding the risks. Only in this manner can the couple cooperate and partner fully with each other to solve their problems as they meet them. Openness allows the possibility of pursuing reasonable challenging projects and ambitions. Secrecy, distortion, deception, twisting, and spinning, on the other hand, erode and rot a relationship.

A very busy spouse may tell the other that they filled out the college financial aid papers for their son or daughter when they really just completed half of them. The recipient of this information may assume that the forms have been submitted only to learn a month later that they are actually still not quite completed. If the end result is that their son or daughter receives less financial aid, the one spouse may blame the other for the delay and may be embittered by the deception. Trust, which is critical in a close relationship, is eroded and the couple becomes less able to withstand the next test that they face in the future.

Whether at the micro level or macro level, name-calling as a substitute for mature conversation and negotiation is another way of twisting the truth. Throwing derogatory names at one's spouse or child blocks communication and increases the distance between the parties. To call people savages, racially loaded terms, dumb, lazy, treacherous, terrorists, insurgents, guerillas, pinkos, feminazis, satanists, infidels, and heretics is to hide whatever might be inferior in the name-caller as well as whatever is human or good in the person being castigated. Furthermore, it drives the person being castigated away and into the arms of the other side. Name calling stops thinking, hides information about the other side, and ensures destruction.

The fuel for twisted fear: hatred and prejudice

Negative prejudging and stereotyping often form a basis for discriminating against people and treating them unequally and inequitably. Some argue that prejudice is a fairly modern phenomenon. The argument contends that in pre-modern times strong groups or nations simply took from others by force whatever they wanted without giving any excuse. But in modern times when we are supposed to be more civilized, we need a justification when we take other peoples' lands or coffers. Today, we need justifying myths when we lord it over others. Prejudices generate hate and are, in turn, sustained by hate.

There will always be wars and rumors of wars, and there will always be deception, twisting, and spinning. The world is often described in literary terms as being broken, and inhabited by men and women with feet of clay. Christianity expresses this dark side of the human condition as sin and evil. But we know enough today to lessen conflict and suffering significantly. Dispersing the fog of nationalism at the larger level and ego at the personal level and gaining a will to cooperate and partner more will point us in the right direction.

★★★

King Abdullah II of Jordan. 2011. *Our Last Best Chance: The Pursuit of Peace in a Time of Peril*. Great Britain: Clays Ltd, St Ives plc.

Rogers, Jack. 2009. *Jesus, the Bible, and Homosexuality: Expose the Myths, and Heal the Church*. Louisville, Kentucky: Westminster Knox Press.

Chapter 4: Superordinate Goals

THE DIRECT CONTACT model of conflict reduction, which is the cord that ties this whole book together, relies heavily on the concepts of equality and cooperation. The kind of cooperation focused on in this chapter is the kind required when it takes two sides to reach an overarching goal, one bigger that either side can accomplish alone. The contrasting approaches of competition and independence each has its legitimate place and receives more than its share of attention in American culture. Cooperation and negotiation, on the other hand, are frequently seen as weak and, therefore, inferior. Chamberlin's selling out the West in World War II negotiations is indelibly printed on many of our minds.

The truth would seem to argue that cooperation should be rated far higher than it is. The interdependence and connectedness of all life should point us away from over reliance on the masculine, in-dependent, shoot-first-and-ask-questions-later mentality. Without the living microbes under our eyelids and in our digestive tract, humans would be in agony and probably not live very long. We now have the insight that when we take a regimen of antibiotics to kill microbes, we may need to follow up with probiotics to restore the benign microbes. Take one animal out of the predator/prey web of life and imbalances occur. Reduce the wolf population and rodents run rampant. Disregard the critical functions of the coastal marshes to accommodate development and a whole series of ecological mal-functions emerge.

In human affairs, cooperation allows groups to support each other instead of tearing each other apart. Cooperation often enables solu-tions to problems otherwise beyond hope. Instead of seeing cooper-ation as weak, it should be embraced for its strengths. It may require more maturity and skill to follow this path than the old rough-and-tough frontier mentality.

Another roadblock on the way to cooperation is a lack of vision and imagination. When planning and action are buried in a deep rut of thoughtless habit, new horizons are obscured. Imagination and far sightedness can open up far bigger things and better things than ingrown constricted boxes.

It should be noted that direct contact theories were explicitly designed to reduce animosity, hostility, and hatred or prejudice between groups. That is, to de-categorize. The goal is to take workers and bosses, who have inhabited two separate categories for a long time and integrate them into one category—humans. What we are showing, however, is that many of these principles of direct contact are applicable to problem solving in general.

Conflict is common between individuals in the same group or between two or more groups. In the smallest unit of society, two intelligent and generally like-minded marriage partners will have disagreements and differences. Prospects for reducing conflict are enhanced when two disagreeing persons or groups realize they have a problem that neither can solve separately. Sometimes, it is a common enemy that neither side can handle alone. Antagonists may entertain reconciliation when they know that they face a problem that is too unwieldy for either one to overcome.

Remember in the Robber's Cave study in Chapter 1, the two antagonistic groups of boys in the summer camp, the Rattlers and the Eagles, each separately tried to push the water truck to get it started to go into town for a supply of drinking water. Neither side had enough muscle to budge the truck and get it started. By joining forces, they were able to get water and slake their Oklahoma thirst. The superordinate goal, one that neither side could achieve alone, was securing drinking water. The means to the water was getting the truck started. Through pushing together some consciousness started to occur that they did not need to hate each other. If we are working together and it is getting us ahead, we must like to work together.

Behavior apart from initial belief is not always superficial. Behavior can be profound; it leads to new beliefs. This model of learning complements the old classical one that we learn ideas or beliefs first and they lead to behavior.

A community organizer, Saul Alinsky, used to say that "a deal is based on a common need, you care for the other guy when you need him." This is hardly altruistic motivation, but it is often very realistic. Reconciliation has a good chance of occurring when we realize that we need each other.

For superordinate goals to be effective they must be triggered by a mutually perceived threat that is very real, substantial, and undisputed. The goal must be seen as having a very good chance of succeeding. When antagonists fail to reach an over-arching goal, they tend to come to hate each other even more and blame each other for the failure.

What must follow after a clearly and mutually perceived threat has been agreed upon? How is the situation moved from a threat to a goal? Once antagonists perceive a problem fully shared by both sides and well beyond the scale for either side to solve, a search for a common cooperative solution would seem to be the next logical step. Not so. It is commonly thought so, but that is a great error. Before moving quickly from threat or sensing a problem to go on and seek a solution, one must stop and be certain all parties are defining the threat the same way. Different definitions or framings of the same factual problem can be so diverse as to make any movement toward solution unlikely.

The primacy of problem definition

In a participative approach to management, at this juncture, the leader needs an open conversation about how to define the problem. What are the variables and the parameters to be included in the problem? Take the problem of obesity and its impact on heart disease. This is obviously a complex and many faceted problem. We need to simplify in order to illustrate the power of defining the problem. If you were on a national sub-commission limited just to the issue of the consumption of red meat (your task is further limited to cattle only) and its fatty content connected to the undesirable type of cholesterol, how should the problem be defined? Would not all the following be possible legitimate definitions:

1) There is no control over the breeds of cattle entering the market having higher fatty tissue rather than lean.
2) There is no control over breeding beef cattle for lower fat content.
3) There is no legislation or incentive to start substituting buffalo for beef cattle.
4) We do not have an adequate national education program to educate people to eat less beef.
5) There is no educational program to teach people to radically drain and squeeze the grease from cooked beef.

Imagine how radically different the problem might be defined depending on the individual's commercial or civic interests. A beef grower and processor might dismiss the problem entirely or suggest cooking and preparation techniques are at fault. A buffalo grower and promoter would make a definition to further the growth of that industry. A public health official might opt for the lack of education. Forcing the definition will probably not be politically possible and will not gain the full cooperation of the various constituencies. A total ban on beef conceivably could be possible some day if there emerges a mass consciousness as in the case of the recent non-smoking trend. But this is very unlikely.

If family relations are strained because one spouse, let's say the wife, is away on business much of the time, the nature of the problem needs further definition. What is the exact nature of the deficiency or complaint? Is she a good communicator when at home but negligent when she is away? Is she preoccupied even when she is at home and out of touch with the family dynamic? When she is home, does she try to compensate for her absences by being overly possessive, overly controlling, or overly permissive? These hypothetical definitions of the problem represent very different problems and certainly point to different goals and solutions. Trying to force one definition on the wife will be counterproductive. Neither spouse knows enough for a unilateral decision. Forcing a decision will disempower and insult the dignity of the other person. The definition needs to be worked out in a way that both sides feel fully supported to articulate whatever might be involved. Because this kind of truth seeking is potentially threatening, building trust and long-term strength of the relationship is critical before beginning to define the problem in an open manner.

Contrived superordinate goals

The Robber's Cave camping study and a study by Cook (1970) about running a simulated railroad were both contrived in the sense that they were field experiments. The superordinate goal in the Cook study was to run the railroad smoothly and efficiently and to create positive feelings between white and black participants. The Cook study was impressive because the participants worked at the simulated task several full days, and it was conducted at a southern university at a time when racial interactions were taboo. The goals in the camping study were to reconcile two groups of boys that had been experimentally influenced to dislike each other. Even though contrived, these studies meet the standards of the model in that the goals must be substantial, realistic, and have a good chance of realizing success.

Outward Bound experiences have goals that meet the above requirements and approximate real life problems more fully. The activities are typically rappelling, crossing a dangerous body of water, swamp, or desert. The Outward Bound approach takes individuals from two frequently opposing groups such as white and black, labor and management, design and manufacturing departments and places them in a survival experience. Rappelling is commonly used. The superordinate goal is for all members of the small group to get to the top of the cliff safely. All climbers are novices and would not be able to make the climb alone. The task becomes possible only when members support each other with interdependent lines or ropes. If one person should slip the others serve as a safety net. A complementary superordinate goal is to get to a food drop at the top and be able to make dinner and to get the tents and gear to stay overnight. One's safety and life depends on everyone faithfully following the climbing procedures together and the necessity of taking a chance on trusting each other. The task inherently requires full cooperation of all the members regardless of prior affiliation, status differences, and prejudices. Everyone becomes functionally equal during the task.

Superordinate goals presenting themselves naturally

The goals we could be working on are endless. Impediments like pride, greed, lack of knowledge, short-term thinking, and a lack of vision and imagination block the way. One political party claims to champion family values and infers that the other party does not care; they both obviously care about family at some level, but to cooperate would seem to diminish the family values plank of one party. Cooperation on education, science, employment, business reforms, and scarcity of natural resources could have great potential.

Marriage and family goals

Take a hypothetical example of a husband who is a sales representative for a pharmaceutical company. He makes moderately good money and has good benefits, but his personal vehicle is old with high mileage and increasing repair bills; it is critical to maintain his income. The problem is his car is unreliable. They have worked out a system where he pays for certain specific family expenses and she pays for the others. There is no way he can afford a new or even good used car out of his salary alone and still pay his share of the family expenses. She certainly cannot come up with the monthly funds to replace his car.

However, by each person's curtailing some discretionary items and combining funds for the car, they will be able to purchase a replacement. They both expect some increase in salaries in a year or so. Acquiring a reliable car is a superordinate goal because neither spouse can afford it by themselves. The car is critical to their common well being, and it will be possible by combining sacrifices and resources. If there are children involved, they can play an important role in making this kind of cooperation work; they need to be included in every step of the process to some degree, depending on their age and maturity. When there is little family cooperation, cohesion breaks down, hostility builds up, and, unless addressed, a breakup or even separation and divorce may occur.

Education

Early education is finally getting on state and national agenda more substantially. President Obama has been calling attention to it, and the Mayor of New York City is boldly sticking out his neck to support it with a 5% tax on residents with incomes over a half a million. Current research reports show that Head Start helps underprivileged children catch up significantly, but they seem to lose the cognitive gains by the time they reach third grade. An encouraging finding is that long-range benefits have been documented: more pursue higher education, are more fully employed, and have a more positive relationship with the law than those not exposed to Head Start. Estimates of financial benefits to the nation rage from 3-to-11 dollars return for every dollar put into early education.

After-school activities are usually inadequate in lower economic neighborhoods. Part-time summer employment has shrunken. Too many youths with no constructive activities are likely to be involved in destructive behaviors, misdemeanors, felonies and permanent scarring. If small communities cannot afford indoor cold weather activities and sports centers, a coalition of communities may be able to convince foundations or governmental agencies to find financing. Often, there is no vision beyond one's own limited horizon. Funding agencies pay attention when imaginative, cooperative, and well-constructed plans are submitted. These are illustrative of superordinate goals.

Technical and vocational training has received less funding over the last few decades because the training was not always geared to the changes in the market place, and more and more youth were directed toward college. Pittsburgh had two fine vocational high schools several decades ago. An entirely new national venture, Year Up, is having good success in taking at-risk, underprivileged youth, specifically, and putting them through an intense year of boot-camp-like basic education. Year Up shows that we could save many of our youth from being wasted and, at the same time, help our businesses. Year Up has a 75% success rate of youth completing the program and being placed successfully.

The school-to-prison pipeline shuttles kids from school to prison for bad behavior rather than crime. It is good for the lucrative prison industry but inhumane for our youth. There are as many black kids in prison today as in college classrooms, and there are as many blacks in the criminal justice pipeline as there were in slavery during the 1850s. We are putting about as much money into prisons as we put into higher education. Black youth are imprisoned about 10 times more than whites for the same drug charge. These are festering and unconscionable injustices. Wasting 15 billion of our youth in poverty should cry out as a superordinate goal for our nation, a problem requiring maximum cooperation. Most poor youth will never have the opportunity to advance.

Colleges, universities, and governmental research agencies are being underfunded increasingly in the national budget. Research drives innovation and application in business and industry. There are great examples of universities cooperating closely with business and industry often creating start-up companies. Carnegie Mellon and the University of Pittsburgh are major examples where superordinate goals are being tackled in applied research. The University of Pittsburgh's membership in America Makes (a 3-D manufacturing institute) places it in partnership with government, private industry, and other research institutions. Claims for 3-D manufacturing may prove to be a bit too enthusiastic, but this particular partnership gets kudos for imagination and stellar cooperation.

Cutting edge brain research is another example making news as a widely shared venture. The Martinos Center for Biomedical Imaging in Boston is a joint project of Harvard University, MIT, and Massachusetts General Hospital. Fine-grained images of the brain reveal an overall grid like structure similar to lower animals but immensely more elaborated. At the deeper molecular level, six humans have been mapped showing 20,000 protein-coding genes. This represents a mass of data collected in one electronic site called the Allen Brain Atlas. The Atlas is available to researchers around the world in a wide-open spirit of cooperation. The brains are from recently deceased people, and the seed money of some 29 million came from one wealthy donor.

On a radically smaller scale, and in a far more humble context, the collaborative student/faculty research in liberal arts colleges is an outstanding model of tackling superordinate goals. At many fine liberal arts colleges, a continuous two-semester piece of empirical research is required as a capstone study, that is, a final demonstration of scholarship. Faculty and students work on these projects as a team. Faculty in liberal arts colleges have full-time teaching loads with very limited time for research. Students, on the other hand, have scheduled time and structure, but are lacking in experience and knowledge. By students' searching and organizing the research literature on topics, spending the hours necessary to collect data in the lab or in the field and then investing more time in analysis, and by the faculty giving a relatively minimal amount of time, but watching and guiding with a critical eye, incredible products are generated and realized. The status of a faculty member and a student is very unequal formally, but very close to being equal functionally. In fact, a student will come to know some things about the topic that a faculty member may only know at a distance. A nice example of a recent senior study that was both rigorous academically and commercially relevant was "Precipitating barium and strontium from Marcellus shale produced water." Both agents could be environmentally harmful, but commercially profitable, and the study was a small step to treating these two elements more soundly. Neither faculty nor students could complete this kind of research without dynamic teamwork (see Murtaugh).

Cooperative learning made visible inroads in elementary and secondary education over the last several decades. The definition of the supcrordinate goal in this movement is more abstract. Apparently it is that all children will learn better and more, especially, by working together and developing group skills. The reward structure in public education has been either independent (all students theoretically could achieve any grade) or competitive (only so many could get As, graded on a curve). Independent and competitive reward structures prevailed in public education for a long time and precluded cooperative structures. Some of the cooperative learning models have come directly from the kind of research reported in this book.

Overarching goals for business and industry

The examples of productive cooperation among businesses, government, and private research firms cited above in the section on education should be models for business and industry generally. Johnson and Johnson recently announced that they were making all of the data from their clinical trials available to researchers anywhere. This is unheard of and commendable. Proprietary possessiveness usually blocks cooperation that can lead to better and cheaper pharmaceuticals. The Marcellus shale industry fights hard not to disclose proprietary mix of chemicals used in the fracking process regardless of the potential threat to natural water sources. There was a time when Levi Strauss Company arranged for their denim suppliers to be tapped directly into that portion of their computing system that logged daily sales, item by item, across the company. The free access to daily sales data helped both Levi Strauss and the suppliers to better complement each other's needs.

But cooperation and vital innovation is overshadowed by greed and power. One of the fathers of free enterprise, Adam Smith, surprisingly warned against greed. The spirit of the anti-trust laws was to curb excesses within the capitalistic system. This need was clearly recognized as far back as the Sherman Act of 1890, the Clayton Act, and the inauguration of the Federal Trade Commission in 1914.

If we needed business constraints, then, in a somewhat simpler world, how much more do we need controls now? In response to the national and international financial depression of 2009, the Dodd-Frank Wall Street Reform and Consumer Protection Act was passed in 2010. It is doubtful whether it is enough or whether it can be enforced. Opposing parties are endlessly trying either to gut it or strengthen it. At least, it shows the need for balancing powers. The larger financial zeitgeist is the law of the jungle. In 2012, the head of Boeing made 20 million, and the overall ratio of executive to average worker pay was 314 to 1. Meanwhile, the workers were forced to take nearly no wage increase in the long term, reduction in health insurance, and a pension freeze. Over at Oracle the pay ratio was 1,287 to 1, at General Electric, 491 to 1, at AT&T, 339 to 1 and Lockheed Martin, 351 to 1. (*New York Times*, February 3, 2014, page A19) Partly as a result of this kind of greed and blindness at the top, the middle class that drives economic demand is diminishing significantly. VPs and next layer of executives share the greed of the CEOs such that the 1% or so represents a sizeable number of people taking resources from the people below them. Perhaps, more devastating is that this greed also means that money is diverted from building and developing the companies.

Regulating giant international businesses may never be possible any more by the countries of their origin alone. Countries are afraid that international laws may threaten their national sovereignty. The United States ignored international law regarding the use of unprovoked military force in Iraq. It will be difficult to change attitudes, but that is what may occur in the long term. We may need enforcement by many nations combined to control some of the behemoth international business enterprises that are usurping the power of nations. For example, international companies threaten to sue governments for interfering with total business freedom.

We have allowed gigantic firms like American International Group (AIG) to evolve to the point where it threatens much of the global economic stability, as seen in the 2009 depression. It is like having a nation within a nation and spread across many other nations. AIG insures nearly 200,000 businesses and corporate entities. It has over 100,000 employees in 130 countries from the United States to Europe and through Asia. It supplies insurance to U.S. municipalities' pension funds, and provides protection for many 401 (k) plans. This company owns properties in 50 countries and operates 950 airline jets. At least many, if not a majority of economists, contend that its failure would set off intolerable de-stabilizing consequences around the world. It is too big to fail. International policing and regulating efforts have lacked teeth for the most part in the past. The day may come when more imaginative world leaders devise an overarching way to cooperate.

The AIG example indicates the broader international task of imagining new economic forms. Are there new creative ways to regulate and moderate the most vicious forms and practices of capitalism without vitiating the incentives of free agents? And which of the old correctives have we forgotten and need to revitalize?

Natural resources, water especially

Our Great Lakes go through cycles of pollution, clean up, and subsequent pollution again. One of these cycles unfolded in the 1970s. Raw steel and steel production was active in the industrial center around Gary, Indiana, and across the waters 200 miles away in Sudbury, Canada, as well. Many pollutants were dumped into Lake Erie by American mills that eventually polluted the shores of southern Ontario. Likewise the Sudbury mills were dumping into Lake Huron pollutants that eventually reached the eastern shores of Michigan. Air pollution from these sites was another problem that we shared in common between the two countries. Lakes Huron and Erie are basically separate, but air space across the two countries has no barriers. Air pollution and acid rain was freely shared across the boarders. Companies like Diamond Shamrock in the Cleveland area demonstrated that by capturing polluting agents profitable by-products could be realized. The oil contaminated Cuyahoga River, known to have caught fire, became a refuge where bird and fish returned when it was cleaned up.

Contemporary pollution in China would seem too distant from the States and of little immediate concern to us. Yet, it is of immediate concern to us. Environmental scientists tell us that Chinese particulates and toxins can be reliably detected on our west coast 7 days from the time the air currents move them off the Chinese mainland and that 10% of the pollution on the California coast comes from China.

Extended droughts, unusual to an area, can displace millions and cause suffering, stress, and social unrest. One hundred million farmers in northern Syria have recently been forced to abandon their dried up farms and flee south into a country, causing great civil turmoil. Climate change is entering the conversations in Syria even when energies are consumed with the civil war. In our own country, we have overbuilt in arid lands. When extended droughts occur in California, as they are now, the flow of the Colorado River is overtaxed and water becomes a source of conflict. The great city of Phoenix grew up out of a desert with little thought about limited water. It would seem that extensive regional planning and controlled development is a crying need.

Unless technology can eventually and economically produce desalinated water from our oceans, the national and world water problems will increase. It is amazing that as far back as the 1950s Israel was moving far ahead in water management, both acquisition and conservation. In 1962 when a major earthquake killed more than 12,000 people in Iran and destroyed their wells and water system, Israel came to their aid by drilling state-of-the-art artesian wells and building water systems. Also amazing is the fact that Israel was so far ahead in desalination that they not only met their own demands but also were able to build dozens of desalination plants for Iran beginning in 1968. (Today Israel desalinates over 50% of its water supply.) This cooperation between Israel and Iran abruptly ended with the revolution in 1979, which ushered in the anti-Western lurch toward a theocracy under Sharia law. Had the American CIA and the British M16 not launched the *coup d'état* to overthrow the democratically elected Mosaddegh back in 1953 Israel and Iran might still be working together and Mid-Eastern history may have unfolded differently.

We have already come a long way along the road of water demand and costs. If someone said they were going to sell water fifty ears ago most people would have laughed. It is free and it belongs to the public, right? Not any more. About ten years ago Bechtel, the giant international construction company, was well on its way to buying the water supply for a town in Bolivia called Cochabamba. The peasants could not afford the water rates and feared the rates would be increased even more. The peasants revolted in mass, barricading the streets and bringing the city to a halt; Bechtel relented and departed. Fresh water supplies need to be on the international agenda of superordinate goals.

Employment and economically useless people

How to regain purpose in life for the massive sea of marginal people around the world should be receiving our endless attention. It seems unrealistic and utopian to suggest it for the world agenda at this point. Millions are useless economically, supernumeraries, excess humans. The very young and the very old are most affected. We live in a day when so much can be made so well by so few in such a short period of time that a lot of people are simply not needed. Societies will always need service functions, and the conditions of these could be improved, but automation and robotization will shrink employment even further in this category. Worldwide support of schools, training centers, universities, and internships might strategically replace half of our 160 some military colonies around the world. In our own country, it is high time for public education to replace prisons and time for the country to investigate a whole new category of vocations and jobs.

Surely, capitalism can be enriched and humanized enough to build in ways to utilize all our people and to create meaningful vocations that would offer some dignity to life. Unemployment in marginal U.S. groups is double or more than the national average, and unemployment around the world is often over 50%. That spells huge trouble and a real threat to our national security. Scarcity is not so much the problem as allocation and priorities in our abundant nation. We have the will to power. We have the will to wealth. Someday we may move toward the will to be human and to live more humanely in terms of finding a useful life for all people. Utopian? Unrealistic? Some effort to move in the right direction is not too much to expect.

Global Warming and Health Care

The overwhelming majority of scientists agree on the evidence that substantial and ongoing global warming is occurring. Naysayers point to a few select instances where the opposite is happening. This should be not surprising in something so complex. The body of science is also agreed that the rate of increase of this phenomenon is more alarming than previously thought. Two major reports in the spring of 2014 ratcheted up the intensity of the alarm substantially (one by the UN and one by the American Association for the Advancement of Science).

Crop loss is already resulting from erratic temperature patterns, and fish and wild life are showing disturbed patterns. Even though the oceans have risen only a little over 3 inches in the last twenty years, the trend is inexorable and the rate of rising is increasing. Poor people in the undesirable low lying coastal areas will suffer most and most quickly. All poor people, having limited resources and limited mobility, will suffer disproportionately. Our whole national economy and world economies will become radically unsettled. Food supplies, water supplies, and overall health conditions will be challenged. Poor people more than ever will need good national health care.

We desperately need good national and international coopera- tion on these major issues. Unfortunately, the wealthy of our nation have so effectively propagandized a good segment of the population into total disregard of the scientific evidence that progress has been stalled. Propaganda disparages any long-term responsibility for the commonweal. There are ways to address carbon emissions, and there are serious legislators and scientists presently pursuing lucid proposals. One serious proposal called "cap and dividend" would auction carbon permits that indeed would increase consumer prices substantially, but the income generated from the permits would be returned to every citizen in generous dividends (see James K. Boyce).

In a similar positive vein, high quality national health care could be achieved and at a lower price if we could work together (see T. R. Reid). Mr. Reid visited several developed countries and actually used their health services as an international guest. He found single-payer national health insurance in France, Germany, Japan, England, and even in India, to be quite adequate to meet health needs at about half the price of our pre-Affordable Care Act costs. Various reports indicate that overhead costs among major HMOs may run as high as 13% or more; whereas, Medicare and Medicaid may be as low as 3%.

Cultural exchanges and modeling aid cooperative problem solving

In 1989, just before midnight and the official demolition of the Berlin Wall, Leonard Bernstein led an ethnically mixed concert com- posed of members from both sides of the Wall in Beethoven's *Fifth*. It was a deeply moving occasion showing the common bonds of all people, even though their governments are often incapable of such a unified and uplifting expression. In 2014, Pittsburgh Symphony was planning a concert in Iran but it has been put on hold. This will be our first major cultural exchange since the concert by the same group in

1964, which was before the 1979 revolution and the 444 days of holding U.S. hostages. These events may not change history in a dramatic leap, but they lessen tensions, reassert our common humanity, and provide a model for more lasting cooperation and finding superordinate peaceful goals. These events model approach instead of attack.

Simple modeling should not be discounted to help increase cooperative behavior. A supermarket study in an area where many carts were discarded anywhere after being emptied by customers showed that if one person returned her cart to a holding area, it doubled the returns by others. Groups and individuals are always being watched. Even individuals who may feel insignificant are making an investment in the human bank of development or destruction depending on what they model.

Surely there is no scarcity of challenges that cry out for cooperative efforts by people who do not always agree. Imagination is needed to formulate solutions in cooperative terms, and then the will is needed to follow through.

★★★

Boyce, James K. 2013. *Economics, the Environment, and Our Common Wealth.* Cheltenham.UK: Edward Elgar Publishing Limited.

Gray, David B. 1985. *Ecological Beliefs and Behaviors: Assessment and Change.* Westport, Connecticut: Greenwood Press. Common insights into the biological basis of the connectedness of all life and the need for a more pervasive understanding of cooperation, in Chapter 1.

Miller, N., and Brewer, M. B. 1984. *Groups in Contact: The Psychology of Desegregation.* New York: Academic Press. Two of the leading early researchers in this country on the shared coping or direct contact model.

Murtaugh, Danielle. 2014. *Use of Experimental Design to Minimize Coprecipitation Of Barium and Strontium from Produced Water from Marcellus Shale.* Undergraduate senior research. Westminster College, New Wilmington, Pennsylvania.

Reid, T. R. 2009. *The Healing of America: A Global Quest for a Better, Cheaper, and Fairer Health Care.* New York: Penguin Books. Convincing international evidence about the advantages of single payer health insurance.

Smith, Douglas K. February 3, 2014. A New Way to Rein In Fat Cats. *New York Times.* He proposes a salary ceiling for all governmental employees and all firms doing business with the government.

Worchel, Stephen, and Austin, W. G. 1986. The Role of Cooperation in Reducing Intergroup Conflict. In *Psychology of Intergroup Relations.* Chicago: Nelson-Hall. A clear read on reducing barriers between groups.

Zimmer, Carl. February 2014. Secrets of the Brain. *National Geographic.* Full color photos of upper level grid structures of mass orderly connections as well as photos of chaotic patterns at the deep molecular level. A similar report appeared in *Science*, November 1, 1014.

PART II

Rules, Compliance, and Independence

A LEADER WHO wishes to bring antagonists together in working teams must believe strongly in the rule or norm of cooperation and must exemplify it in his or her actions. The norm of cooperation is facilitated by open social and physical structures; whereas, closed structures will vitiate cooperation. Furthermore, the structural effects will be far more powerful than individual independence for the majority of people in most situations. However, individuals who have deeply internalized and integrated belief patterns rise above structural determinants much of the time.

Chapter 5 Norms Supporting Cooperation

Chapter 6 The Effect of Structures on Conformity and Independence

Chapter 7 Individual Strength and Independent Behavior

Chapter 5: Norms, Rules

NORMS ARE RULES that groups live by. They are not necessarily written, but are often very binding. A norm of an urban gang may be that "we do not rat on each other ever," or, "if a member of another gang disses one of us, that's time to kill." And the more one identifies with his or her group, the more the internal compulsion and the external group pressure will be to adhere to the norm.

The norms for different kinds of car manufacturers might be comfort and luxury or style and muscle, or economy and reliability. A fast food firm might value taste and price, but speed may be the paramount norm. A paint manufacturer might develop the mentality that "we make the most durable and lasting outdoor paint." Thus, durability would be the norm. A family may declare that members do not hit. Members help. Businesses may rule that they maximize profits and minimize all else. Or the monthly bottom line is all that counts.

A leader's commitment to a norm

One of the criteria in the overall model for everyone's winning is that the boss or leader must truly believe in the norms of the group or in the norms that he is trying to establish for a group. He or she cannot fake it and cannot be hypocritical. If a machine shop is to be known for its precision, then the boss can never approve a product to ship out unless its tolerances are perfect. Otherwise, the workers quickly get the idea that precision is just a sales slogan and not really the rule. The leader of the group must really believe in and have a deep commitment to the norm of the group. Martin Luther King, Jr.'s norm in the civil rights groups he led was justice. His belief in that norm was unwavering. He was willing to go to jail and face threats to his life and the life of his family. So, when he quoted the Old Testament (Amos 5:24) and proclaimed, "Let justice roll down like mighty waters," all people knew that was the rule he lived by. His fellow demonstrators were then willing to be beaten, jailed, and killed for the rule, the norm.

The author's father was a farmer with a very strong work ethic. I think his basic norm, which he followed and taught his family, was "hard work." The work was sometimes hard, dirty and dusty over long hours, but at other times, pleasant. Hard work was simply a way of life. Yes, hard work was instrumental in raising good crops; they, in turn, sustained the family, plus earned him recognition in the larger community. There were certainly times for fun on the farm and in the family, but that was icing on the cake, as it were. The cake, the real stuff of life, was work. If he had preached hard work but had been lazy, the norm would not have been effective.

Some of the rules that families have are really norms. If the parents are dead set on things like, "We do not hit, we do not cheat, and we stick together," we are talking about norms. And if the children have internalized these rules, then they are norms the family lives by. The rules will have to be discussed and will often be strongly challenged; this will help the children see their value and will help to internalize them. But beyond that, the norms are not negotiable.

Frequently there is one word that captures the essence of a group's norm. For the political right, it is *austerity;* defund the government and let private interests move freely in the supposedly free market place (a market place ruled by the 1% who have the wealth and power). For the political left, the word is *invest;* fund the government so it can help to rebuild a frayed country.

The word *ubuntu* signals the ancient attitude and behavior of the Xhosa people of South Africa and the legacy of Nelson Mandela. Translations often leave much to be desired. Sampson in his biography (page 12) of Mandela says *ubuntu* means mutual responsibility and compassion. Bishop Tutu elaborates by saying, "It refers to gentleness, compassion, to hospitality, to openness to others, to vulnerability to be available to others and to know that you are bound up with them in the bundle of life." *Ubuntu* conjures up interdependence and cooperation rather than the modern mentality of independence and competition. Also a starting point for this ancient way was to see the best in other people. This frame of mind was radically shaken by the intrusion of the modern western world, although never lost entirely. Apparently, the definitions of *ubuntu* in this paragraph capture quite a bit of the norm that guided Mandela, the ANC, and their achievements.

President Obama seems to leave a confusing trail in regard to any overarching norm. It seems to be a norm of looking good from a progressive perspective. He promised transparency and openness, but he strengthened the intrusive Patriot Act, spied on our trusted allies, and threatened whistle blowers as much as or more severely than prior presidents. He received the Nobel Peace prize for conciliatory rhetoric followed by the expansion of a wrong-headed war in Afghanistan. He has stuck his neck far out on the Affordable Care Act which should help many thousands not previously insured and has frequently affirmed fairness and an even playing field. In his second term, he has more boldly declared that inequality is the defining issue of the times; how hard and how effectively he will fight for these will eventually be known.

The psychology department at Westminster College, a small liberal arts college in western Pennsylvania, instituted a required two-semester continuous senior research project over three decades ago. When the requirement was instituted the norm among the students was rejection, "We sure do not want that." The study had to be either a rigorous empirical experiment, or, at least, a systematic measurement of critical variables within a formal model containing predictions. There was considerable latitude of venue, either in the laboratory or in the field. Broad application studies were allowed. Advanced statistical analyses and conclusions were reported in a formal written paper and presented orally to the department in the form of a mini-science conference.

There is a strong tradition (an area norm) of this activity among the colleges in western Pennsylvania. At an area undergraduate psychology conference, students demonstrate speaking and presentation skills. They get to compare their performances with other competitive schools. After about two years of this work, students at Westminster no longer questioned senior studies, but asked, "What will my senior project be?" The students saw the merits of independent research with all the logistic, analytic, and reporting skills it entailed. Senior studies became the norm. The chair and the lead faculty members were fully committed to an activity, which was obvious to the rest of the faculty and students. The faculty fully embraced the new norm. This raises the question of how to change norms which is a different topic and beyond the scope of this book, but it is largely a group issue and not an individual one.

There is a most unusual contemporary evangelical Christian leader who gives voice to the belief that the church is responsible to act politically, but not partisan, to call the nation to care for the least of these. Jim Wallis leads a following that subscribes to the *Sojourner Magazine* and encourages national legislators to support the poor. He led a several day hunger strike in 2012 when federal benefits where threatened. His group also produced a DVD of the story of four poor families and hand delivered a copy to each of the legislators in Congress. For many days, groups took turns reading the some 2,000 Biblical passages that attack the abuses and oppression of the rich over the poor and the need to champion children, widows, the poor, aged, handicapped, and all in need.

Another hunger strike for immigration reform was completed more recently by Sojourner participants. Children of immigrants who are born here become citizens, but their parents are often illegal and sometimes get deported and separated from their children. The groups worked out of a tent on the Mall and succeeded in having the President and the First Lady and some of the legislators visit the tent. The church at large is silent about the plight of the poor and the way the income gap exacerbates the problem for both the poor and the middle class. A small percent of the nation has garnered vast wealth and with wealth, vast power, meaning that the rest are rendered more powerless. Wallis directs us to one of the reasons for Jesus coming when Jesus declares in his early preaching (Luke 4:18), "The Spirit of the Lord…has anointed me to preach good news to the poor. He has sent me to proclaim release to the captives, recovering sight to the blind, to set at liberty those who are oppressed."

While Wallis affirms the separation of church and state, he is one of the few churchmen who is crying out that the church is complicit in the national neglect of the poor, and, even more, that we need to cure the causes of poverty not just the symptoms. He leads by fully observing "water only" fasts. There is no doubt about his commitment to the norm of justice.

In South America a special norm was established about the poor by voices within the Catholic Church. This was a radical departure from the centuries-long stance of the church's blessing oppression by the rich. Priests like Gustavo Gutierrez argued that Jesus' gospel has its origin in and for the poor and oppressed. There is no discrimination about the gospel's being for all, but there is condemnation for the abuses of the rich over the rest. All beginnings in Christian practice and theological conversation are with the needy because the Divine is a Being of Compassion. This is obviously a radical norm that rubbed the religious and secular power structure in the wrong way. This was all happening in the latter half of the last century. Gutierrez was tried for heresy in Rome by the Catholic hierarchy but could never be entirely condemned.

The fact that norms can change is evidenced by Gutierrez having been invited to Rome by Pope Francis, apparently as a friend and old South American colleague. The 1960s and 1970s was a dark period when many bishops, priests, nuns, and Catholic laity in South America were killed or disappeared. The norm never substantially penetrated the church in North America. Daniel Migliore's book on liberation theology from Princeton Seminary represented an important, but minority, voice in the overall church. The North American church continues to adhere to the norm of either blessing the rich or, at least, being complicit in ignoring their abuses; it is safe to stay out of the public square and remain limited to private piety.

Strength of identity with the group

In addition to the strong commitment of the leader to the norm, the degree of identity that all the participants have with the group is a critical factor. The degree to which an individual feels duty-bound to follow the group norm is largely influenced by how much he or she identifies with the group. How important is the group to that specific person? Does the group strongly define the individual's identity? This is why the question of what a person does, his or her work or profession, is a personal and psychological question. If a person says, "I belong to the local carpenter's union" or "I belong to the Shalom Synagogue" or "I just completed my bar examination" or "I am a member of the well-known Kossuth (Hungarian) family in town," they are saying quite a bit about who they are. The more they reveal this identity with pride, the stronger their bond is with the group and the more they gain their personal identity from the group. Group membership is a powerful thing because it dispenses meaning, significance, and security to its members.

A study at a rehabilitative youth institution in Western Pennsylvania dramatically revealed the power of group identity. The researcher found that when youth came to the center from dysfunctional urban communities, they brought the norm of survival and violence with them. The institution was using a behavioral modification system such that the young person learned that life could be much more pleasant there by adapting his behavior to the norm of cooperation and nonviolence and that non-compliance resulted in deprivation. The adjudicated youth not only learned the mechanical contingencies between behavior and reward but also, in varying degrees, seemed to internalize and personally own the new norm of cooperation. This could be demonstrated, for example, by observing them helping each other in norm-compliant ways that they never bothered to record for reward points. Unfortunately, as the youths' sentence at the institution started to draw to a close, their behavior started to deteriorate. As they anticipated the return to their old community their old norms apparently started to re-emerge (see Benasr).

The psychology students mentioned in the section above develop group cohesiveness by the time they reach their upper levels. They work together in the labs collecting data, analyzing, and writing into many late nights together. Because they identify with the senior psychology group so strongly, they put their heart and soul into the norm of senior research. They mentor and reinforce the norm with the freshmen and sophomores. The senior research has become a group norm that is valued as a function of their group membership.

Even though ethics has traditionally been in the bailiwick of philosophy and religion, social psychologists started to study helping, or pro-social behavior, several decades ago. They assumed, from surveying the literature of world religions, that there was a universal norm for helping people in need. Other than during a period of warfare, when a person was in need, one should help. In regard to group membership and identity with the group, an amazing thing happened about helping to hide and save Jews during the Holocaust. After the war helpers and non-helpers were interviewed. Helpers said things like, "Jews are part of the human race. I couldn't do anything but help." Non-helpers said things to the effect that Gentiles and Jews are different; Jews are not part of us. In other words, helpers identified with one category, human. They could not help themselves. They had to help. But the non-helpers saw two distinct groups, them and us and, of course, identified with "us," the Gentiles of the Fatherland. Both groups said they had no choice, it was automatic; thus, we see the power of group membership being perceived differently by two subgroups.

★★★

Ashmore Richard D., Jussim, Lee, Wilder, David. (Editors). 2001. *Social identity, intergroup conflict, and conflict reduction.* New York: Oxford University Press.

Benasr, Lela. 2000. *The Effect of Group Identity On Adjudicated Boys in a Treatment Facility.* Undergraduate senior research. Westminster College, New Wilmington, Pennsylvania.

Brown, Robert McAfee. 1990. *Gutierrez, Gustavo: An Introduction to Liberation Theology.* Maryknoll, New York: Orbis Books.

Migliore, Daniel. 1980. *Called to Freedom: Liberation Theology and the Future of Christian Doctrine.* Philadelphia: Westminster Press.

Monroe, Kristen Renwick and Epperson. 1994. "But What Else Could I Do?" Choice, Identity and a Cognitive-Perceptual Theory of Ethical Political Behavior. *Political Psychology*, Vol. 15, No. This is one of the records of interviews comparing Gentiles who helped Jews survive the Holocaust to those who had the opportunity but did not help.

Wallis, Jim. 2005. *God's Politics: Why the Right Gets It Wrong, and The Left Doesn't Get It.* New York: HarperCollins. One of a minority of religious voices contends that the church should not be silent in the public sphere because silence signifies complicity in the wrongs of society.

Chapter 6: Physical and Social Structures

AMERICANS CHERISH THE belief that we are free agents and we make up our own minds. Freedom, independence, and self-reliance are fundamental values embedded in our Constitution and founding documents and celebrated in the legends of our rough-and-tumble frontier days. The question here is how free we really are, how determined or conditioned we are, and how these affect our behavior in the workplace and our lives as citizens. How do social and physical structures either squelch or free creative and productive acts?

The power of social structures

There is no question in my mind how critical the values of freedom and liberty are in a democratic society, as well as in groups where we value cooperation and where we want everyone to win. However, as critical as these values are, behavioral science research indicates that to a considerable extent, they are an illusion. The short of it is that they are goals, targets, directions, but at the individual level, at least, we tend to allow ourselves to be boxed in, determined by the social currents swirling around us. In experiments on conformity in which half of the participants are placed under pressure to give a certain answer compared to a control group not under pressure, the pressured group made conforming responses well over 50, 60, and 70%. The social pressure is experimentally created by a majority of group members being instructed in advance to give one unanimous answer to a question or an issue. This conformity effect occurs even with intelligent and successful participants, not just with people who may be down and out, as it were.

Our groups shape and form us far more than we imagine. If we are Shiites, we are not likely to become Sunnis, at least not overnight. If we run with people who identify with the Tea Party, we are most likely to tow the party line and are unlikely to switch in any short period of time. If we are misers, we do not easily become generous. If we are forced to be part of an inner urban gang, we are not likely free to seriously consider joining the choir of the local church. If we are born into a culture where babies have babies, we are not likely to defer childbirth to 30 years of age. We are deluding ourselves when we overemphasize our freedom and deny social channeling and conditioning.

What makes us this way? Why are we in boxes, in categories, and contained by impermeable walls? We do not choose them. Babies do not choose to be born to a crack mother. We do not choose to be born into a billionaire family and all of that lifestyle. In large, we are born into boxes and socialized from birth. In spite of changing thinking about gender roles, at least some progressive parents still seem to favor soft pink things for baby girls and toy trucks and diggers for boys. I guess it is why we instinctively get it when we ask people where they were born and raised. It tends to be a big part of who we are.

It is further enlightening to compare the power of internal personality effects to external social conformity effects. It is a slightly different way of posing the same question, "Do we control ourselves, or do the forces around us have control?" Some of the conformity research shows that the forces around us have as much as four times the influence that we have ourselves. These findings are profound and humiliating, but require a lot of elaboration. The detailed nature of the social pressures makes a great difference. If we have a great deal of knowledge about an issue, we are less likely to conform to pressure; whereas, if we are ignorant and lack knowledge about the complexities of an issue, we are likely to conform easily. For example, if we have very little knowledge of the history of our national debt and the relative dollar numbers placed in a broad perspective, we are more likely to say it is the biggest problem our nation faces today when placed under pressure. If we have knowledge, we are more likely to know the national debt is large, but not overly serious and not overwhelming. A high level of knowledge is critical for an individual or group to make good decisions.

The relative importance of the people pressuring us makes a big difference, which should be no surprise. There are some people we want to please very much and other people may matter very little on a given issue. Pressure to conform declines dramatically when at least one other person breaks from the unanimous majority. This has huge implications for leadership and group decision-making, which we will discuss later. The role of a single dissenter to break a unanimous majority in a small group setting is profound. The support of another single person has the potential to reduce conformity many times over. When one wants to express an opinion contrary to what everybody is saying in the group it takes great courage. You will be punished. Whistle blowers may have their lives destroyed. To dissent may seem useless but may very well provide the support that some other person needs badly to express a minority view.

While most people seem susceptible to conformity in the studies, there are strong individual differences; that is, some conform almost always, some moderately, and some never or hardly ever. The non-conformers are often called independents. Independents may very well have more than average knowledge about the issue at hand as we have already noted and, thus, can withstand pressure, especially when there is a moral dimension to the task at hand. Then the degree to which a person has a highly internalized and integrated belief or value structure enables resistance to pressure. If an army division has conquered a town and the victors are committing mass rape, it is unlikely that a soldier with a deeply internalized belief in the dignity of all humans will engage in that mob behavior. More on this will appear in Chapter 7 on individual strength.

David Gray

The power of physical structures

The structure and arrangement of physical spaces shape us as well as the social pressures just discussed. For example, the physical round table of the Camelot tales told those seated that one person was as important as the other. There was no end of a long table to suggest a special high status position.

Centralized and impersonal physical structures

Constraints of simple physical structures should be obvious. In an airport lounge, the chairs are lined up in long rows. The shoulder-to-shoulder arrangement is in a sense a "cold shoulder" setting that discourages eye-to-eye contact and lowers the likelihood of conversation. Although crowded together, the arrangement gives a sense of privacy. We go to the airport to travel, not to hear about some stranger's story. Likewise, in less expensive homes for the aged, chairs are frequently lined up along a hall corridor similar to the airport setting. The physical setting is telling the residents to vegetate or sleep, but not to interact. The old traditional classroom or lecture hall presents an authority figure at the front with students placed in rows to receive the truth with the expectation of passivity.

The physical structure of the early medieval cathedral gave a clear message. Most worshipers were uneducated and illiterate; they stood in a nave with no seats. As the status of the worshipers elevated through the centuries, benches first appeared, then pews, then padded pews. The cathedral was the place of the bishop who sat in the seat of authority, the bishop's chair or *cathedra* up on an elevated platform. When the supreme head of all the bishops issues an important directive, he speaks from the chair or *ex cathedra*. It is not a setting for discussion. It is an intensely hierarchical scenario where one commands and all others obey. One is great in status, and others are lesser, depending on their descending rank.

The whole medieval concept of inequality and idea of dignity emanated from the extreme hierarchical structures of church and state. The precious vestments of the pope, bishop, or king represented dignity, and the wearers of the vestments were the great dignitaries. Peasants in their homemade clothes or rags had little or no dignity. The inherent dignity, and thus equality of all humankind, was a long way off in the struggles that later unfolded in the birth of modern democracies.

The ecclesiastical power of the priests was concentrated in the priest's power to turn the elements into the actual body and blood of Christ (trans-substantiation). Administering mass conveyed eternal life and withholding it (excommunication) dammed one for all eternity. This model of power is a classically centralized one. The Protestant reformation movement certainly was not thoroughly democratic; however, it powerfully laid the groundwork for a departure from medieval hierarchy and helped to lay the groundwork of democracy.

Hierarchy and centralized power will never die. The high priests of today are the CEOs of the multinationals, the heads of private equity and hedge fund groups, members of Congress, most of our bosses, and on down to those husbands who still dominate their households.

Office size, office appointments, furniture arrangement, reserved parking places and executive lavatories all reflect status, power, and degrees of hierarchy, or inequality. When the regular citizen could still walk through the Pentagon rather freely, in the pre 9/11 days, it was easy to observe the increasing richness of wood and intricate paneling on the doors as one progressed from the lower officers to the generals' offices. If a leader intends to democratize the workplace, the physical structures should be in harmony with that end. Sharing decision making, sharing goal setting and planning, sharing quality control, and valuing creativity will be helped along by deemphasizing status differences.

Office size is just one a many factors to consider when downplaying formal status, and emphasizing functional equality. All offices being the same size operationalizes equality. Besides, the traditional array of increasingly bigger offices corresponding to official rank is unnecessarily expensive in construction and in the cost and disruption of moving every so many years. Offices of the same size convey a message of equality, unity and teamwork. The higher-ranking person has a higher salary, possibly with bigger benefits, and has a higher official and formal responsibility. He or she does not need to worry about loosing that earned formal status. But when it is time to go to work, it is the functional equality that counts and generates free flowing sharing and teamwork.

Andy Grove, the founder of Intel, had the same size office as all the other workers but with an extra office of the same size next door for small meetings. When Union Carbide exited its Manhattan offices for more reasonable real estate in Connecticut, they designed all offices to be 13.5 feet by 13.5 feet for all white-collar personnel top to bottom. This is a real break from tradition and a serious expression of democratizing and giving all workers more equal status. The integration of workstations and play or relaxation areas in a Google office complex display anything but a formal hierarchy heavily laden with status markers. The physical Google-like structure conveys communication, which says to work and interact in order to produce.

There is a better way than a command-and-obey structure. Decentralization and democratization in the home and in the workplace serves us a lot better. It is always the right time to abandon the model of the bishop's chair and work again on the model of Camelot's roundtable. The literal physical structure of the round table conveys a message that all the participants are equal. What does that mean? It means they have an equal responsibility and opportunity to perform to the best of their unique skills or talents. As we have discussed before, it does not mean that all members would be the same. Quite the contrary, one may be strong in one thing and weak in another. Personality and aptitude profiles would and must vary greatly if we hope for creativity. Kurt Vonnegut's denunciation of a mass dumbing down type of mediocrity and holding brilliant people back is well taken. His short story, entitled "Harrison Bergeron," begins by saying,

"The year was 2081, and everybody was finally equal." It proceeds to describe a Handicapper General who makes sure that no brilliant person overcomes a mediocre one by actually applying handicapping weights to the star performer.

The rationale for physical structures that convey equality

Formal status and power would also be unequal and would still be concentrated in a central figure. Formal status would still vary, but functional status would be equalized. The leader would be respected for his or her appointment and position, the older members for their experience, and the newer members for their up-to-date savvy and fresh ideas. All members would have the equal right to speak, the right to initiate proposals or projects for group evaluation. In fact, all members would have the responsibility to speak and contribute, to reinforce others as well as critique them. The task of the leader would not be to squelch the neophyte or anyone else, but to assure that everyone was protected and encouraged to contribute. For a leader to do less is to lose talent, abilities, and unique facilitating perspectives. Any business leader would be chastised for losing track of a thousand tons of coal or steel, but thousands of tons of skills are lost and repressed without their superiors raising any alarm. Hierarchies are wasteful and, therefore, not really conservative or wise.

Admittedly there are working members who are anti everything. They seem anointed with the mission of throwing the monkey wrench into every turning gear. Proposals that seem far out need to be given a fair hearing, but monkey-wrench ideas are poorly developed and not worthy of a group's time. The open democratic leader probably needs to switch to a very direct and firm method of shutting this person down. If the disruptive person is acting out of a need for attention, there may be a creative way to meet that need.

This fundamental paradigm shift is going from control to release. The traditional leader feels he or she must have control and is afraid of losing it; therefore, he tends to discourage initiative by tactics of condescension, fear, and intimidation, playing members off against each other. The weaker and more unskilled the traditional leader is, the more he or she is likely to try to manage by an external show of force. Heavy-handed leadership may be a sign of internal weakness and felt inferiority, or perhaps just a lack of understanding of a better way.

In the shooting sports, including bows and guns, the release determines accuracy. Almost any archer, if using an appropriate weight of bow, can draw the bow to full draw position and hold the bow steady on the target. It is more difficult to make a clean release. When the bowstring slips off the releasing fingers, it is so easy for the archer inadvertently to twist or torque the string ever so slightly. An absolutely smooth release makes a great archer. Likewise with a gun, holding it steady is, of course, critical, but without a perfectly smooth squeeze of the trigger, the aim will be pulled off target. There is no place for yanking the trigger. If we begin by believing that all of our workers have potential, then the challenge of the leader is to learn the skill of encouragement and accurate feedback in an atmosphere of security and safety. Attention is given to releasing talent and willingness. The opposite approach begins with not believing in one's employees, and assuming they are out to get you. Consequently, constant surveillance is needed, and there is a prevailing threat of punishment.

If the labor market is bad for the workers and they have nowhere else to go, external compliance by the workers is likely, but they will not give their heart and soul. And if they have job choices, they will flee a company. Hiring, acclimating, and training new people is expensive, but that is not an issue for the company in slow times. In fact, it is one of the motivations of the corporate world to keep jobs scarce and unemployment high. A really smart and internally strong leader will work to release the workers, giving them more power, discretion, and benefits.

Hierarchical mentality assumes that only the top person has the wisdom, vision, knowledge and overview to call the shots. If that is truly the case, it may very well be that that condition exists because data, knowledge, and training have been denied the workers. If the workers care only for their own narrow domain of interests, it is because the structure has walled them into that narrow channel. They have been told to mind their own business.

In a very small organization, the lowest level of production may indeed be able to contribute to the highest decisions of the company if invited to do so. But in a larger organization, the democratic model is appropriate mainly at and within one's own work level or department. At whatever level of an organization, it is integrity, honesty, truth, and quality products that are fostered by democratization in the workplace.

Absolute truth, relativism, and diversity

In spite of living in a day when spin, denial, deception, and cover-up are the order of the day, truth and transparency are still necessary for integrity and vitality. What kinds of truths are we talking about here?

Truth

In order for everyone to win, we will value truth highly, but will avoid the trap of absolutism. A famous case unfolded in Youngstown, Ohio in 1995. Mickey Monus, CEO of the Phar-Mor pharmaceutical chain of stores, cooked the books in order to look more profitable and falsely generate phony revenue. It was done by mass movement of inventory from store to store to create the picture of high sales and profits. It was, of course, one great lie and led to the end of the company and prison time for Monus.

Contrary to fundamentalist thinking, there are usually exceptions to every rule and, often, some contextual element to every principle. Nevertheless, the principle of truth telling is far more often sound and complete than not. On January 28, 1986, the spacecraft Challenger exploded 73 seconds into flight. Most of America witnessed it either live or a short time later. All seven-flight members were lost, including Christa McAuliffe, the teacher who was to broadcast back to her students the news of the flight and results of several science experiments she was to conduct. Space activity was frozen for 33 months. Several of the engineers of Morton Thiokol, the manufacturer of the critical "O" rings, warned NASA the night before the launch that the rings were unreliable at temperatures below 52 degrees, which was the case that night. One of the chief engineers, Allan McDonald, refused to sign an engineering green light document. A top NASA official fired back, "I am appalled at your recommendation." Picture 16 inch battleship guns turned on the engineers and blasting away as it were. The weight and volatility of a prestigious arm of the government coming down on one's shoulders was enormous, yet the engineers held their ground. The authorities castigated the lowly engineers and wondered if they wanted to wait till April. McDonald was removed from his position and demoted, but was restored later. Whistleblowers and dissenters do a great service but pay a painful price. The truth was told, but the authorities wanted none of it.

The 2013 premature ill-prepared launching of the national health-care website apparently could have been avoided. The attempt to bring health support to our people and catch up to other advanced nations who have had national care for many years brought frustration and great disappointment to thousands. Responsible persons constructing the site sent memos written in capital letters warning of the un-readiness and impending disaster. Critical information resided at the level of the action, the builders of the site, but was not accepted further up the line. Somewhere higher up in the levels of government denial and fumbling occurred. It would seem that this is another case of greater ignorance further up the chain of command rather than down the line. Contrary to the style of traditional management who think they know it all and that their subordinates are not too bright, people at the bottom often have large amounts of critical information and truth.

Misinformation is not always intentional; it may result from faulty accounting, unintentional errors in planning or organization, mis-judging costs, or demand. A good friend was an important executive of a new transport company filling a unique niche in the market and realizing handsome but reasonable profits, only to find that their accounting software had a flaw which masked costs and erroneously calculated gains. The company failed suddenly.

A welder in a non-union shop paused to wipe the sweat out of his eyes. The boss came over and said he saw no sparks and the man was fired. A friend of the boss took the welder's place later. It did not build trust or productivity.

Before the Japanese economy unraveled in the late 1980s for a variety of reasons, that country presented a model of lifetime employment, constant improvement and perfection of products, and thoughtful treatment of the employees. Instead of giving employees brief economic reports biased and distorted to make the company look like it was struggling in order to make the workers produce more and be more compliant, the companies regularly posted unbiased and detailed production, sales, and profit reports. Furthermore, the companies trained the workers at all levels to understand accounting language, categories, and techniques. This use of the truth served them well for a very long time.

The Japanese development of quality control was also a vital expression of telling the truth. One of our astute statisticians, W. E. Deming, finding no interest among American companies in the old booming economy of the 1950s, was warmly received by the Japanese. Objective standards were constructed for a given product using a band of error, which was tolerable, and below which the product was rejected, or the line shut down for improvement. Due in part to this method, a Honda sedan emerged which became widely recognized for its all around quality and durability.

And it was more than incidental that a worker could shut down the line if he or she saw something wrong that a superior did not see. The great expense of shutting down the line was compensated for by increased quality, fewer rejects, and truly empowered workers. Workers' perceived importance and empowerment was elevated by this responsibility and trust extended to them by the company. Thus, quality control was shared with all the employees as well as an overseer.

In some cases of intentional fabrication or fraud, truth may be fairly easy to establish. In other cases, truth may be more illusive. Different data sets, different measurements, conflated time periods, and other uncontrolled variables may present what looks like conflicting truths. This is the stuff of rational discourse and science. The Curries conducted some 5,000 experiments before the reality of radium could be substantiated and accepted. Science is filled with contradictory results, especially in the beginning phases of investigation. Furthermore, even when a scientific finding is empirically supported, it is always open to new investigations and alternative explanations. This does not mean that you cannot trust science or that total relativism is the end result of open inquiry. It means that we always need a better-educated citizenry that can discern the relative support of a given scientific principal, or political argument for that matter.

If reason, analysis, and science do not produce absolute and totally certain truth, where shall we turn? Many turn to religion and claim they have absolute truth. People set themselves up for mental anguish when headed in this direction. There may be absolute truth. Some Christians believe, for example, that absolute truth resides in a Sovereign God. The critical distinction that is often missed in the formulation of this belief is that while the absolute truth may exist, we can never fully access it; we see through a glass dimly, in the expression of St. Paul. Humans cannot capture God; he is beyond us. The anguish for fundamentalists is that they must stringently defend the tenants of truth when they are threatened. If the challenge to the tenants is strong enough, the very existence and mental and emotional security of the person is threatened. Socrates' paradox seems to be more healthy and realistic. On the one side, he said, "This I know that I know nothing." Humility was expressed and he had nothing to defend desperately like absolute truth. On the other side, he was grounded enough in his belief that to question is to be human and even to die for his commitment to make the youth of his day think rather than blindly conform.

When members of any faith or politicians of any stripe fail to make this distinction, a fundamentalist belief system is what is likely to follow. Fundamentalists tend to believe they have the absolute truth and believe that it can and must be captured in a set of closed and unalterable principles or fundamentals. Many moderate Christians may agree with many of the items on the list of religious fundamentalists. The difference is that they do not believe the list fully captures God or absolute truth. The list is subject to reformulation and interpretation over different circumstances and over time. Lists are the best approximations that we can make and are open to change, although the absolute truth that the list tries to represent never changes.

The dynamic of political fundamentalism is similar to the religious version. Grover Norquist's pledge of no new taxes under any circumstances does not have the divine absolute dimension, but it is intended as a human categorical imperative. Conservative Congressional members are pressured to sign it as a certification of true political belief. It would seem to me that most of the signers are not really fundamentalists but a minority of the extremists who have dogmatically tied themselves in knots about "no new taxes." There is no wiggle room with a fundamentalist. And almost all the members of one of our major political parties have signed, but a few have deactivated recently.

A tiny, but fanatical, fraction of Muslims believe that they have the only absolute truth and are duty bound to commit physical jihad against all infidels. Occupation of their lands and violation of their civilians increases their fundamentalist fervor.

Exceptions to the rule of truth must be noted. A central part of some group sports is deception, misrepresentation, and faking, all perfectly sportsmanlike and legitimate. Slight of hand is the art of the professional magician. Secrecy, disguise, and deception are practiced by all nations engaging in international intelligence and espionage.

Relativism

Where does that leave us in regard to slipping into relativism? If we are always open are we not committed to relativism? No. It is not so neat, and it is admittedly paradoxical that the open-minded person is grounded in certain verities of practical living. One example is a working definition of truth. Lies and deception are not just as good as truth. Cheating on a term paper is not just as good as doing one's own work. Consider other verities, killing is not just as good as helping. Stealing is not just as good as not stealing. Wrecking a family is not just as good building one. Putting an innocent man or woman in prison is not just as good as getting an innocent person out of prison. The notion of value-free education is absurd. It is not just as good to bully and beat up a fellow student as it is to encourage a fellow. Science is anything but value free.

Biases and fads influence science and the problems they work on and the techniques they use. Therefore, it is critical that their results can always be questioned and examined from other angles with alternative techniques. It is a rule in the behavioral sciences that any bona fide researcher may request the raw date from another scientist's study for re-analysis or refinement. Raw data should be kept for sharing for seven years. Open, honest inquiry is a *sine qua non* in the sciences.

It is interesting that as social psychology ventured into an area formerly reserved for ethics, the question of helping others in need came under the social microscope. Hundreds of laboratory and field experiments and assessments have been done to chart the conditions that determine if a bystander will help or pass. One of the many factors studied examined was how much a person had internalized the universal principle of helping people in need. There is a universal principle of helping. Drawing on the world religions and the age-old thought patterns that have influenced us, there is a ubiquitous norm or social obligation to help people in need. In other words, in spite of how contextual ethics has evolved, some things seem fairly anchored. It is not just as good to push a person farther down into the mud as it is to help him or her get up.

Diversity

Though disparaged as a vapid politically correct topic, the concept of diversity is huge. It really should have little or nothing to do with political correctness. Biologically, it is essential. In the animal kingdom, both human and infrahuman, inbreeding within a limited gene pool tends to magnify infirmities. Marrying between cousins and the incest taboo raise this red flag. The author's home is sixty miles north of Pittsburgh in the heart of a rather large Amish community. Some years ago the concern about inbreeding was prevalent within that community. The need to reach out to wider communities in other states for marriage partners was recognized and the problem has been resolved.

In the plant kingdom, monocultures are dangerous. The dust bowl was due in part because as the price of wheat elevated, more and more sod was broken and wheat predominated the crop of the Great Plains. Tree lines were obliterated in order to enlarge fields for large farm machinery, and meadow crops and pasture were sacrificed for wheat. Add extended drought to this mix and you have the terrible dust bowl of the late 1920s. The natural prairie sod consisted of a large number of types of plants with different depths of root systems. With this variety, if one plant could not withstand a time of natural stress, such as drought, another plant would pull through and the stability of the plain was preserved from drought and winds. The potato famine in Ireland in the mid-nineteenth century could have been avoided if the farmers had developed a greater variety of edible crops. When the potato blight wiped out the main food source, millions starved.

Cultural diversity apparently fosters a higher level of vitality also. The main argument for the rise and fall of empires in Chua's book entitled *Days of Empire* is that, among many factors, tolerance and openness to the influx of people from different tribes or nations correlates with growth and prosperity. Decline of superpowers is related to drawing inward, shutting others out, and trying to preserve ethnic or national purity.

Empires such as China and Persia and Rome flourished during periods when their doors were open to the exchange of ideas and people as well as the exchange of merchandise on the Silk Road. When they turned in on themselves and excluded cross-cultural exchanges, they declined. When countries build walls, they shut off the supply of new blood and different cross-pollinating ideas and skills.

The character of the Mongol empire has been maligned as unbelievably barbaric and ruthless. Most of us, I dare say, have the picture of Genghis Kahn's mounted hordes burning towns wholesale and committing mass executions, looting, and rape. The western record of civilization has distorted the story of the Mongols. Since recent scholars discovered the *Secret History of the Mongols* and other relevant ancient documents, a different image appears. When approaching a new town or city in their western expansion, three primary demands were monetary tribute, loyalty, and sharing some of their most skilled citizens. If they complied on these three things, they were not harmed. If they refused, Genghis sent his troops back and wiped out a city in toto. To be fair, the record also admits that occasionally he wiped out towns in rebellious areas in order to create complete terror and obedience.

The record apparently indicates a substantial degree of tolerance and openness. If his subjects complied with the three demands, they were not only free of religious persecution or pressure of any other kind, but they were counted as nearly potential equals, that is, they could rise through the ranks to high levels of leadership. Meritocracy and social mobility existed in an age when Europe was mired in endless religious wars, frozen class boundaries, and rigid hierarchies. A big part of Genghis Kahn's genius was utilizing the brains, wisdom, skills, and insights wherever he found those kinds of riches. The result was the largest empire of the day, one of the largest ever.

The decline was just as sad as the accomplishments had been notable. After Genghis died some of his sons and grandsons became soft, lost the vision of unity, and the kingdom devolved because of inner conflict and decay. The high status of women had been remarkable during the days of Genghis; many held positions of high command. During the decline of the empire, a dismal reversal of the status of women occurred.

Another ancient model of dynamic diversity was the Lithuanian-Polish Commonwealth of the 1500s and 1600s. The Empire was one of the earliest and largest European ventures in shared power (limited to the nobles to be sure), open trade, and laws of toleration for different faiths and peoples. Business was conducted in a half dozen languages in Warsaw and learning and the arts were celebrated. Much later it was carved into three pieces by three major Western powers, and then reappeared as a proud united nation before the Second World War. When that war broke out, Warsaw still had the highest concentration of Jews of any city in the world other than New York City. The relationship between Jews and Gentiles was never a love affair, but they knew how to tolerate each other; it had been a matter of law. This was in acute contrast to the uncivilized pattern of Western Europe where differences were met with butchery and wars lasting a hundred years, all based on hierarchical notions of royal blood and the divine right of kings.

Having honestly confronted the best parts of the model of the Mongol Empire and the Lithuanian-Polish Commonwealth, we would do well to seek out the best in other cultures and regions of the world. Of course, we should celebrate our unique strengths where we are exceptional. But to parade as globally exceptional is simply inaccurate because any nation's overall strengths must be tempered with the overall weaknesses and dark sides. It is embarrassing and humiliating to admit that Genghis Kahn was likely more tolerant and progressive than our Puritan forefathers in the Massachusetts Bay Colony when they punished heretics, killed native Americans, and burned so-called witches at the stake or lobbed off the ears of devout Quakers in the public square or sold them as slaves to the Barbados because they did not have an orthodox view of holy communion. Intolerance ruled supreme under McCarthyism. It ruined many productive American lives, falsely accused of traitorous affiliations with communists. Intolerance of Native Americans, Catholics, Jews, Blacks, Irish, Chinese, Mexicans, and Iranians has never been scarce in this country. We could have learned valuable knowledge and wisdom from these people down through our history, but they were not only written off, but also castigated. This recognition of our dark side is another seldom-recognized but critical part of what diversity means.

If we put our arrogance in check and learned from others, we might advance at a more rapid rate. When very recent modern European models of health care and general welfare were suggested as being able to help inform us, there was a pattern of closed mindedness. Too bad for us; we lose out regarding effective problem solving. Benchmarking, or learning from other's products, should make great sense. When the Japanese were rebuilding their industries after the World War II, they rented three floors of the Pan Am building in New York City, filling them with the best American products of all kinds for analysis and industrial intelligence, as it were.

Examining others' products and including other kinds of people are all critical parts of diversity. Improving immigration policies may be as complicated and as intransigent as national health care in the United States, but we have always benefited from brains from abroad. Streams of so-called foreigners have enriched us in abundant measure. Eugene Kleiner escaped Nazi Vienna in 1941 and teamed up with physicist William Shockley in Bell Labs to develop the transistor. Kleiner went on to develop the commercial integrated circuit out of silicon. He was a moving force in generating what we have come to know as Silicon Valley.

Another immigrant, this one with a heavy Hungarian accent and a hearing impairment, developed microprocessors. He and his colleagues called their company Integrated Electronics and eventually flooded the computer market with the Intel chip. His name was Andy Grove. *Time* magazine featured Grove as Man of the Year in 1979 and attributed his leadership for transforming the end of the last century as the Industrial Revolution changed the prior century. It would do us well to remember how many ignorant Hunky jokes we used when talking about Poles and Hungarians. We could have missed Andy Grove.

These examples of vital innovation are not exceptions. A young Russian student, Sergy Brin, along with some friends, started what we know today as Google. Google employs several thousand people and enables users across the web to access immediate valuable information. Sun Microsystems was launched by two immigrants from the Continent of India. Key architects of the world-wide web came from England.

Of course, reasonable immigration restrictions need to exist; we obviously should reject terrorists dedicated to destroying our nation. We expect that immigrants will be willing to learn our language, accept our currency, and pledge loyalty to the Constitution. Loyalty to and interpretation of the Constitution leaves the gate open quite wide for interpretation but forms a minimal groundwork. The values of freedom and equality are surely well embedded in our democratic documents. All of these elements together form a core of our culture. Diversity is crucial to continued vitality, but a nation needs some commonality or glue to hold it together.

Structures that are open physically and psychologically encourage fresh thinking, alternate ways to frame and solve problems and adapting to rapidly changing conditions. Open structures lead one to learn from what others are doing and thinking without aping or following blindly. Closed structures that block out diversity, on the other hand, discourage the vitality of robust innovation, critique, and exploration.

★★

Asch, S. E. 1956. Studies in Independence and Conformity; A Minority of One Against a Unanimous Majority. *Psychological Monographs*, 70, (9, Whole No. 416). This report and the Crutchfield one below are two classical foundational reports of conformity research by social psychologists.

Crutchfield, R. S. 1955. Conformity and Character. *American Psychologist*, 10, 191-198.

Chua, Amy. 2007. *Day of Empire: How Hyperpowers Rise to Global Dominance—and Why They Fall*. New York: Doubleday. The significant role of diversity in vitalizing great nations invites thought.

Davies, Norman. 1982. *God's Playground: A History of Poland, Volume II, 1795 to the Present*. New York: Columbia University Press. A premier chronicle of that period of Polish history.

Weatherford, Jack. 2004. *Genghis Khan and the Making of the Modern World*. New York: Three Rivers Press. A more positive account based on the release of a long suppressed book entitled *The Secret History of the Mongols* and other newer manuscripts.

Chapter 7: Individual Strength

THE GREAT PERSON theory of leadership still captures some people's admiration. It is a somewhat dated idea in formal organizational thinking. It is certainly true that the transformational, charismatic, turnaround leader is still sought out and paid excessively. There is some basis for this strategy, but, all in all, the success of the great leader usually depends on the conditions of the time. Lee Iacocca turned Chrysler around many years ago, but if he appeared on the scene today, he might or might not be matched to the nature of today's problems. JFK moved our spirits and raised and refined our aspirations. This is not to disparage figures that in one way or another make a difference. A more balanced and realistic approach is that a great leader's impact depends on the circumstances of the time. If Martin Luther King, Jr., returned to our scene today, he probably would not find the national culture, which has lurched far to the right, to be very conducive to equality and justice. Of course, he met great resistance in his day, but overall, the timing was right because the secular populace and religious bodies in general passed the point of tolerating segregation.

We argued in the Structures chapter that the external forces around us usually influence us much more than we think, in fact several times more than the internal influences of our own personality. There are strong individuals who are the exception.

The message of this chapter qualifies and moderates the main idea of the Structures chapter that spotlighted the power of the forces around us, rather than within us. It contended that the amazon-like currents around us might influence our behavior as much as four times that of personal characteristics. As a sweeping generalization, it is arguably true that personality strength has been overstated. In countless laboratory and field studies, formal measurements of various personality variables seldom correlate with behavior more than about .30 (on a .00 to 1.00 scale), which explains about 9% of why participants in a study behaved differently. Personality is an important, but usually modest, part of explaining behavior.

The relative strength/weakness of personality seems to be related to age, experience, knowledge, and the degree that one has internalized dimensions like his or her attitudes, values, and worldview. The younger and less experienced person is likely to conform more than the older experienced one. The more superficial one's beliefs are the more the conformity. Conformity is also likely when the person under pressure has a lot at stake, like re-elections or job advancement. None of us can be renaissance persons anymore; the exponential explosion of data and knowledge means that any given person, regardless how well educated formally or informally, will come up ignorant on many topics. Thus, we are often vulnerable to persuasion, even persuasion that should not warrant a positive response.

There are times, however, when personality is salient and unshakable. It is when a certain well-integrated belief system has been deeply internalized and ingrained in a person. In those cases, personality reigns supreme regardless of unfavorable circumstances. The old Hebrew word "shalom" captures a good part of this type of person. The person's peace comes from the wholeness of life; all the parts have been put together harmoniously. The parts of the person have substance, and they are integrated and intertwining. The person is integrated; the opposite is obviously disintegrated, conflicted and fragmented. The water is sweet in wells that are deep and well constructed.

Who are these people who are well integrated, healthy, and strong. They are not the majority, but many ordinary folks undoubtedly fit this description quite well. To get an overview of how many people are independent versus conforming, we might expect that the list of independents could fill a large volume, but the conformists could fill a room full of books. An important qualification needs to be kept in mind. To conceptualize people into two categories of conforming or independent is to put people in artificial boxes. The point is that people may be independent about issues they are well grounded in, but very compliant in problems about which they know little.

The more celebrated independent figures illustrate personal strength because they are familiar. A few exemplary leaders will be paraded out in this chapter. The list is arbitrary. But we will start with Moses.

Moses

A very early figure of towering inner strength comes to us through the Hebrew literature called the Law--the first five books of the Old Testament. The story begins with Moses being born into mortal danger under the rule of a Pharaoh. Moses was hidden in the bulrushes in the River Nile and discovered by Pharaoh's daughter. He was adopted by the royal princess, highly educated in all the wisdom of the Egyptians, who were among the most learned in the civilized world. Moses was privy to the ways of the royal court, the practice of law and justice, and all the ways of Egyptian civilization. He remembered his Hebrew origins and identity, and when he saw an Egyptian overseer beat a Hebrew slave, impulsively, he killed the overseer and buried him in the sand. Fearing Pharaoh would kill him in turn he fled the land. Eventually, he felt called to be the leader and deliverer of the Israelites, who had been in slavery in Egypt for a long time. The life of the slave was to manufacture bricks of clay mixed with straw and baked in the hot sun, in addition to all the other onerous duties.

Moses chafed under the harsh treatment of his people, and with the help of an assistant, named Aaron, he planned an exodus back to the Promised Land by the Jordan River. The story is that Moses stood up to one of the greatest powers of the then known world, looked him straight in the eye and cried, "Let my people go!" He did not just ask for a few more food stamps or a day off once in the while; his was an ultimatum to the king, "Let my people go!" Pharaoh refused; the ten plagues then descended on the Egyptian people. Finally, the

Israelites departed toward the Red Sea and home. Because he himself failed to keep the circumcision of one of his sons, and the people fell away to worship idols from time to time and grumbled and mumbled about God not caring, Moses never reached the Promised Land himself. God condemned the people to wander for 40 years in the wilderness. Through all the rebellion and ingratitude of the people, Moses remained faithful to the divine imperative and eventually to the Ten Commandments and the mission to bring his people to the River Jordan. His learned background in the courts of Pharaoh would have enabled him to write the books of the Pentateuch, the first five book of the Old Testament. The actual authorship, however, is roundly disputed. In the story, he is experienced, solid, deep, and well integrated. The greatest power on earth could not make him conform. Internal strength trumped external pressures.

Martin Luther

In the early 1500s, this scholarly priest sought basic reforms within the Roman branch of the Catholic Church. He was disturbed with the debauchery and ignorance of many priests, the abuse of indulgences, the barring of the Christian laity from direct access to God, and abuses of the powers of the priests regarding mass. Against his desire, he found himself being more and more alienated from the hierarchy who resisted his pleas for reform. Although historians dispute parts of the story, he supposedly tacked 95 theses or propositions on the doors of the church in the town of Wittenberg in southern Germany in 1517 with the appeal that they be publically debated. Luther contended that every Christian was a minister or priest and could take his prayers and devotion directly to God. This was a flagrant challenge to the sole and powerful doorkeeper function of the priesthood over eternal life. It was a massive threat to the absolute rule of the Pope and the hierarchical layers of cardinals, bishops, and priests. Salvation by faith alone also was a frontal attack on the Catholic Church's considerable reliance on salvation by works and a treasury of merit.

Various trials ensued in which Luther felt the full weight of the Holy Catholic Church pressuring him to recant his beliefs or be excommunicated, meaning that he would be hopelessly cut off from salvation for all eternity. That had a ponderous and sober meaning in that religious age contrasted to what it might mean in our more secularized world today. Threats of vile hatred called for his life. Legend has it that the trials concluded with his words, "Here I stand. I can do none other. God help me." He was excommunicated in 1521.

Using his scholarship and the aid of the invention of the printing press, he was able to translate the Bible from the Latin into the German vernacular. His explicit teaching of the priesthood of the individual believer, coupled with direct lay access to the Bible, laid the groundwork for people to escape the bonds of absolute authority and begin to formulate modern attempts at democracy. The Reformation, as it was called by Protestants, was a fundamental turning point from the divine right of kings and popes to governments of the people. Unfortunately, some serous black marks attach to Luther in his later life. The peasants' grievances and revolts were undoubtedly inspired to some degree by his teachings, but he, by no means, blessed all of the abuses of those revolts. Also, Luther's relationship with Judaism soured badly in his later days, which darkened his record.

All in all, Luther is a giant who had the strength to remain independent at the price of being denied the comforts and blessings of the Church. His anguish had to be extreme. It would be little wonder that he apparently became somewhat paranoid and neurotic. It is my perspective that our founding fathers, Washington, Jefferson, and Lincoln among others, built partly on the legacy of Martin Luther to no small amount. His wide scholarly strength coupled with practical experience apparently enabled him to integrate a strong, stable, deeply internalized belief system, nearly impervious to pressure.

Abraham Lincoln

Just before Lincoln took office in 1860, South Carolina led a rebellion and seceded from the Union. By his Inauguration day of

March 4, 1861, six other Southern states had withdrawn from the Union. Subsequently, four more departed, for a total count of 17 states. It is hard to imagine a more hopeless beginning for a new President.

An entire way of life and privilege rested on the institution of black slavery. Southern power and privilege was not to pass lightly. Slavery and a belief in the categorical inferiority of African-Americans formed the groundwork of the institutions in the South, and plenty of that belief prevailed in the North as well. Lincoln was inundated with a rejection no other President has ever experienced. It is common for cartoonists to vilify, and for Presidents to lose on major legislative conflicts, but all these political wounds seem to be nothing alongside half of the nation's formally disowning the Union. Amplifying the trauma was the formation of an opposing hostile nation, called the Confederacy. A crowning crisis for the President and the Union came with Confederate guns firing on the Union garrison at Fort Sumter on April 12 1861.

Many of his biographers contend that Lincoln was mostly concerned with saving the Union and secondarily with freeing the slaves. This rank ordering of the two is apparently accurate, but in his Senatorial debates with Douglas, it seems clear that he considered slavery a moral issue and totally wrong. Lincoln's passion was to prove that a people could govern themselves without a king and the right of decree. We forget in our modern era that democracy was a very young and unique experiment in the United States in Lincoln's day. The ideal was a government by all the people, not just the nobility, as had been experienced in the ancient city-states of Greece and in the Polish-Lithuanian Commonwealth. It was not just that two nations might be the outcome of the conflict, but that democracy would be discredited throughout the world. Layer upon layer of grief and despair descended upon this President. He had no allies in Europe to buoy him up as our leaders count on today. In fact, the English Empire would have been only too happy to see their rebellious breakaway colonies fail. Russia was the exception in providing some naval aid.

The uncertainty of the outcome of the four-year war and the conflicting forces raging all around him pushed him toward physical and mental collapse. But he endured, I believe, because of a deep grounding in learning in the law, in the Judeo-Christian scriptures, in his deeply internalized respect for human life, and in an abiding sense of Divine Providence. Of course, he had help from personal supporters and the military, but he carried a crushing weight alone. He was anchored, shaken, but not moved. The Union was saved, and the slaves were freed, with the hope of malice toward none and respect for all.

Rachel Robinson, Jackie Robinson, and Branch Rickey

Here are three people who worked together to resist enormous pressure through mature and heroic character. Jackie Robison started at first base for the Brooklyn Dodgers at Ebbets Field in April 1947. He was the first black ever to take the field in Major League Baseball. His teammates signed a petition refusing to play with him. The fans shouted streams of racist abuse at him. The manager and the players of the Phillies at one game shouted, "Nigger, go back to the cotton fields."

Racial abuse was not new to Jackie. While in the service in the Second World War, he refused to go to the back of the bus when the driver ordered him to do so. He was court martialed and harassed shamefully by the military, but finally acquitted. He foreshadowed Rosa Parks in his behavior and, of course, was a forerunner of the wider civil rights movement to follow later in the 1960s.

Branch Rickey, President and General Manager of the Dodgers, stuck his neck way out in seeking Jackie and getting him signed. Rickey had seen the effects of discrimination in sports and detested it. He felt it was inconsistent with his Christian faith, and, up front, he also candidly expressed that it would be profitable for all concerned. Branch Rickey prepared Jackie to expect merciless harassment and insults. He was thoroughly trained and commanded not to answer back or to act out in any way ever. His answer to the insults had to be through his outstanding performance coupled with effective restraint.

Leo Durocher, the manager of the Dodgers, squelched an internal mutiny decisively with harsh words against the rebels. Branch Rickey was a pillar of support. A scattered few of Jackie's teammates were supportive. During one of the racial episodes, the Dodger player Pee Wee Reese put his arm around Jackie in solidarity before the packed stadium. Perhaps his most solid rock was his wife Rachel, whom he met during his student days at UCLA. She was a well-educated, mature wife who helped him through those many trying times and provided a castle, a family, and a secure and loving home. Jackie, Rachael, and Branch Rickey all knew what they were about and were fiercely independent in achieving it. The value of justice and inclusion must have been deeply embedded in their belief systems.

Martin Luther King, Jr.

Like Moses, King spoke unequivocally to the highest of powers and said, in effect, "Let my people go." Blacks had been freed by the emancipation proclamation in 1862 and more completely by the victory of the Union forces. The Union won the War but not the hearts of the Confederates as well as many others. Reconstruction was undermined by discriminatory hiring and voting, intimidation by the Klan, lynching, terrorism, and peonage. Blacks made great strides in education, business, and government by the end of the 1800s, only to be met with a rising anger and revolt precisely because of their success. A dramatic illustration is the violent overthrow of the fusionist (integrated) city government of Wilmington, North Carolina, in 1898. Armed white militia roamed the city on election day threatening all Blacks that if they showed up at the voting poles their bodies would be piled so high as to clog the mouth of the Cape Fear River. Blacks were driven from their homes permanently. They hid in the swamps and eventually fled to safer parts. A Gatling gun mounted on a wagon moved from one polling location to another to terrorize and kill. The

Black newspaper office was burned to the ground. The next morning an all white racist city government seized total power.

The oppression of the Black population in the South continued after the Civil War and on into the 1900s. It was the challenging inheritance of a new black civil rights leadership. Martin Luther King, Jr., and other leaders and groups, started with appeals and marches for relatively small changes like integrating lunch counters, rest rooms, and buses. Then came bigger things like voting rights, integrating schools, and on into the pocket books of the Southern establishment to pay the garbage workers decently. His cries for "justice rolling down like mighty waters" eventually extended into overall economic reform and restructuring of capitalism in order to recapture equal opportunity for all, one of the two great pillars of democracy. The famous "I have a Dream" speech on the Mall was given at the occasion of the March on Washington in 1963. The focus was on reducing prejudice and, thus, enhancing work opportunities. The "I have a Dream" portion of his speech was abstract, idealistic, perhaps romantic, highly inspirational, and generally fairly safe in the eyes of the larger public. While these topics were relatively controversial and provocative, they were nothing like the systemic critiques which came later in King's development.

By 1968, King's Old Testament type of critique of the nation became more comprehensive, reaching into the Viet Nam War and our total economic structures. His definitive speech in this vein was given in 1967 at the New York City Riverside Church, entitled "Beyond Vietnam: A Time to Break Silence." He accused the military of killing a million innocent Vietnamese, including many children, for no just cause. Furthermore he condemned the massive dollar cost, money that could have been spent on improvements for the impoverished at home. He said our policies were leading us to "spiritual death." He charged the U.S. government as "the greatest purveyor of violence in the world today." He was far ahead of his time on this. Even a centrist might be able to say things like this today and not catch too much flack. This was three years before Daniel Ellsberg and his colleagues leaked the so-called Pentagon Papers indicating that we were losing in Viet Nam. *Life* magazine called the speech at Riverside "demagogic slander that sounded like a script for Radio Hanoi." The *Washington Post* stated that King had "diminished his usefulness to his cause, his country, his people." The country was still in denial at that time, and King was seen as skidding close to being a traitor or, at least, as a malcontent and misfit.

King was arrested over 20 times and imprisoned 13 times. After one of his arrests, he was taken on an extended 300-mile ride in the night blindfolded with no explanation. It would not have been entirely out of the question that he feared it was to his death. The lives of his wife and children were endangered when their house was bombed. Death threats to his life were common. The stress, anguish, and fits of fear must have been an overpowering reason to pull back, tone down, postpone, and even quit. His extensive reading and synthesizing of philosophy, theology, literature (Tolstoy, for example), the Judeo-Christian scriptures, and the study and visits with Gandhi served as an internal anchor which could not be moved by any amount of external pressure.

The visit with Gandhi in India in 1959 immensely enriched and deepened his belief in non-violent resistance. Gandhi's method of *satyagarha* embraced the principles of courage, truth, and non-violence. The march he led over 200 miles to the sea to make salt defied the British Empire, which made it a crime to purchase salt from any other source than the British. His leadership of national resistance was pivotal in gaining Indian independence in 1947.

On March 29, 1968, one year exactly after the Riverside Church speech, King was shot to death on the balcony of his motel in Memphis, Tennessee. The cost of dissent, deviation from the majority, and threatening fundamental interests of major powers is always substantial. The reward is that we get closer to the truth and closer to democratic strength and everyone's winning. Short of an assassin's bullet, King could not be moved.

Daniel Ellsberg

It seems that when whistleblowers or government officials leak information, they think the populace should know something that threatens them. The press does little to print an accurate character sketch of the person. Rather, perhaps indirectly, the suggestion comes across that the person may be of somewhat questionable character. How could any patriotic citizen leak something that might bring the charge of espionage or treason? I remember that when Daniel Ellsberg leaked the so-called Pentagon Papers in 1971, the popular press gave the impression that he was less than highly desirable person and of insignificant status. Nothing could have been more inaccurate.

Ellsberg was a gifted child in both the arts and math. He completed Harvard *summa cum laude* and topped it all off with a scholarship to study economics at King's College, Cambridge University. He served three years in the Marine Corps, including duty in the Suez Crisis of 1956. In decision theory, he pioneered papers on the conditions under which people violate their own declared values. After military service his path led back to Harvard to complete a doctoral degree in economics.

He worked for the highly respected RAND Corporation on military strategy in the Pacific Theater. During the Cuban missile crisis he was called to Washington to assist in analysis for the National Security Council. In 1964 the Defense Department put him to work drafting top-secret plans to escalate the war in Viet Nam. He worked on site in Viet Nam for two years. Back in the States, he continued working for RAND on a document on "decision making in Viet Nam from 1945-1968," later to be known as the Pentagon Papers.

Ellsberg was in the midst of top level Viet Nam planning and information. He knew we were not winning the war. He became increasingly convinced that like the Gulf of Tonkin fabrication, the war was built on lies and endless unnecessary violence against the people and country of Viet Nam. As early as 1969, he began photocopying the complete 7,000 pages of the document. He first offered it to the *New York Times*, which was stopped from printing it by an injunction, and, then later, to the *Washington Post*. The Supreme Court ruled that newspapers could publish the Pentagon Papers without censure.

Lower courts charged him with conspiracy, theft, and espionage. The charges were finally dropped and a mistrial declared because Nixon had mounted a campaign to smear Ellsberg by breaking into his psychiatrist's offices, hunting damaging character information.

The public, the government, and the courts vilified Daniel Ellsberg. He realized in advance that he very likely might pay for releasing the papers by going to prison. There seem to be two things that motivated Ellsberg. One was the comprehensive, long-term, and first-hand information he had about the war. He had worked virtually for the duration of the war in central and sensitive government positions rather than peripheral ones. He knew mass warfare was not working against a guerilla war, and he knew that endless reinforcements would potentially flow forth from China. He knew unequivocally that we were losing and continually lied about it.

But there has to be another bigger motivation because many other top military and government officials had the same information but did nothing to launch a voice of opposition. He apparently was anchored in a body of ethics that did not square with our actions. He was inspired by other war resisters and the works of Gandhi and Martin Luther King, Jr. The growing sense of the immorality of the war became something he could not escape. He could have denied guilt or found a diversion, but he had the courage to act on his conviction. His action carried great personal costs and pain. He had to consider his family: a wife, three children, and five grandchildren. He had to possess uncommon courage in great supply. His extensive experience, deep and broad learning, and, above all, his deeply rooted value system, anchored his immovable internal resolve.

Nelson Mandela

The year the Berlin wall was coming down in Europe, 1990, Nelson Mandela was finally leaving the walls of his 27-year-old prison. Seldom does such a man who possessed such a rare congeries of accomplishments and style honor us. In his tribal setting, he was a royal child. Somewhat arrogant and vain, Mandela completed his education with a law degree. Perpetually moved by the brutality and injustice of apartheid, he used the law to pursue justice but was stymied. He tried violent armed conflict but later such behavior morphed into a more powerful exemplary avenue of compassion, reading and learning, and endless debate, persuasion, and patient diplomacy.

Southern African tribes share a belief and practice of collectivism in contrast to modern Western individualism. Solidarity, interdependence, mutual responsibility, and compassion mark their way of life. Being taught to cooperate rather than compete, they tend to see positive things in the other person rather than negative. Throughout Mandela's life he reflected on the old ways of the Xhosa tribes as a rich coveted age of equality devoid of exploitation. His 1999 biographer, Anthony Sampson, quotes one of Mandela's speeches before his prison sentence. Of their way of government, he said, "The council was so completely democratic that all members of the tribe could participate in its deliberations. It was so weighty and influential a body that no step of any importance could ever be taken by the tribe without reference to it."

Alex Haley tells of a similar finding among his ancestors in Gambia, West Africa. There was a chief who became heavy handed and dogmatic. Custom dictated that the tribe would warn him twice. If he reformed, his old faults were forgotten. If he still persisted to dominate, the tribe would pack its belongings one night while the chief was sleeping and move on, leaving the chief with no people. If he found them and truly changed his ways, no one was ever to speak of it again. They had mastered humane political correction, balance of power, and political forgiveness. These tribes possessed rich human relations and practices, but the Europeans in their ignorance could only focus on their lack of artifacts, like cathedrals as indices of progress.

Even though some of the English forces in Africa recognized advanced indigenous ways, as early as 1835, the white man destroyed the collective ways by dividing people into artificial groupings and began the process of subjugation. Apartheid, a modern form of oppression, was instituted when the National Party took power in 1948. The African National Congress (ANC) was a response to the inhuman destruction of the tribal peoples. Mandela played a key role in the early days of the ANC, assertively protesting the oppressive policies leading to his Treason Trial, lasting from 1958 to 1961. He was found not guilty. Rebuffed repeatedly by the government while seeking redress, the ANC became more militant. Mandela was arrested in 1962 for leading a bombing campaign against government sites and for sabotage to overthrow the government; thus began his 27 years as a political prisoner in the Robben Island prison and other prisons toward the end of his incarceration.

Robben Island held many political prisoners, irate about their people's suffering and driven to more fully understand their situation and what they might do about it. Mandela, apparently, was evolving from reliance on protest and force to other more effective means. Whites in the country were a minority, but they held all the power. They were adept in wielding it brutally. There had to be a path of building sophisticated knowledge among the prisoners and gaining the sympathy of the outside world. Pressure from the Red Cross and the outside world gradually brought about an atmosphere where prisoners could interact and even discuss issues with the guards. Books were devoured and shared, including the classics. Seminars were held. Vigorous, intense, but disciplined debates were endlessly exploring what constitutes good government. Also thorough study occurred to understand their oppressors.

College students in the Western world were occupying presidents' offices in universities and colleges demanding divestment of corporations that were complicit in Apartheid. After much time in which the Black population became more and more restive and the outside world increasingly outraged and applying active sanctions, the South African government began to reconsider Mandela's imprisonment. He requested and gained negotiating sessions with President de Klerk.

After much struggle, in a monumental speech in early 1990, de Klerk promised to free all prisoners not guilty of violent crimes, legalize all political parties, including the ANC and the Communist Party, cease all executions, and the unconditional early release of Mandela.

The standing government leaders were surprised and impressed by the stature of Mandela and his close associates, the sophistication of their ideas and arguments. They were further surprised by their positive unifying vision for all the peoples of the country and lack of vindictiveness. After Mandela was released, he visited many of the former government leaders who were responsible for his captivity. His very presence and demeanor conveyed his affirmation of equality and, at the same time, an attitude of wanting to build together. He was released from prison in 1990 and elected President of the new nation in 1994. His tribal ways of reconciliation and respect carried him to the top.

This chapter was roughed out the day before Mandela died, December 5, 2013. The most impressive commentary to me was that Mandela supposedly said that when freed form prison, he would not really be free unless his hatred toward his tormentors and a natural inclination for revenge could be entirely vanquished within himself. Then, he would be free entirely. That, in turn, allowed his grace and conciliatory behavior to win the hearts of blacks and whites. His genius was in enabling everyone to win, old friend and old foe. Dan Rather called him the greatest leader in the last half of the 20th century. Past President Clinton said that Gandhi, King, and Mandela were the greats of the century.

These men are examples of people who were stronger than the currents around them. They were selected because of the centrality of the belief and practice of equality and their commitment to them. People like Julian Assange, Glenn Greenwald, Edward Snowden, and many other whistleblowers in business and industry could be added. Time will probably lessen the controversy around them and elevate their value of speaking the minority voice. Hopefully, none of us will ever have to bear the weight and conflict these have born. And in every major example cited above, they were immersed in the values of justice and fairness displayed in the Judeo-Christian teachings and in the great literatures of the world. Liberal learning is not sufficient for independence, and may not be categorically necessary, but all the examples above were immersed in it.

★★★

Bainton, Roland H. Original publication, 1950, reprinted 2012. *Here I Stand, The life of Martin Luther.* Forgotten Books. Reliable account by a prominent late church historian

Ellsberg, Daniel. 2003. *Secrets: A Memoir of Vietnam and the Pentagon Papers.* New York: Penguin. Valuable, compared to many other accounts, because it is his own

Fischer, Louis. 2002. *The Essential Gandhi: An Anthology of his Writings on His Life, Work, and Ideas.* New York: Vintage. The collection lets Gandhi speak for himself.

Frady, Marshall. 2002. *Martin Luther King, Jr.: A Life.* New York: Penguin. Has special attention given to his legacy, as well as his whole story

Haley, Alex. 1976. *Roots.* New York: Doubleday. The famous true story of the author's research tracing his family roots back to West Africa via old sailing records, and the culture he discovered.

Holy Bible: New International Version. 1984. Grand Rapids, Michigan: Zondervan.

McPherson, James M. 2009. *Abraham Lincoln.* New York: Oxford.

Robinson, Jackie, and Duckett, Alfred. 2003. *I Never Had It Made: An Autobiography of Jackie Robinson.* New York: HarperCollins. A first-hand account of his struggles against racial hatred, abuse, discrimination, and overcoming them.

Sampson, Anthony. 1999. *Mandela, The Authorized Biography.* New York: Knopf. Covers historic and contextual materials and stories not in Mandela's autobiography of 1990 *Long Walk to Freedom.* It chronicles the release in detail, the development of the constitution and national planning, and Mandela's presidency and subsequent statesmanship.

PART III

The Meaning of Equality, and Its Demise

THE BELIEF IN equality as defined in Chapter 8 is an umbrella set of beliefs supporting the central idea that human abilities and potential are widely distributed in the human population. The demise of equality in Chapter 9 focuses on the decline of equal opportunity and a withering of equal protection under the law. Three major personality measures are examined in Chapter 10, all of which portray worldviews of inequality. Finally, in Chapter 11, we examine how equality has fared down through a long span of time, including some insights from select animal behavior.

Chapter 8 Belief in Equality as an Attitude

**Chapter 9 The Decline of Equal
Opportunity and Equal Protection**

Chapter 10 Three Personality Measures of Inequality

Chapter 11 Cooperation Through Time and Place

Chapter 8: Belief in Equality as an Attitude

The definition of equality

EQUALITY AS AN internalized personal belief is different from looking at equality as equal protection under the law or as equal opportunity. The belief in equality captures a set of attitudes or beliefs that human abilities and potential are widely distributed in the population in contrast to an aristocratic view that ability is constricted to a limited few from privileged or noble positions. Belief in equality assumes that most people have the potential to contribute significantly to their social, work, and civic settings.

This belief is in contrast to the notion than only a few people are inherently equipped to make much difference even in their families and organizations. The belief in equality taps a positive view of human potential; most people are capable of fine accomplishments if given the nurturance and enduring opportunity to grow and mature. If the Churchills, Eisenhowers, and Nobel winners had been born into dysfunctional families and abject poverty, the probability is very low that they would have been high achievers. The probability is high that they would have been hard working poor cooks, truck drivers, laborers, or even unemployed or drug traffickers. This is, of course, not to deny that some children may rise out of deadening environments to accomplish good things. They are exceptions and usually have had someone along the line to encourage them and point them to higher aspirations and opportunities. In a series of seminars on poverty in our community, a young woman who had lived in her car for extended periods was now a senior in college and on the rise because a high school counselor helped raise her aspirations radically. Any one of us could be homeless, alcoholic or otherwise addicted today if we had been born into a destructive childhood.

A slightly different, but supportive, way to view the belief in equality is to cast it into a simple equation. Each human being = 1 unit of human worth. Every person = 1, no more, no less. The forklift operator who makes $30,000 a year has the same value or worth as the hedge fund trader who makes $30,000,000. The literature of the secular humanities would be comfortable with this equation. That is, each person is fully a human being, a full member of the human race, not an 0 as we counted Blacks and Original Americans at one time, or 3/5 as the 1787 Compromise determined. A king, president, or emperor is not worth 1,000 times more than a cleaning person. The king is not entitled to 1,000 units of worth. Economically or militarily, they may be worth more in the affairs of nations. But their humanity just equals 1 full unit. In direct combat, the soldier may have to shoot the enemy. The soldier may have to de-humanize the enemy emotionally in order to be brave and stay sane, but the one enemy combatant is still worth 1 full unit of humanity. In all the secular halls of justice, truth, and compassion, each person has a full value of one.

In the Judeo-Christian tradition, the equation is the same, but the justification or proof is different. In addition to being seen as part of the created animal kingdom, we are seen as a little lower than the angels but, indeed, seen as children of God, made in the image of God. We are his offspring regardless of how long it took through the eons of evolution. In the beginning, God made man and woman, not kings and slaves. He did not put different numbers on us. We all have a full human value of 1. There are no 8s or 1/2s. In Chapter 11 on Cooperation and Equality through Time, we will try to, at least, open the argument that significant roots for equality reach clear back to the Exodus story and even throughout the governmental discourses in the book of Deuteronomy. And, of course, we will note the equality theme from the prophets through Jesus and, with considerable clarity, in the letters of the New Testament.

Exceptions and qualifications

The belief in equality obviously recognizes that some are born with marked deficiencies, deformities, and severely limiting diseases and other limitations. In these cases, expectations have to be especially tailored to fit the special persons. But even within this small percentage of the population (traditionally considered to be about 2%), these persons can make significant contributions if we are open to them. For example, the Downs Syndrome child is often abundantly capable of demonstrating genuine affection and loyalty, often missing in many persons. In our own family, a grandchild bore extreme limitations of mitochondrial disease; he moved many to exceptional levels of love and compassion.

On the other end of the ability spectrum, the gifted are in some sense beyond our conception of belief in equality. The belief in equality does not deny exceptional musical ability, quantitative reasoning, athletic prowess, and artistic imagery, to name a few dimensions. The top two percent at the top of intelligence scales constitute a small part of the population.

Genetics has an especially singular determinative impact at each end of the population distribution; whereas, for the mass of persons in the middle, the genetic impact is not nearly as singular or salient but rather unfolds in a dynamic interaction between genetics and the environment. The environment plays a large role in turning genetics either on or off. This is a not a denial of the incredible power of genetics; it is to say that their function is not always static, but dynamic. The effects of genetics are not denied, but even though opportunities do not affect the genotype of actual DNA, they do impact the phenotype, that is the real person who develops. Opportunities facilitate or diminish any person's development. Gladwell's analysis of outliers shows that even for persons who may be exceptionally genetically endowed, opportunity plays a critical role.

The belief in equality also does not mean that we are all made the same or develop the same. The middle ninety-six percent of the population that we are focused on here have a full array of individual differences, whether pre-wired or acquired. Our profiles of abilities and characteristics are richly diverse. One person is strong in one area, and another in another area. So we should approach a group of people assuming that they all have a rich and varied repertoire of abilities, or the potential for such. The attitude has an affinity for the current conception of intelligence as being multiple rather than single. A person may measure high on one type of intelligence but not very high in another.

The practical gist of the belief-in-equality argument is that we should approach an individual or group with the assumption that the right circumstances at the right time makes a big difference. This assumption holds regardless of appearances, like missing teeth, crude clothing, impoverished speech, and a bad attitude. James A. Garfield articulated this assumption forcefully. He likely would have made a noted and accomplished President if he had not been assassinated only four months into his term. From his roots in poverty, he rose to be a recognized university professor and later a member of Congress. Kind, warm, highly intelligent and generally capable, he is credited for the following affirmation and expectation of potential in all people: "I never met a ragged boy in the street without the feeling that I may owe him a salute, for I know not what possibilities may be buttoned up under this overcoat."

Reality check

But is the belief in equality a flight into idealism divorced from reality? Aren't many people hopelessly cranky, selfish, lazy, duplicitous, and careless. Anybody who has done a stint in the labor force has met many of these people (or in any segment of society for that matter). They do not care about quality, honesty, producing, or taking care of the customer. They have a generally bad attitude. They care about when their break comes, getting the easiest job, and finishing and going home. They demoralize the workforce and poison the atmosphere.

How did they get that way? Why no loyalty to the company, no work ethic? Could it have something to do with the disloyalty of the company toward them? Part of the unraveling of society, if indeed it is decaying, is the abandonment of the people by the corporations. The bottom line is maximizing profits in both the short term and long term. Much of corporate America has written the worker off as dumb labor, a commodity, not different from a drill press or a load of coal. Something to get the job done to maximize profits. It is perfectly understandable that many workers are sour and fewer of them have a work ethic. When we treat people poorly they respond poorly. It is a rational response.

Belief in equality impacts expectations.

The term "self-fulfilling prophecy" has become common language. Some may take the term lightly, but the phenomenon can be very real. Numbers of experiments indicate that if a coach, teacher, or boss is told that a new group of charges are exceptionally promising, and other leaders are given no such expectations for their groups, the resulting performances differ greatly. Positive expectations can explain as much as half the variance in task success. A study in a welding school suggested to certain instructors that their new class had very high potential to be great welders. Nothing was communicated to a similar set of instructors. The first group performed 50 percent better that the control group.

When leaders expect that their groups have potential, they give better instructions, demand more, and provide better feedback about performance. Result? These groups do better. When the initial expectation is that a leader's group is inferior, the leader's behavior is the opposite. He or she explains assignments less well, gives less feedback, sets lower standards or demands, and over controls.

When one is pulled over by a police officer, if one expects courtesy the officer is more likely to extend courtesy. If one expects belligerence, one is more likely to get it. In the world of sports, anticipation and other aspects of the mental game are very real. The Zen influence on archery leads the archer to forget a bad shot and picture the next shot as perfect. The archer is coached to imagine that the next arrow is blazing into the heart of the target. Of course, expectation does not explain the whole world, but it is one of many vital influences. How many kids are told that they are worthless and are nothing but criminals? It sure helps them on their way to destruction. In stark contrast, other kids are told that they can do and become any thing that they want. Raising their aspirations raises their expectations and motivates them toward higher goals.

If we could take all the dirty, sullen kids in school and see potential, we would be further along to unlocking that potential and turning them around. If the belief in equality has the merit claimed, apparently hopeless kids may very well come to demonstrate as much potential as the class leader in a prestigious school. If we could take all the un-kept, sloppy, perhaps belligerent, or, maybe, dull-looking adults and consider them worthy of stimulation and opportunity, what treasure we would uncover? Just to have a meaningful job and living wage would be a significant encouragement for many. A caveat, of course, is that once something is broken, it is often very hard to fix.

Consequences of believing in equality, for leaders and followers

If leaders believe that their workers have valuable skills and potential, then, they will treat them very differently. Old terms, like mutual respect, mutual dignity, and mutual loyalty, have a chance at a comeback. Democracy in the workplace, which captures these old terms, was beginning to have a significant emergence in the form of profit sharing, group decision making, and distributed quality control in the late 1960s and early 1970s. The widespread value of the worker was reflected in national governmental protections in civil rights enforcements, environmental protection agencies, and consumer rights agencies.

Because of these new protections for the common person, big businesses became alarmed and felt their rights were being seriously infringed upon. The result was that communications, like the Lewis Powell memo of 1972 to the national Chamber of Commerce, raised a battle cry for big business to unite and mount a countercharge. The new protections for the common man were explicitly called a threat to the "American system." In other words, protecting the dignity of the common person was seen as a threat to the privileges and entitlements of big business.

A plethora of right wing foundations were born to protect the "American System" as Powell called it. Foundations, such as the Heritage Foundation, Coors, and Cato, all came to the aid of unfettered capitalism. Powell urged corporations to go on the offensive against education and the media. Colleges and universities got the message and became more cautious about their liberal public image, adopting a more careful and conservative tone. Illustrative of this impact on one well heeled liberal arts college is its slogan "Where Faith and Freedom Matter." Equality is absent. At another school, the name "Liberty University" conveys the same sentiment. Equality is so eradicated and erased from the public relations pages that an "Equality University" would sound absurd.

President Reagan assigned a book to his cabinet called the *Manifesto* to reassert legislation and propaganda to put regulation agencies to sleep (defund and depopulate) and put big business on the top. This book was a response to and continuation of the spirit and concerns of the 1972 Powell memo.

A systematic and planned redistribution of wealth and power had been launched by think tanks and legislation. This is not to say it was a centralized conspiracy. Many independent foundations and powerful figures made their agendas known separately. The crushing of the Air Traffic Controllers union triggered the intentional destruction of unions widely. In the ensuing four decades or so, organized labor went from thirty some percent to around eleven percent of the work force. This meant that workers had little chance to negotiate the terms of their labors, contributing to the yawning gap emerging between the powerful one percent and the ninety nine percent. Middle-class people were stripped of power and stagnated economically, and the poor were crushed in growing numbers. Of course, other forces, probably more powerful and pervasive, were at work to dehumanize the regular person on Main Street: fraudulent finance at the highest levels, shipping jobs abroad even when greed was the motivation rather then true global competition, raiding corporations that remained at home by some of the less principled private equity groups with the short term goal of profit maximization, regressive tax structures, and funding and nurturing groups set against any form of common welfare, such as a the so-called Tea Party.

Shared decision-making

Lopsided power in any organization at any level is likely to dehumanize. Some sense of shared power (and wealth) has great potential to engender human respect and dignity. Leaving the scenario of the devolution of the quality of life at the national level and coming down to smaller structures, how will a leader who really believes in equality treat his or her workers? Rule by fiat, command and obey, fear, intimidation, and deceit will be replaced by sharing decisions at appropriate levels. Shared decision making will be data-based with data widely shared rather than being secret and, thus, more easily manipulated and misrepresented.

During the build-up and before the downturn of the economy in Japan, all workers were privy to and actually trained to read the production and fiscal reports of their units and their companies. Lifelong employment was cultured in a climate of mutual respect of management and workers who had the unified goal of continual improvement. Japanese management assumed that the workers were intelligent and had the potential to understand the functioning of the company rather than assuming that the workers are dull, dumb, and uncaring. With a greater understanding of the workings of the company, the workers are more likely to identify with the company and be supportive, as well as being more likely to become whole-hearted active participants with management at their particular level of work.

The skeptic may say this is nonsense. Admittedly, many or perhaps most people in some organizations do not care a fig for the company; they will do as little as they can, sometime engage in a bit of sabotage, pilfer what they can, with little concern about making mistakes or demonstrating any form of responsibility. Some come to work partially stupefied from abused substances. This is a picture of poisoned waters. When companies and corporations undercut and generally mistreat workers, it should be no mystery that the workers will be hostile or, at least, apathetic about their jobs. Just as poisoned bodies of water take time to clean, so changing the culture of a sour workforce takes time and understanding. And quite possibly what is once sour may never be sweet again. In a decaying organization, it is no wonder that the skeptic would say that the possibility of shared power is fatuous.

But, in fact, if a modicum of trust can be established, the result will be that workers will appreciate having some sense of control and will come to feel that the organization respects them. Self-respect does not guarantee better performance, but it certainly opens the way for that outcome. Leaders may be vulnerable when they step off the unilateral throne of commanding and open some of the protected company information needed to do group problem solving. The genius of doing this, however, is that the company conveys trust and lays the groundwork for the worker to return that trust. Capitalism is simply cruel to the common person unless it is tempered with some degree of caring. Maximizing profits kills workers; whereas, making a reasonable profit can include the welfare of the worker.

Ongoing training

We are assuming here that when leaders start with a new organization, it may be open to transformation. If the leader believes in the potential of the worker, and the leader wants to share decision-making, then training will be a very high priority. If vital managers are constantly learning to remain at the cutting edge, then workers who share in problem solving must also be constantly learning. Ongoing training adds value to the worker and mutual benefit to the worker and the company. When this happens, the company is likely to produce a better product, and the workers will gain some satisfaction from the company investing in them. The worker is also likely to find the training to be stimulating and invigorating. Training becomes necessary if companies want to move back toward long–term employment and commitment to the worker. Unfortunately, the corporate desire for employee longevity is absent in the current scene. Sad to say, training is one of the first things to go during cutbacks and downsizing. It is not considered essential, even though in reality, it is crucial to competitiveness. Ironically, when democracy in the workplace had some presence in the early 1970s, a slowdown in company production was used to increase intensive training instead of reason for laying off workers.

Technical training may be needed even in the fundamentals of STEM, as specific high tech training will be necessary to bring our country up to speed. On the other hand, the soft side of leadership is even more likely to be neglected. Many have lamented that we can put a person on the moon, but we do not know how to get along with one another. Positive group problem solving is likely to make a group far more effective in resolving conflicts and working through interpersonal barriers. Negative group dynamics are too often the order of the day; the leader may not even be aware that he or she is alienating workers.

Goal setting

We are raising soft considerations here that are at the very front end of problem solving. A front-end issue is the activity of goal setting. If the boss sets goals, why should workers feel any personal and internal investment in them? In fact, unilateral goal setting is likely to result in the workers and leaders having opposing and different goals.

In our case of national conflict between the debt reducers and the investors, a stalemate is likely to continue unless goals can be brought closer together. This is especially true if both sides remain politically strong. The outcome will probably not be cooperation but rather one side's overpowering the other and promoting its own goal. That may not be unusual in national politics. But in relatively small work groups when a cooperative dynamic is valued, the tactic of overpowering will be counterproductive. When people are ignored, they either fight or withhold their very best. When the total group establishes a clear consensus on goals, actual problem solving can begin and can be productive. This is radically different from when the boss comes into a meeting saying, "Here are our goals. Let's get busy and meet them."

Another example of the critical nature of human resources research is the nature of dissent in group problem solving. Looking at all aspects of a problem, not just the most unpopular options, will go a long way in avoiding destructive or inferior decisions. The much-studied debacle of the Bay of Pigs invasion was hatched in a bandwagon atmosphere with almost no dissent. None of us likes dissent because it threatens our comfort and perception of reality. Nevertheless, if we value truth and the highest integrity of data and decision making, we must not only learn to tolerate criticism, but also must create an atmosphere where it is welcomed, invited, and required.

Waste

Running pell-mell for immediate profit maximization is wasteful in the long run. Not only will workers be less satisfied and less productive under heavy-handed leadership, but also the leadership will waste expensive resources. The most expensive resources, the ideas and creativity of the workers, will be lost to the company. Neglecting the soft side of problem solving occurs at great cost. Corporations so discount the value of the worker that colossal loss goes unnoticed, unreported, and unaccountable. No one is responsible for this loss. If $100,000 is missing in a small firm, someone is going to be accountable. The loss will be considered great. If 100 barrels of oil disappear from inventory, an investigation will follow, and someone will lose a job. But when untold quantities knowledge and intelligence of workers is lost, management is often too blind and profit driven to notice.

Egalitarian expectations not only make our approach to an individual more positive, but also change our approach to the structure of organizations from hierarchical and centralized to democratic and decentralized. This is a radical shift. Traditional organizations of all sizes cherish strong control by very few at the top and very little power or control passed down through the several layers of a firm. The shift is profound, but does not necessarily have to be either/or. The military requires an intensely hierarchical structure; however, a general should value the knowledge that his lieutenants and soldiers in the trenches have. The general knows a lot more than the private overall, but the private has valuable information that a general, sitting in his protected headquarters, can never have. Generals have to make the final decision about an issue, often instantly, but war councils and information from the trenches at other times can save generals serious blunders.

Not only does waste tend to be greater in hierarchical structures than in democratic ones, but safety is more likely compromised as well. It is reported that 70% of airline crashes are due to human error. A version of cockpit training originated as far back as the 1980s by Blake and Mouton when they introduced democracy into the dynamic of a flight crew. Many years ago a commercial flight crashed into the Potomac shortly after takeoff. It had de-iced but sat on the runway too long and built up more ice. If the whole crew had been expected to look at icing from different windows, the pilot may have been advised not to take off. In the case of the South Korean airline crash, July 6, 2013, deference to authority prohibited the lower-status co-pilot and engineer to question the senior pilot's decisions. Even in highly pressured situations where life and death demands rapid decision making, a flight crew can deliver various observations to the pilot in split seconds. The pilot still has the authority and responsibility to make the final decision.

Shared benefits

Good companies pay the worker as much as they can, bad companies pay them as little as they can. It would seem that we have a lot of bad companies. The class warfare and redistribution of wealth upwards by corporations over the last forty years has created a tiny, but very powerful, one percent and a disempowered ninety-nine percent. This is the exact opposite of profit sharing. Before corporations intensified their paradigm of maximizing profits, there were serious attempts at profit sharing designed to distribute some of the benefits of increased production to all people up and down the production line. At least, health insurance and pension plans had been the old normal even if profit sharing was more often experimental. Now, in the phony guise of global competition, needed flexibility, and the technology revolution, benefits have diminished profoundly. The current formula calls for freezing wages, withdrawing benefits, and pumping profits up the ladder in a way that is, in my opinion, truly obscene. Hoarding benefits is unwise for our businesses in the long run and unwise for our nation.

Measuring the belief in equality with the *BE* scale

Psychologists are wont to measure everything. Can something like the belief in equality be empirically quantified? There is a measurement device called the *Belief in Equality* (*BE*) scale. It has been demonstrated to have both reliability and validity. It consists of a set of 32 statements and has been administered to many participants in four different countries. People respond to each item on a 5-point scale ranging from strongly disagree to strongly agree. Here are some example items. "All individuals are worthwhile to society." "The different forms of creativity of employees are beneficial to a business." "When you look at the masses, there is a sea of untapped talent there." The inventory is very reliable. If people were measured multiple times, the measurement would be very nearly the same each time. Reliability is reported on a scale ranging from .01 to .99. *BE* reliabilities were all in the nineties, measured over many studies in four countries.

Validity of a psychological measurement is more complicated and difficult to establish. An examination of validity ascertains whether the measurement actually measures what it says it purports to measure. Predictive validity is one of the more common and useful forms of validity. Being able to predict types of leadership behavior from *BE* measures would be evidence of predictive validity. Participants typically complete the 32-item *BE* scale and then indicate their choice of leadership strategies to solve simulated group problems. Simulated life-like problem scenarios are used dealing with issues such as budgeting, delegating, assignment of working tools, marketing, production, and the handling of status symbols. Varying degrees of autocratic or democratic approaches are presented from which the participants could choose. The basic predictions were that persons who scored high on the *BE* scale (strong belief in equality) would choose a democratic rather than an autocratic approach to solving the simulated work scenarios.

The *BE* scale predicted leadership choices validly and consistently many times over across a wide range of ages with samples from United States, Germany, Poland and Russia. All research materials were translated into the languages of the latter three countries, and then back translated to check on accuracy. Even in the former Soviet countries, belief in equality predicted the choice of leadership styles.

★★★

Gladwell, Malcolm. 2008. *Outliers; The Story of Success.* New York: Little, Brown and Company.

Gray, D. B., Ageyev, V., Djintcharadze, N., and Bovina, I. 1996. Belief in Equality and Democratic Leadership Behavior in Two Russian Samples. *Political Psychology,* 17, 473-495.

Gray, D. B., Czapinski, J. and Fialkowska, M. 1995. The Effect of the Belief in Equality on Democratic Leadership in Poland. *Polish Psychological Bulletin*, 25, 201-221.

Gray, D. B., and Mizner, D. S. 1996. The Effect of the Belief in Equality on Democratic Leadership Intent. *Journal of Applied Social Psychology*, 26, 652-656.

Kahneman, D. and Tversky, A. 1984. Choices, Values, and Frames. *American Psychologist*, 39, 341-350.

Chapter 9: The Equality Barometer

THE EQUALITY BAROMETER has fallen and bad weather is here. When the value of equality (equal protection under the law and equal opportunity) is passively diminished or intentionally deleted from democratic society, democracy stumbles. When one of the two pillars of democracy is destroyed, the freedom pillar alone will not hold the structure.

Freedom and equality as a pair are the *sine qua non* of democracy. "General welfare" and "Liberty" are the goals that the Constitution declares it will promote, and the Union will strive to realize these goals in the context of "justice" and "tranquility." This declaration is in the very Preamble of the Constitution. Freedom and equality are also linked in Lincoln's famous address at the Gettysburg cemetery, and they are the two rubrics often used in delineating types of political systems.

But the pillar of equality has been bulldozed. Political, corporate, and populist rhetoric is all about freedom. Supposedly governmental regulations are strangling the economy; more freedom is the only thing to save the day. Apparently the financial world should be freed in order to plunge us once again into a great depression. Many of the Tea Party types of movements like to use the word "freedom"; none uses "equality." Modern Presidential speeches are laced with the word "freedom." Our current President has used references to a "level playing field" and "playing fair" in his presidential speeches and only recently has declared that inequality is the defining issue of the day. Shunning the word "equality" has become a litmus test by political fundamentalists.

When policies in support of equality are substantially reduced, people on Main Street are consigned to a lower status, i.e., unequal. They are logically, socially, and economically recast as inferiors. They have less and less power, which is a function of less and less wealth. This is the falling equality barometer. Those in power say, "Who cares? Life is not too bad for many middle class people, and the many who really suffer are voiceless and too weary to be heard."

Some of us care. We care because the weather connected with this falling barometer has taken on severe storm proportions. Some humans become exponentially more valuable and some even are above the law, while others have lost their dignity and have become less than human in the economic storm. Among our youth alone, 15 million or 25% are being left out of the American dream. Unlike a real wind burst, the effects of this economic and social storm are gradual and kill silently. The superior are entitled. And the rich turn this truth on its head by saying that "entitlements (meaning only to the poor) must be reduced." It is entirely appropriate to track this story with emotion as well as analysis.

Too many people still do not get what inferiority means, what forced inequality means. It means that the original Americans were not equal to the invaders from Europe. The original Americans were uncivilized heathen savages. Forced inequality means that mill owners saw laborers in our early industrial age as nothing more than lifting machines. Forced inequality means that the eugenics elite during that same period, late 1800s and early 1900s, could sterilize thousands of American citizens because they were "shiftless." That characterization was actually the basis for many of the sterilizations. Inequality and assigned inferiority means that women were not permitted to vote or openly participate in business, assigned only to reproduction by destiny. Inferiority and inequality meant that Jews, Slavs, the mentally challenged, homosexuals, and Gypsies could be incinerated *en masse* by Hitler. Imposed inferiority means that Blacks could be sold like a bale of cotton.

And now the superior ones are appearing again and are telling us who the inferior and unequal ones are. The political fundamentalists proclaim that 40% of us are takers and not makers. A rising presidential aspirant suggested that the food stamp program fostered laziness in able-bodied men and women, but he avoided the hot button word laziness. He used the metaphor of the hammock, which conveys the on-the-dole mentality of people using food stamps. Food stamps supposedly make people complacent and dependent.

The campaign against supposed negative effects of food stamps and other social support funding ignores the fact that well paying jobs are not out there. Furthermore, the vast majority (two-thirds) of beneficiaries are children, aged, and specially challenged persons. These are not takers. Some of the beneficiaries are working poor juggling more that one job. Other beneficiaries are recent vets. Of course, there are cheats just like there are in government, business, and industry, but the percentage is reported to be as low as one percent.

Equal protection of all citizens and equal opportunity for all

In the last chapter we looked at equality as an attitude or set of beliefs that abilities and potential are widely distributed in the population as a whole. The aspect of equality attended to in this section has to do with equal protection under the law that should enable all citizens to have equal opportunity. Equal standing and protection under the law as assured in the 14th Amendment should mean that we are all so treated. Supposedly we have equal justice. When will our society admit openly and honestly that we are far from it? For the same class of drug related crimes, Blacks are still sentenced ten times more frequently than Whites. Of course, middle class Americans do not want to believe this; it sounds like careless reporting and radical ranting. At every point in the criminal justice system, a Black, on average, will be treated less favorably than a White. Blacks are more likely to be apprehended, wait longer in county jails for hearings and trials, are sentenced more harshly and longer, are more likely to get the death sentence, are less likely to get parole, and are treated more harshly while on parole.

Overall, poor people of all backgrounds are generally treated badly in the criminal justice system, which has become a vast lucrative industry. The poor are subject to public defenders that may not have the time to do a good job; they may be more pressured to make a plea bargain even though it will carry the liability of a felony for the rest of their lives. Our prisons, to a considerable extent, function as substitutes for the age-old poor house.

In the world of industry, a company can demand the workers take pay cuts or relinquish health care under threat that it will be financially forced to close down. The worker has no say. The worker does not have to be shown the financial proof of the company's difficult finances. With the skewering of organized labor, the workers are powerless and have no voice. So what is the value of the worker? Do they have a voice with management? They are simply expendable. Back in the industrial age, when unions did exert themselves in extended strikes and unions and management both used violent tactics, the law was always on the side of management. The National Guard never protected the workers against company lockouts or the abuse of the coal and iron police

The poor and minorities are protected by the 14th Amendment *de jure,* but not *de facto.* Why? Because we have allowed the poor, minorities, and lower level laborers to be viewed as inferior and, therefore, treated as unequal. Most of the nation does not care, and they do not care because the victims involved are considered to be of a lesser sort. The poor and lower level laborers are often seen as losers, lazy, criminal types, immoral, and insignificant. If the elite see the poor at all, it is as cheap labor. They are an income stream for corporate farms, fast food companies, cleaning services, and the whole established criminal justice system: law enforcement, the courts, the law firms, construction companies, and equipment suppliers.

Equality means not only equal protection under the law, but also equal opportunity. Equality never means equal outcome in our society, but an equal chance. When one percent of the nation has a near monopoly on wealth, and thus power, control, and opportunity, the ninety-nine percent do not have equal opportunity. Our great wealth disparity carries with it opportunity disparity.

Lincoln declared eloquently that our forefathers had launched a new nation "conceived in *Liberty* and dedicated to the proposition that all men are created *equal*." It was a speech honoring all the dead equally because they fought for a government "of the people, by the people, and for the people." Lincoln saw the great task before the nation to be a rebirth of freedom for all people. Surely, Lincoln was envisioning equality of citizenship and equality of opportunity for all people of the land, not one percent.

The denial of equality is followed by the assertion of superiority

People who deny equality set themselves up as superior. It is a widely shared observation that young MBA graduates from the Ivy League schools who enter high finance jobs consider themselves superior and look down their noses at their peers who go into manufacturing, sales, or research. Even though these peers have equivalent MBAs, they are not the peers with whom the financial people will build lasting relationships. Manufacturing or research graduates are nobodies. They are not worth keeping in one's smartphone directory.

Can you imagine how bad it is for the single mother with a child, working two low level jobs? She is truly nobody and invisible. These vast pools of people are deleted from the consciousness of the captains of Wall Street and the chiefs of the multi-national corporations. For superior people today, maximizing profits has replaced equality entirely. Maximizing profits minimizes all else, including the lower workers who ironically make companies function.

Self-appointed superior people feel entitled to be "hogs at the trough," continuing to get big bonuses on top of multi-million dollar salaries. Mr. Robert Benmosche, chief executive of AIG (American International Insurance Group) compared criticism of bonuses to lynching in the old South. Stephen Schwartz, Chair of the Blackstone Group, one of the world's largest private equity groups, compared the criticism of their relatively low tax payments to Hitler's invasion of Poland in 1939. These people are superior and entitled. And they magnify and attack the miserably little entitlements of the poor. These are the people we bailed out of their fraudulent misery.

The "superior" assign inferiority to all the rest, and then abuse them.

To be assigned to an inferior category is totally contrary to the egalitarian ideals of democracy. It is much worse than just "too bad!" It is destructive. To be classified as inferior is to be condemned to low status, powerlessness, helplessness, poverty, and total insignificance. The scene it set for either pervasive neglect or overt abuse. Ninety percent of the benefits and profits of the bailouts of the Wall Street bankers have gone to the one-percent. The ninety-nine percent have been neglected or, at least, used, if not abused. It is not just individuals that lord it over others. History is replete with whole groups subjugating other groups.

It would be easy to say this is the American way, but that would be inaccurate. There have been periods of generosity and good will among American tycoons and their subordinates and between groups. For example, in the 1960s and 1970s, in a sizable minority of companies, there was mutual caring and loyalty; it was called democracy in the workplace. That movement is dead now. Maximizing profits rules the corporate world; workers are minimized. On balance, the powerful have too often been predators. But I believe that within the heart of the American people as a whole, there is still a great generosity and caring. And, on balance, we recognize there are undoubtedly generous people of integrity among the 1%.

Making workers inferior

In very current history, how often have we seen the powerful treating the workers like dirt. For example, private equity groups buy companies, hike dividends during the first year through laying off workers, double work loads, and curtail research and development. Private equity officials sell a company for millions but leave it debt ridden and stripped of its bone and muscle. It is not uncommon for these supposedly superior people to make 50 million in the transaction. It is legal but intensely evil. This is what happens when one-percent have all the power and the ninety-nine percent have none. It is not just bad. It destroys our industry, our jobs, and our people. This is a current form of selling humans as commodities. When the populace conceptualizes what is happening more lucidly, there may be a better chance of massive resistance.

Workers who are not organized to negotiate with their employers are powerless, low status nothings, who apparently deserve to be abused by management. Recently, a western Pennsylvania chain of hardware stores secretly decided to close one store. The workers had no say in the decision and were not even extended the courtesy of a meeting or expression of regret by the company. Employees went to work on Monday morning to find the doors locked with a notice of "closed permanently." Guards were posted to protect the property. When equality is denied, superiors skewer inferiors. It is management "of the superior by the superior and for the superior."

Our history of the powerful considering workers' insignificance, powerlessness, and inferiority is long standing. During the three massive strikes or lockouts (textiles, railroads, and steel) in Pittsburgh in the late 1800s, workers were always seen as the troublemakers, ignorant, lazy, revolutionaries, and idlers. Of the railroad strikers of 1877, a professor in a Presbyterian seminary said the avowed objective of the workers was "the destruction of that divinely ordained order of society wherein individual men by various personal gifts are made by God superior to others, and invested with power over their fellows." The church of the day, influential leaders, and upper middle class people propagated this fatuous nonsense.

We know the classic explanation of why the poor are poor. It is that "there is something wrong with them." It is a worn out and untrue explanation but it persists today. Paul Ryan's recent two-hundred-page report on why the war on poverty supposedly failed has the same old refrain. It is the mentality of "kick the stray cat, whip the slave, and blame the poor." The truth is that many lower class jobs have disappeared via automation and corporate raiding and that those lower level jobs that remain are being filled with workers with more education. "Men with a high school degrees earn a third less in real terms than they did in 1979," according to Eduardo Porter (2014).

More and more men are just not marriageable economically. This is a significant causal factor in why 36% of births are to unmarried white women, and double that for black women. To attribute poverty to moral decay of these poor women and families is an ugly dodge. We can point our finger, feel superior, and relieve ourselves of all responsibility. This supposed "value decline" started in the 1970s and is correlated with the policies favoring the privileged. Correlation does not prove causation, of course, but all the other evidence points to unfavorable economic structures more than anything else.

Making many unfit, and targeted for elimination

The eugenics movement was dedicated to the proposition that any individual with any kind of deficit was flawed genetically and should be weeded out of the population. This could be done positively by "good breeding" or negatively by sterilization or segregation. The leaders tended to be from the very prestigious Ivy universities and were supposedly dedicated to the improvement of society by reducing poverty, mental inferiority, and defective character.

There were two fundamental errors in the movement. One was that nearly all misfortunes or deficiencies were considered to be of a static genetic causation and, second, was that the impact of the environment, opportunity, and privilege were entirely disregarded. So men who went to work when they were 12 years old and put in very long days of drudgery became early school dropouts and appeared to be dull and stunted. They were written off as mentally deficient. The elite eugenicists with degrees from Harvard were devoid of any insight that if they had lived in the impoverished environment of the workers, they too would have looked dull and stunted.

The ambitious plan was to sterilize millions of unfit and undesirable persons. Fortunately this ambition was never realized. However, sources estimate that around 60,000 were sterilized without their knowledge or against their will. Many geneticists, apparently, easily accepted the Godlike responsibility of deciding who was unfit and unworthy. By current standards, the list is beyond belief. Many from the asylums and prisons, epileptics and others, suffering many kinds of diseases. Children whose parents possessed some deficiency, who were homeless, vagrants, or unemployed, they considered to be shiftless. Even persons with imperfect eyesight were included. We might have an ounce of sympathy for the perpetrators because the germ theory was not well established during the early days of the eugenics movement leading them to continue to believe that manifest diseases issued out of inferior "protoplasm," to use their term.

As most national histories are written to leave out the dark sagas, so it has been with our early historians and textbook writers. To this day, many of our citizens do not know about the broad reach of the eugenics movement. It is not widely known that in spite of the "lady of the harbor" saying, "Give me your tired, your poor, your huddled masses, yearning to breath free," many immigrants from Eastern Europe were denied entrance because of supposed mental retardation based totally on invalid intelligence tests. The eugenicists had a significant impact on national policymaking regarding immigration. The long arm of the movement, indeed, reached Germany and provided the pseudoscientific foundation for the Nazi elimination of all whom they considered unfit: Jews, Slavs, homosexuals, Gypsies, and the mentally challenged. This exporting of the goal of creating a super race from the United States to Germany may seem to be a sensational stretch to some readers. It did to me at first. But it is there for any reader to verify for himself or herself.

It may occur to the reader that the abuse of the worker during the days of the early industrialists was unfolding concurrently with the eugenics movement. How much the notions of the eugenicists influenced the industrial and business leaders of the day may be indeterminate. We, at least, know that the zeitgeist of the country, to a large extent, lionized the entitlement and superiority of the rich and powerful, and, in contrast, degraded the scrub lady, the ditch digger, and common mill worker.

The use of force and brutality on the one hand, as well as generosity and compassion on the other hand, are both paramount in our national history. Denial of the brutal side of our story will not clearly inform us about moving creatively into the future. Far before the scenario of the mill laborer working in unsafe and inhumane conditions or the misdirected crusades of the eugenicists, America's reliance on force, brutality, and deception was substantial. The degradation of the original Americans and of the African American slaves is as much a part of our story as is our prosperity and achievements.

Making original Americans inferior

Who took the first scalp? Who fired the first shot? It is not accurate to say it was the American Indian. The Massachusetts Bay Colony probably would not have survived the first winter without the welfare extended by the Wampanoag people. Lewis and Clark apparently would have perished without the support of the original peoples. It would be more accurate to say that the real savages were the devious, greedy, ignorant, and ungodly people from Europe. Most native tribes were more generous, cooperative, closer to God the Great Spirit, and more in touch with God's creation than the pale-faced invaders.

The uncivilized whites made many treaties of peace and cooperation with the Indians, then, turned around and broke them all. The whites broke the treaties whenever it was convenient and economically desirable. When they wanted more land, they simply drafted the American Indian Removal Act of 1830. The Act was also correlated with the discovery of gold in Georgia. Treaties were broken when gold was discovered in the sacred Black Hills. And when we needed flood control in western Pennsylvania, we sacrificed the Seneca lands, and when we needed the uranium in South Dakota, we took the lands of Sioux. But the people we mistreated were a small minority of supposedly inferior and truly disempowered people. It is amazing what can be done with people when we make them into inferiors.

It may be a bit of a stretch to call our brutal treatment of the American Indian genocide, but it certainly tilts strongly in that direction. The Trail of Tears and placing of native Americans on reservations in least desirable tracts of land and breaking all treaties with them comes as close to genocide as one can get without calling it that. At least, we have reduced them to a tiny minority with a tortured culture and questionable standing in American society. But amazingly they have endured and still have great wisdom, which could enhance our materialistic culture.

Data about numbers of original Americans in 1492 is uncertain, to say the least; estimates range from 1 to 12 million, with some sources saying around 4 to 6 million. In contrast to the explosive growth of the white population since pre-Columbian days, the Indian population is stuck at 2.9 million, not quite 1% of our population. Is this close to genocide?

Making African Americans inferior

A number of professional societies, such as the American Psychological Association, have been on record for several decades stating that there is no scientific data indicating that Blacks are genetically inferior in intelligence. It took a long time to get to that conclusion.

As we all know, Africans were forcefully taken from their homelands, often separated from family, and packed into slave ships for a brutal voyage across the Atlantic. They were bought and sold like infrahuman animals. They were whipped, lynched, and barred from education or hope. Good Christian men got rich from the slave trade and slept well at night because white society declared the slaves to be not fully human, inherently and thoroughly inferior.

Half of the nation embraced their inferiority and slavery with such tenacity that a great war took more American lives than any other war. The Emancipation Proclamation finally set the African Americans free, but policies of subterfuge led to new forms of sub-servience, such as share cropping, peonage, discrimination, continued intimidation and lynching, and even a violent municipal *coup d'etat* to overthrow a successfully integrated city government in Wilmington, North Carolina in 1891.

Not until the 1960s in the South were Blacks served at lunch counters and allowed to use regular rest rooms. But the price was that houses were bombed and civil rights workers were beaten and killed. Martin Luther King, Jr.'s house was bombed and he was imprisoned 13 times. He was accused of being a communist and was finally killed by a sniper.

If one believes that the concept of individual and corporate evil remains useful to describe the human condition, then, a common form of that evil or brokenness must forever be to put other people down in order to raise oneself up. And one powerful way to put the other down is to ascribe inherent inferiority to that person or group.

Our culture has limited and controlled one group after another in this way. Not just American Indians, laborers, African Americans, but women, Irish, Slavs, Jews, Chinese, Mexicans, homosexuals, and the poor.

Up until 1920 women were considered to be too emotionally un-stable to enter stressful roles in business or politics. They were openly labeled the "weaker sex." The dominant culture put them down for long time, and women will forever have to fight to maintain their equality. Compare the large numbers of single mothers slipping back into subsistence living often through no fault of their own, but being blamed for their "immaturity, immorality, and general incompetence." And for the more prosperous, the good old boys and the glass ceiling will have dominion for a long time.

The Irish were commonly labeled the "dirty Irish' and were assigned the lowest, dirtiest, most menial jobs. Fleeing the potato famine and coming to America with nothing, they often couldn't afford soap, detergents, running hot water, and changes of clothes. They were considered inherently inferior. It is a mystery that they became some of our great leaders in business and industry and politics, even President of our country.

Eastern Europeans, such as the Poles and Hungarians, were castigated as being slow. Comedians thrived on jokes about the dumb Polish laborers. These jokes have finally disappeared. People like Andy Grove and his production of the Intel chip, and many other outstanding Slavish people like him, finally put charges of inferiority to rest. The list of derogatory labels goes on: emotional dagos, wetbacks, towel-heads, etc. Erasing this list and striving for justice and equality will continue as an ongoing challenge.

★★

Black, Edwin. 2012. *War Against the Weak: Eugenics and America's Campaign to Create a Master Race.* Wshington, DC: Dialog Press.

Carlson, Elof A. 2001. *The Unfit: A History of a Bad Idea.* Cold Spring Harbor, New York: Cold Spring Harbor Laboratory Press.

Edin, Kathryn, and Nelson, Timothy J. 2013. *Doing the Best I Can: Fatherhood in the Inner City.* Berkeley: University of California Press. Intensive interviews with over a hundred inner city youth over extended periods of time retires the tired old idea that "there is something wrong with them."

Gerard, Phillip. 1994. *Cape Fear Rising.* Winston-Salem, North Carolina: John F. Blair Publisher. This is a detailed description of the only metropolitan coup d'etat in American history, in Wilmington, Delaware in 1898. A brutal story of racial hatred, fear, white domination and the negative economic consequences to both sides from squelching diversity.

Greenwald, Glenn. 2011. *With Liberty and Justice for Some: How the Law is Used to Destroy Equality and Protect the Powerful.* New York: Henry Holt and Company. The origins of elite immunity are developed and a depressing catalogue of injustices benefiting the rich and harming the poor and middle class by both political parties is fearlessly set forth. The author is assisting in releasing the Snowden papers.

Hirsch, James S. 2002. *Riot and Remembrance: America's Worst Race Riot and Its Legacy.* New York: Houghton Mifflin Company. Especially Chapters 3 and 4 depict the extreme de-personalization of the African American in the early 1900s in Tulsa, Oklahoma such that torture by red hot pokers, cork screws, and flogging laced with tar could be inflicted on the victim of the lynch mob.

McKinney, William W. (Editor) 1958. *The Presbyterian Valley.* Pittsburgh: Davis and Warde, Inc. Chronicles the history of this one denomination where its members were more concentrated that in any other part of the country. The positive accomplishments and well as the complicity of the denomination in injustice.

Millard, Candice. 2011. *Destiny of the Republic.* New York: Anchor Books. A little told story of the promising, bright, compassionate presidency of James A. Garfield, cut very short by the near fatal assassin's bullet. Interwoven is the account of the assassin's belief in having the absolute truth, and the arrogance and domination of the head physician who increased the likelihood Garfield's death.

Porter, Eduardo. 2014. Time to Try Compassion, Not Censure. *New York Times*, March 5.

Sidanius, James, and Pratto, Felicia. 1999. *Social Dominance: An Intergroup Theory of Social Hierarchy and Oppression.* Cambridge: University of Cambridge Press. A systematic analysis of gross one-upmanship from the perspective of an integrative major theoretical framework called social categorization theory.

Chapter 10: World Views of Inequality

THREE PERSONALITY MEASUREMENTS are presented in this chapter: Machiavellianism (*Mach*), Social Dominance Orientation (*SDO*) and Right Wing Authoritarian personality (*RWA*). In varying ways, they all are designed to measure traditional views of hierarchical and heavy-handed leadership, submissive followership, and inequality. All three correlate negatively with the belief in equality as described in Chapter 8 and measured by the *BE* scale. As belief in equality increases, scores on these other three scales decrease. The three have very different histories and measure somewhat different things. All three of these traditional sets of beliefs will tend to stifle the creative, open problem solver who strives to rise above blind group conformity. The strong characteristics of great historical people set forth in Chapter 7 were presented as most desirable; whereas, the characteristics of people subscribing to the tenants of the three measures in this chapter are seen by the author as undesirable and anachronistic, but subscribed to by a nearly half of the participants in empirical studies.

These three sets of beliefs are not formal comprehensive worldviews; they were never intended to be that, but they embody a rather broad spectrum of assumptions about human nature and the social/political world. While formal worldviews tend to be detailed and comprehensive, the three views dealt with here are more selective. Nevertheless, they have considerable breadth in that they all attempt to tap into the proclivities of human nature and various conceptions of power. These three views are presented as models to be avoided.

The questions about world-views running throughout the three measures are the following: what is the world like, and what are people like? Each of these measures reflects stereotypically masculine beliefs and behaviors. The assumptions support a bloated Pentagon and the military-industrial complex that General Eisenhower warned us about. These beliefs support a predisposition for going to war, even when it is in reality unwarranted and unlikely to have a beneficial result. Politicians are only too ready to stoke the fundamental fears that support these kinds of believers, e.g., the belief in the domino effect in Asia and, more recently, weapons of mass destruction.

A pervasive assumption in the *RWA* scale about the world is that it is a dangerous place, and the way to keep order is by strong authority and force. The reality and ubiquitous presence of danger and the enemy are exaggerated. This assumption places an excessive reliance on punitive attitudes and the use of physical power. One cannot have enough guns, a country cannot have enough prisons, and military might comes before diplomacy, views which are actually a cop-out and dangerous. These beliefs lead to our imprisoning somewhere between 10 to 20 times more frequently than most other developed countries. These statistics sound unbelievable. Hordes of non-violent offenders are saddled with a felony status; that status makes rehabilitation back into society as a productive member much less likely and has a gerrymandering effect in term of voting rights.

The opposite worldview would acknowledge that there are many real dangers in the world, but not the overgeneralized idea of a dangerous world. It would recognize that force is the answer sometimes when the opposition understands nothing but brute force. But it should always exhaust the multiple creative measures of national and international influence first, which is one of the stipulations of the concept of the "just war." Diplomatic measures may take years and are prone to buckling to the demand for a quick and immature "shock and awe" mentality. An alternative approach would place much more effort on redressing the roots of aggression, violence, and addiction and, thus, prevent much of it in the first place. This alternative view would have profound fiscal and budgeting differences in allocation of resources.

The second question is what are people like? It may seem an inane question because it is so over-reaching. But beliefs and perceptions are real and have substantial behavioral consequences. When leaders with a jaundiced view of people view an individual or group for the first time, there will be a negative tendency to see the masses generally as not very bright and unable to understand issues with any depth, not caring, and not remembering the issues with a passage of time even if they do care. So people are dull, gullible, preoccupied, swamped in a sea of superficial trivia and entertainment as they struggle to survive. They are easily persuaded by half-truths and propaganda, easily duped. Workers are in no way equal to the boss.

Managerial principles, based on evidence, show these assumptions about human nature are unwarranted and are counterproductive. Of course, many people are lazy, untrustworthy and unfaithful, but they were not born that way. It is not genetic. The old human breeding argument is mostly silly, but subconsciously, it is probably still active. If people have not been damaged or spoiled, they want to work and get the social and material recognition and security that work can bring. Reciprocity and self-fulfilling prophecy studies show that we treat others the way we have been treated, and we treat them the way we expect they will behave, not according to their potential.

These three large research traditions conceptualize negative views, measure them, and indicate their behavioral correlates. An example of a correlate is that if a leader thinks people are inherently untrustworthy, he or she is more likely to install cameras throughout the place of business, or other types of surveillance mechanisms, rather than nurturing and training the employees.

Machiavellianism

This Italian political participant, thinker, and one-time adviser to the leadership of Florence in the 16th century set forth his views in *The Prince*, originating in 1523, and in *Discourses*. His protocol followed a gradient from supposedly benign to threatening to ruthlessly destructive as the occasion warranted. He proposed government of complete opportunism, without a shade of principle. Any Prince who manages by principle will be an ineffective weakling. However, the successful Prince will always begin relating to his people in gracious manner. It is best to be loved. He will know his audience and will pander and please. He will say anything and do anything in the way of speech and manners to make the people like him and, at the same time, please them. If his people believe that the devil rides a purple horse, he will say that the devil rides a purple horse. He will tell the American Indians their ways are greatly respected when one really thinks of them as throwaways. He believes nothing of what he says because he believes in nothing except manipulation and power for his own gain. Illusion, flattery, and masterful deceit become the first tools of the Machiavellian. He may feign feeling and even empathy for the concerns of his subjects. But, internally, he is cool and detached (a classic boarder-line psychopath), but he will try to remain in sheep's clothing.

If ingratiation does not work, then the tactics change to slightly harsher communications. Mild threats will be followed by stronger ones and finally threats inducing potent fear caused by promised punishment or terrorism. A phony, but moderately mild fear message, might be, "If you do not increase production, we will have to cut benefits," or more harshly, "This plant will have to close." There may be no economic basis for such a statement. Or, another empty deception is "If you vote for them, they will take your guns away." Harsher threats may foretell apocalyptic disasters, as the deficit scolds prefer. To avoid paying for investment and rebuilding of our nation, some scare us by saying our deficit is so great that our grandchildren will be paying our bills. Former Vice President Cheney came as close as he could come to labeling any critic of the Iraq war as being a traitor. It was silly, but it quelled a lot of criticism. It was classical Machiavellianism. If these noxious psychological tactics fail, the only fallback is force and violence. The wise Prince must be ready for the use of force.

David Gray

Some example items from one of the Mach measurements are as follows: "Flattery is a good way to win people over and get them on your good side." "It is okay to fool others as long as it helps you get what you want." And, "White lies are essential and often deceit is necessary in everyday affairs." These are not the words of Machiavelli, but the interpretation of the scale writers.

The *Prince* has been a popular field guide of Western leaders throughout the period of colonialism and up to the present day. We made gracious treaties with the American Indians only to break them all. We threatened confinement on reservations, and when they resisted, we slaughtered them or drove them on a trail of tears. We advocated democracy and promised to be on the side of those who have democratic elections, but pulled support from them if the elections did not suit us, as happened with the Palestinians. We did not like the free elections in Iran in the 1950's so we overthrew the government, and the waters are poisoned to this very day. This approach vitiates the social capital of trust so critical for any modicum of cooperative behavior. Trust comes from the truth and keeping one's word. Deceit and breaking one's word erodes trust and prepares the way for strife and worse.

Contemporary works on Machiavelli would attempt to clean him up and have him pictured as a realist (see Michael Ignateiff). He writes: "The Prince must get dirty for the preservation of the state, and therefore for the good of the citizens." Too often the deceptions are to preserve the power of the dictator and his chances of staying in power. President Johnson lied to us about Vietnam and classified the documentation of the war top secret for the sake of "national security." That too frequently means the goal is the preservation of power and protection of a so-called legacy. Obviously, great leaders stand in overwhelming crosscurrents, and some of their decisions will betray their ideals. But that needs to be the exception. Mandela was not without shrewd political craft, but his moral compass pointed reliably to the good of all peoples and away from his own personal power.

Social Dominance Orientation

This psychometric (*SDO*) measures how much the individual desires that his or her group ––country, profession, church, etc.— dominate and are superior to all other groups. Social domination is a master value holding hierarchies very high and seeing equality as being against the course of nature. The overarching belief in superiority, very similar to the concept of exceptionalism, ignores all negatives and sees only the good things of one's group. There is nothing wrong with recognizing the strength and great achievements of one's group, but to deny the reality of an underbelly which every group has, is inaccurate and leads to grief, grief in the form of spending energy defending one's group, and grief in dealing with the hostility caused by putting other groups down wholesale. Exceptionalism suggests superiority in everything; that is never accurate.

As we have noted in the Equality chapters, once universal superiority is established in the minds of believers, then, domination of other groups seems to be justified. It assumes, "They are not capable of leading themselves. That is why they are on the bottom; therefore, we will have to lead and take care of them." Domination is legitimized and justified in more detail by a series of prejudices about inferiority, such as in racism, sexism, classism, ageism, nationalism and pseudo-patriotism. Rush Limbaugh saturated the airwaves on his talk show with hatred toward assertive women by calling them feminazis. A major respected mainline preacher broadcasted that all psychology is totally self-centered. The old cry of the Nazis, "*Deutschland uber alles*," put them above all other nations, nationalism at its ugliest. There is an astoundingly strong bias for most people to say that their group (even in a fictitious nominal group in an experiment) is more trustworthy and moral that the other group. Add to this a group with something really at stake and then add to that a select group of high scorers on the *SDO* and one has a group that believes itself to be pluperfect on trustworthiness and morality.

Positive self-images and up-beat communications are obviously inspiring and needed. Jesus offered unconditional love, but, ironically, on the condition of justice and feeding the hungry and clothing the naked. His love was coupled with profound judgment. Presidents, CEOs, preachers/priests/rabbis, and citizens who never expose evil condone it by speaking of nothing but love and progress.

Excessive concentration on wealth and power are supposedly justified by the arguments that the few at the top work harder and produce the jobs and economic vitality for the rest. When such legitimizing myths are widely disseminated in the population, often cultivated as self-evident truths and subsidized by big money, social change or resistance against the dominating strata is unlikely. Regardless of how much the 99% has become more convinced of injustice, a plethora of legitimizing myths still prevail to soften the protest and stymie progressive legislation. The prejudicial myths act like sedatives that preclude change. The result is a massive number of poor people, the wasting of many of our youth, and bulging prison cells, all in a land of abundant resources.

Illustrative items from one version of the *SDO* measurement reveal part of the mentality of those oriented toward social dominance: " Some groups of people are simply inferior to other groups." "It's probably a good thing that certain groups are at the top and other groups are at the bottom." "It would not be good if groups were equal."

The Authoritarian Personality

The origins of this research was a response to unmitigated evil. A group of scholars at Berkeley who had lost parents, spouses, and other loved ones in the furnaces in Auschwitz, Dachau, and the other places of mass death, asked themselves what kind of personality would commit such extensive and warped crimes? Five years after the World War II, they published their famous answer in 1950, *The Authoritarian Personality*. This thousand-page volume is on most college and university library shelves. Since its publication date, probably thousands of studies have been done around the world on the authoritarian personality. The book is the record of research, including hundreds of interviews and the construction and administration of several personality inventories.

The major measurement emerging out of that research as called the *F Scale*, *F* standing for Fascism, or a Fascist-like mentality. Three components constituted the early formulation—an excessive adherence to convention, an excessive and blind conformity to that convention, and willingness to defend and fight for that convention and its key leaders. This congeries of beliefs is quite opposite to democracy. There is a near hypnotic faith in a strong leader—either being one or following one. Hitler landed at the great nighttime rallies in a bi-plane and created the image of being a "strong arm from on high." The power symbol of the swastika was stamped on 40 foot high vertical banners blowing in the wind combined with theatrical patterns of marching troops, many of them lighting the night with firebrands. He came at a time when the nation was down, out, and broke, with little hope.

The convention that Hitler created, embellished, and propagated was one of a great Fatherland populated by pure Aryans. He embittered the people about the reparations levied on Germany after World War I and claimed the nation was seriously eviscerated by Jewish bankers. The Fatherland had to be cleansed of all impurities, which included the Jews first and foremost, but also the retarded, the homosexuals, Gypsies, and, later, millions of gentile Slavs.

The authoritarian mentality perceived all things in black and white with no room for ambiguity or complexity, nor room for independent thought or discussion, just blind and unreserved obedience. The exact opposite of all things democratic were enshrined. The world-view reflected in the *F Scale* is one of hero worship, development of a super race, and absolute obedience and conformity. This had to have special appeal to a terribly discouraged people caught in widespread unemployment and inflation. Here was real leadership that would bring prosperity in an occult-like 1,000-year reign. There was extreme stress on appearances and external muscle and little room to appreciate inner strength or character. The stress on purity of race ruled out the richness of diversity. Here was a Reich with absolute truth and zero tolerance.

The authoritarian personality formulated by the Berkley researchers should not be confused necessarily with those who lead with authority and may tend to be heavy-handed, an autocrat. Their inner character may or may not be that of the authoritarian personality. Authoritarian style and authoritarian personality are correlated moderately, but they are two separate conceptions and realities. The authoritarian personality will always be authoritarian, preferring domination or submission, but the autocratic leader may or may not be an authoritarian personality.

A more current version of authoritarianism is called *Right Wing Authoritarianism*. It shows very similar correlations with legitimizing myths as with the *SDO*—high *RWAs* score higher on racism, sexism, nationalism, and are against assistance programs for the needy. Example items from the *RWA* inventory are the following: "Our country desperately needs a mighty leader who will do what has to be done to destroy the radical new ways of sinfulness that are destroying us." "Obedience to authority is the most important thing we can teach our children." "The only way our country can get through the crisis ahead is to get back to our traditional values, put some tough leaders in power, and silence the trouble makers spreading bad ideas." Note that there are reasonable notions contained within these statements and they serve as hooks to lead the respondent to acquiesce.

The profile of the high authoritarians would generally reveal closed-mindedness and distress when faced with ambiguity. They are uncomfortable in open discussions, preferring to be told what to do or believe or to dictate to others. Black-and-white thinking with little room for differentiation or gradation and ample use of boxes or categories with impermeable boundaries are evident. Authoritarians tend to be brittle, rigid, non-flexible in their thinking and deny their own faults while over idealizing their own groups. Several of these characteristics would seem to describe the extreme right wing of the Republican Party today. This is a picture of a political fundamentalist who defends a set of a few conventions with a totally closed mind as though they had captured the absolute truth for all time.

A fairly large sample of state legislators in the United States, 549 Republicans and 682 Democrats, were measured using the *RWA* in the late 1980s (Altemeyer, 1988). The scores could potentially range from 30 to 270. No one in either party scored lower than 90, and no one scored higher than 210. Republicans scored dramatically higher (more Authoritarian, at a mean of 180) than the Democrats (mean of 140), although there was significant overlap of the two parties as well. The Republicans were far more homogenously bunched around their mean while the Democrats were widely distributed. These same measures today would probably be quite different, with the Republicans more dispersed.

All in all, high scorers on the *RWA* would seem to have a pernicious worldview, which would make life uncomfortable for them because of the anxiety of having to hang on to their belief system so desperately and protect it from any change or attack. This worldview obviously makes it miserable for all those who are considered less desirable and less capable, those too young, too old, too sick, too poor, and unemployed. Much of this worldview is shared with the high *SDO* scorers as well.

All three of the worldviews just described handicap the average person from ever rising to independence or resistance to dictators or the crowd. The dictator or domineering leader may rule by fiat and appear to be free of conformity, but, in actuality, his choices are limited, and he is unlikely ever to have a widely loyal people for a long period of time and is perpetually at the risk of being deposed. It is not surprising that paranoia stalks this type of leader, a paranoia that may be largely realistic.

★★★

Adorno, T. W., Frenkel-Brunswick, E., Levisson. D. J., and Sanford, R. N. (1950). *The Authoritarian Personality*. York: Harper and Row.

Altemeyer, Bob. 1988. *Enemies of Freedom*. San Francisco: Jossey-Bass.

Altemeyer, Bob. 1981. *Right-Wing Authoritarianism*. Winnipeg: University Manitoba Press.

Boyle, M. 1995. *Machiavellian Beliefs As Reported in a Bogus Pipeline Condition*. Unpublished senior research thesis. New Wilmington, PA: Westminster College.

Christie, R. and Geis, F. L. 1970. *Studies in Machiavellianism*. New York: Academic Press.

Ignatieff, MichIael. 2013. Machiavelli Was Right. *The Atlantic*, 40-42.

Pratto, Felicia, Sidanius, Jim, Stallworth, L., and Malle, B. Social Dominance Orientation: "A Personality Variable Predicting Social and Political Attitudes," *Journal of Personality and Social Psychology*, 1994, Vol. 67, No 4, 741-763.

Sidanius, Jim, and Pratto, Felicia. 1999. *Social Dominance: An Intergroup Theory of Social Hierarchy and Oppression*. Cambridge: University Press.

Chapter 11: Cooperation and Equality through Time

HIERARCHICAL SOCIETIES AND male domination have characterized the order of things human and infrahuman historically. The male is usually larger, with stronger bones, muscles, and teeth and possesses more weapons. Human males had the edge in defending the tribe, bringing home killed meat, and constructing heavy stone and log shelters. This was especially true when brute force was more critical because the types of tools were primitive and machinery and power tools were undeveloped. Male superiority carried over into the social and political realms as well.

Multiple mates, promiscuity, and abandonment of mates and family also followed as far more the prerogative of the male rather than the female. The female was stuck in her environs because of fewer privileges, less power, and the need to care for offspring. As subsistence conditions slowly evolved into adequate life-sustaining resources and even affluence, jobs also changed from backbreaking work to machinery-facilitated employment. More tasks became brain-dependent rather than brawn-dependent. These changes provided more vocational and financial opportunity for females and males. And with that, there was more affinity for democracy with its tenants of freedom and equality.

While male domination continues in many current cultures, women across the developed world have emerged as equals with men, or are emerging as such. Women in many countries are fairly represented at all levels of society, or at least have moved visibly in that direction. Major business leadership, elite clubs, and top governmental positions are all seeing more and more females represented.

This chapter was written while the 2014 Winter Olympics were in progress. The incredible daring and accomplished performances of women competitors surely helped to celebrate the equal status of women. Greater equality is being operationalized.

Even though in our history, the role of women was indeed bleak, the influence of women has always been significant. It would be an error to hide the power and influence of women in male-dominated societies, then and now. There is a large Old Order Amish community in Western Pennsylvania that remains largely male dominated. As in many cases, one has to look carefully beneath the surface for the relative status of members of a group. Amish women provide for the welfare and provisioning of the family. They not only bear, tend, and raise the children, but also paint and repair the house, make the clothes, raise and can the main foodstuffs, often do barn work, and have a definite say in the major financial decisions of the family.

Aspiring women leaders have looked to ancient societies for examples of matriarchal or female domination. Anthropologists are not sure that any have existed. Nevertheless, the relative power of women varies vastly across different male dominated societies. There is a town here in Western Pennsylvania called Aliquippa. It is named after one of the Indian chiefs who happened to be a woman. The Iroquois confederacy here in the East and the Hopi tribes in the West both accorded women decision-making powers. We are told that for many of the tribes decisions like going to war, picking a new chief, planning a buffalo hunt, and making plans for the winter took the voice of the women into full account.

Religion and equality

One modern Jewish scholar, Joshua A. Berman, presents an amazing analysis of the very early emergence of equality based on comparative studies of ancient secular and religious manuscripts. His conclusion about ancient secular societies is the following: "If there was one truth the ancients held to be self-evident it was that all men were *not* (italics mine) created equal" (page 175). If we maintain today that men and women, in fact, are endowed by their Creator with certain inalienable rights, Berman contends that it is because we have possessed as part of our cultural heritage notions of equality that were deeply entrenched in the ancient passages of the Pentateuch. That is an amazing thesis.

Berman begins by examining Mesopotamian and Ugaritic manuscripts. There he finds a low view of humans; they are created to serve the gods as slaves. The hierarchies among the greater and lesser gods dramatically celebrate hierarchy in the heavens. By extension, it is a divine imperative that human affairs be arranged in hierarchies. The gods have no positive feelings for mankind. Even the kings on earth are slaves, albeit of higher status that the subjects.

In contrast, Jehovah's uniquely different characteristic is his pathos for his people. Another Jewish scholar, Abraham Heschel, develops the pathos issue in great depth. As much as the prophets denounce and lambaste the oppression of the poor by the rich and the injustices of Israel and Judah, they always balance judgment with the love of God for his people and the hope of redemption. Jehovah's relationship with the Israelites as a covenant relationship reveals a connection with some mutuality and compassion. It is an agreement between the Sovereign King in heaven and the lesser kings on earth. The lesser kings are the people of Israel (who also happen to have a leader called a king). The lesser-king concept is probably highly debatable (Berman, pp. 28-29). Much more importantly, there would seem to be wide and long accepted support that the agreement or covenant is one of special acceptance by God of the people as a community coupled with community responsibility. The community aspect unfortunately is nearly lost in Protestantism, and even more obscured in our secular culture. It is unfortunate because community has potential to reinforce equality.

There are some specific exceptions to the low role of women in the Old Testament. Two books in the Old Testament bear the names of women, Ruth and Esther. Deborah and Judith also appear as heroines. In the 15th chapter of Exodus there are two liberation songs. They celebrate the hand of God in freeing the Israelites from slavery under Pharaoh. The first song records that Moses and the Israelites rejoiced in that "The horse and the rider he has thrown into the sea." The second song is shorter, reiterating some of the phrases of the first. It is attributed to Miriam. It is not at all known whether Miriam or Moses wrote these hymns of freedom, but it does, at least, suggest the prominent stature of Miriam as a prophetess. Miriam's position is remarkable because of its ancient setting, several centuries before the time of Christ.

Christian scholars like Kenneth Bailey clearly document that this relatively respectful position of women was severely degraded in the inter-testament period followed by a radical uptick in the life and work of Jesus. The elevated view of women begins with Mary, the mother of Jesus, who recites the first Christmas song (Luke Chapter 1) in praise of the Savior who has chosen the poor and who will put down the arrogant and rich from their thrones and will fill the hungry with good things. This "Magnificat" could be totally spiritualized, but the language is simply too concrete and worldly for that interpretation solely. Mary, the mother of God, magnifies the Lord who comes to preach to the poor (Luke 4) and bring redress and justice.

With a politically astute mother like Mary, it would be no surprise that Jesus would proclaim a radically new justice and would demonstrate an equal status for all men and women. Women were included among his disciples (not apostles), they traveled with him, and some of them funded the expenses. He speaks with women with respect and honor as revealed in six of the parables: the wayward woman at the well, the Syro-Phoenician woman whose faith he honored, the woman caught in adultery, a sinful woman anointing his feet, the lady seeking a just judge, and the wise and foolish young women. He not only dealt with these women in constructive, affirmative ways, but also broke social taboos to do so by reaching across to minorities, gentiles, the promiscuous, and questionable business people. He spoke to women without relatives being present, and he ate with the less reputable. He brought nothing less than a revolution of equality and justice in an age of calcified bigotry and discrimination (see Kenneth Bailey).

St. Paul, who authored the majority of the letters in the New Testament, does not seem to rise above the cultural views of authority or women of his day as clearly as Jesus does. There is the culturally prevalent reference to obeying the authorities because God institutes them. Whether this was a tenant of belief in Providence or living in subservience under the all-powerful Roman Empire, or a mixture, is debatable. When he refers to the husband's being the head of the family, it was balanced by the demand that the husband love the wife as Christ loved the church and gave his life for it. On balance, it may be fair to say that his summary view was, "There is neither Jew nor Greek, slave nor free, male or female, for you are all one in Christ Jesus" (Galatians 3). The New Testament letters are full of the tone of partnership, admonishing one another, and teaching one another. In other words, it is marked by the spirit of cooperation and equality. The primacy of St. Peter (the Pope) was construed by some early believers as *primus inter pares* or first among equals. Eventually that conception morphed into a strict male dominated hierarchy, and the church limped through centuries of Dark Ages until the Renaissance.

Old empires and equality

Some very quick rudimentary searches into a few major ancient cultures may add to our perspective here. The status of women in Persia and Egypt was rather equal and complementary with men in contrast to the ancient Roman and Greek cultures. In Persia and Egypt, women rose to positions of relatively high authority. Many women in Persia rose in the military ranks and were greatly respected as such, while, at the same time, clearly displaying feminine refinement and sensuality. In Egypt, women were equal under the law in regard to property ownership and other business and daily affairs. Women could rise to the seat of Pharaoh but had to have royal blood. In contrast, women in Greece and Rome had a lower status than men.

It is an interesting reflection that here we have four empires, all of them powerful and successful, but two saw women as equals or nearly so, and two suppressed them.

In the 1200s A.D., the Mongols launched one of the largest empires ever with very advanced ideas of meritocracy, diversity, and tolerance, contrary to misleading misinformation bout them. It is certainly true that they burned cities wholesale if they refused to be loyal or refused to pay taxes. Otherwise, the new citizens could rise up the ranks of privilege and leadership. Capable women rose to positions of sole leadership of whole provinces, although they usually did not engage in battle. Later, under the leadership of Genghis Khan's sons, there was a terrible reversal. Women suffered rape nationwide by the Mongol men themselves. This was a very dark era of history in an otherwise unusually advanced time.

Animals and equality

Does the relationship between humans and animals over time have something to teach us about equality? These connections have changed greatly over the last century. In the lore of the Western cowboy, training a horse was seen as breaking the critter. The procedure was the following: lassoing, snubbing tightly to a sturdy center post in the corral, saddling, and riding out the violent bucking session. The horse often fought the shortening of the lasso in the snubbing phase violently. There were often rope burns and sometimes broken legs, even the death of the horse. There was no gradual quieting or assuring the horse that the rider was not an enemy. The horse was often taken from the range, sometimes taken as a wild mustang horse from a wild herd.

The brutal braking approach to training horses has been opposed by the highly developed equestrian traditions in Europe for a very long time. Reaching back as far as 400 BCE, Xenophon's approach to horsemanship was far more cooperative and in tune with the natural tendencies of the horse than the Western cowboy breaking mentality. The rarified dressage training of the Lipizzaner horses, reaching back several centuries in time, exemplifies a very close bonding of horse and rider and a great understanding not only of horse breeding (before the science of genetics), but also an appreciation of the personality of each particular horse. The training was, and is, firm with consistent discipline but never in the form of beating or abuse of any kind. Pressure followed by release, very refined and clear cues, reward, and personal affection were, and are, the avenues to accomplish the demanding graceful, but athletic, moves in the air such as the capriole-leaping in the air, leveling and extending the back legs in a kick before coming back down to the ground. Selective breeding is coupled with years of patient, firm, and sensitive training.

Modern equestrian training in the United States has been revolutionized. It goes under many names, but the word "natural" gets at the heart of many of the modern schools of training. The horse's natural tendency for fight or flight and its robust emotional capacity to facilitate either of those responses are fully taken into account. Fear is one of its pivotal survival emotions. Being alert to a sudden change in the surroundings has been a matter of life and death out on the open range. Because of the innate sense of security gained from living and running in a herd, separation from the stable and other horses requires thought and attention, not shouting and beating. The approach is only partially cooperative because horses are innately hierarchal and follow a pecking order. Therefore, in training, the human partner must become the alpha horse substitute. But the alpha trainer must exert his or her firm, but non-destructive, cues without anger or loss of control. Although a large beast, the horse is sensitive to sight, sound, and touch. A fly on their hair produces a twitch. The mothering behavior of the mare is instructive. When a foal gets too sassy with the adults or wanders too far afield, the mother will nip him firmly, but never destructively, and may immediately accept the suckling response.

In terms of gender dominance, the stallion is incorrectly seen as the overall boss. It makes for great drama, but it is wrong. The dominant mare is the one who leads the herd away from danger and to better pasture and water, and the stallion guards the rear from any attack. These insights have been garnered through hours of observation of horses in the wild by horse trainers of our current age.

Undergirding this change in our behavior toward the horse is the basic feeling about the animal kingdom in general. We have been instructed by the biological sciences that humans are continuous on the phylogenic scale rather than strikingly separate. Furthermore, we have to remind ourselves of our total interdependence with the animal kingdom. We are animals, full of beneficial microbes, and in great trouble without them.

A quick look at the rest of the animal kingdom offers some exceptions and corrections to male-dominated patterns of promiscuity and aggression. Seven years of continuous life and research in the Kalahari Desert by Mark and Delia Owens reveals lions being predators fitting into the web of life, surviving long droughts by sucking the bodily juices of their prey. But the big cats do not kill for killings sake. They kill what they need food. Nature is seen as red in tooth and claw as the Tennyson writes. But there is another side of the big predator that comes out more clearly in their open natural spaces than in the zoo. The best zoos are constrictive and confining, producing unnatural conditions that generate stress and abnormal levels of aggression. In the open spaces of the Kalahari, the Owens observed lion prides caring for each other, and brown eyed hyenas not being solitary scavengers, but caring jointly for their young and even adopting orphan pups. It was not uncommon for the lions to roam through the Owen's tents at night to scavenge some food but not harm them. The Owens were, of course, frightened and knew their bodies were not entirely off limits to the great predators.

A quick search of dominance and mating in the animal kingdom seems to show scant frequency of female dominance. Apparently, some lemurs are female dominant: the mouse lemur, dwarf lemur, and the mongoose lemur. Mating for life is certainly a different issue and does not guarantee mutual compassion, sharing, or general cooperation but would seem to be the context where those elements might be more expected. Quite a list of animals do mate for life, or nearly so at least: the bald eagle, the old faithful love birds, the wolf, Gibbons, swans, black vultures, French Angelfish (equal hunters and always in pairs), turtle doves, and prairie voles (share nesting and puppy raising).

A fascinating research report of prairie voles in *Smithsonian* magazine indicated that a male prairie vole mate spends about 60% of its time in the nest caring for the young. It mates for life or, at least, very long periods. However, some may sneak out occasionally for extra marital affairs. Another twist in this report includes the administration of the hormone Oxytocin (not to be confused with OxyContin). This so-called social hormone accelerates grooming, touching and closeness, in short, what looks like bonding in many animal subjects, likewise in the prairie vole. This hormone, which is receiving wide research attention, is showing up in undergraduate research in our fine liberal arts colleges. Rats become much more social after injections of Oxytocin.

Predatory, promiscuous, abusive, non-caring, or, simply and more subtly, overpowering male domination is deeply ingrained into our consciousness. However, there are significant ancient and far-flung exceptions. Modern reading of the animal kingdom requires a more nuanced understanding. There is substantial evidence of emotion, compassion, cooperation, and even grieving, by horses and elephants, especially. That should temper traditional judgments. Modern Judeo-Christian scholarship argues for a revolutionary theological foundation for equality among humans and among men and women, in stark contrast to the secular culture of Biblical times.

★★★

Bailey, Kenneth E. 2008. *Jesus Through Middle Eastern Eyes, Cultural Studies in the Gospels.* Downers Grove, Illinois: Inter Varsity Press. Source for the interpretation of the six parables of Jesus. Dr. Bailey is steeped in the near Eastern languages and has lived most of his life in that area of the world. His scholarship on the New Testament is recognized around the world.

Berman, Joshua A. 2008. *Created Equal: How the Bible Broke with Ancient Political Thought.* New York: Oxford University Press, Inc. An acclaimed scholar of the Hebrew Bible explaining the Hebrew text in the light of the other texts of the day.

Herschel, Abraham. 1962. *The Prophets.* New York; Harper and Row. A major Twentieth–Century Jewish scholar demanding respect and deep reflection.

Holy Bible, New International Version. 1988. Grand Rapids, Michigan; Zondervan.

Miller, Robert M, and Lamb, Rick. 2005. *The Revolution in Horsemanship and What it Means to Mankind.* Guilford, Connecticut: The Lyons Press. A nice summary of very early alternative training approaches like Bill Dorrance and how they laid the foundation of modern training which is also reviewed well.

Owens, Mark and Delia. 1948. *Cry of the Kalahari: Seven Years in Africa's Last Great Wilderness.* Boston: Houghton Mifflin. A day-by-day non-technical account of observing the movements and behaviors of the lion prides and other species.

Podhajsky, Alois. 1977. *My Horses, My Teachers.* North Pomfret, Vermont: Trafalgar Square Publishing. Cooperation of man and horse by a major figure in the Lipizzaner history.

Roberts, Monty. 1997. *The Man Who Listens to Horses.* New York: Ballantine Publishing. A figure who spent hours of his youth watching the wild horse herds in the western United States and popularizing modern applications from those observations.

Scanlan, Kristina. 2012. The Role of Oxytocin, Vasopressin, and D-cycloserine in Remediating Social behavior in rats with Amygdala Lesions. Senior Research Paper, Westminster College, New Wilmington, PA. In *Journal of Student Research.*

Tucker, Abigail. 2014, February. Voles in Love. *Smithsonian.*

PART IV

Toward Constructive Power and Friendship

THE TERM "POWER" does not play a salient position in the set of conditions required for the shared-coping model to function successfully. The word "power" itself may seem secondary in the model, but functional equality is pivotal and clearly assumes and necessitates the sharing of power. This part begins with a chapter on hoarding power in order to show that it is counterproductive and that, in turn, sets the stage for the chapter on sharing power. At first glance, friendship may seem out of place in this behavioral science model. In fact, the deliberate attempt to recapture a dimension of humanity in the context of problem solving should not be strange at all.

Chapter 12 Hoarding Power

Chapter 13 Sharing Power

Chapter 14 Friendship

Chapter 12: Hoarding Power

THE INSIGHTS OF a book about how everyone can win are certainly meant to apply to our everyday work and family life. Dysfunctional families and work places are likely places where one or a few at the top of the organization are amply empowered and those under them disempowered. The counterproductive effect of hoarding power prevails at every level of society. Hoarding and abuse of power in the political sphere is easier to uncover, which the reader will see in this chapter, than in the domestic realm.

Dictatorial, autocratic power highly concentrated in the office of a king or any form of absolute leader has obviously been a great motivator of oppression down through history. The histories of great powers are generally not pleasant because it is most seldom that one person has the wisdom to rule solo, and paranoia plagues this type of reign because rivals always covet the position. Admittedly plots and assassinations occur within democracies, but the ruler never seems to reach the insane paranoia of a figure like Stalin, who felt that he had to purge thousands to maintain his office. Our form of democracy protects us from absolute power by balancing the three Federal branches of government, a long-standing Constitution, and a body of law. Other forms of accumulating power by various other institutions and individuals are nevertheless still prevalent.

Hoarding power and wealth at the top

Today, the power elite, the 1%, gather massive wealth and, therefore, power. Wealth and power are inseparable. If the poor are relatively powerless, the mega rich are super-charged with power. We are looking here at the multimillionaires and especially the multibillionaires. If any middle class or upper middle class person aggregates all of his or her assets, it is fairly easy to realize a million dollars. In today's currency, a million dollars is not what it formerly was; therefore, modest wealth is not the main focus in this section.

It is nearly a truism that wealth generates power. Opportunities, choices, protection, insulation from the knocks of life, and elite relationships are all multiplied by wealth. The writer of antiquity knew the connection of wealth and power all too well and the abuse of power. Several hundred years before the time of Christ, the Old Testament prophet Jeremiah (Chapter 5) put it this way: "Among my people are wicked men who lie in wait like men who snare birds;... they have become rich and powerful and have grown fat and sleek. Their evil deeds have no limit: they do not plead the case of the fatherless to win it, they do not defend the right of the poor." The degenerate power of the rich is lamented throughout the Old Testament writings. The prophet Amos (Chapter 2) says, "They sell the righteous for silver, and the needy for a pair of sandals. They trample on the heads of the poor as upon the dust of the ground, and deny justice to the oppressed." Jesus spoke the same language. Harsh and unequivocal. This is not to deny that among the super rich are undoubtedly those who are humane and ethical in private and public life.

Wealth supremacists have the power to control those without power. Society turns its face away from the fact that many of the mega rich have gained their wealth and power unjustly, and many of us fail to realize their overwhelming and, in some cases, devastating evil. The mega wealthy pay millions of dollars in ads to place their preferred candidates in office and force office holders to speak and vote their way. Some 12,000 lobbyists in Washington speak for big interest groups that hire them. It is more encouraging that a much smaller number is especially effective. The mega rich buy chains of newspapers, radio stations, and television stations over which they pour out a mix of trivia, prejudice, and venom against struggling working people with characterizations, such as "feminazis" for any intelligent assertive woman, and "pure Marxism" for the critique of capitalism by the current Pope Francis.

Without antitrust and anti-monopoly control to assist the little guy, mega mergers make the large power players more powerful yet. The merger of Comcast and Time Warner will allow the airwaves to favor the biases of the 1% even more. The powerful elite cry for freedom and competition until they acquire control of a sector, then they shun competition and favor monopolies. In the airline industry, what will be the results of contemporary mergers?

What voice do the 99% have against the Amazon of hate, distortion, and distractions? None or just a whisper. The reason why the massive gap between the rich and the poor is so destructive is a power gap and an opportunity gap. Big decisions are made in favor of the tiny super class, and in favor of maintaining the income gap.

We probably cannot argue that we are playing a zero-sum game, but the greater the power gap, the closer we come to powerlessness and shrunken opportunity for the majority. When CEOs make 400 times more than the average worker (who really is the one who builds the company), the chasm causes decay because the company is not being vitalized and renewed.

How the mega rich succeed is not our main topic here, but it is part of the larger picture. Many have gotten to the top not by making things, but by making deals—bad deals in junk bonds, Ponzi schemes, high-risk derivatives, leveraged buyouts by private equity firms, and plundered pensions. Fraud characterizes many of these transactions. As in most things, good and bad are mixed; some of the private equity purchases have been fruitful. The Carlyle Group claims success with companies such as the John Maneely Company, a steel pipe manufacturer, and Sequa Company, an aircraft engine repair firm. Apparently, the Bain Group has had good success with Experian, a giant credit rating firm.

All in all, the history of high finance by organizations, like private equity firms, is dismal from the perspective of the 99%. Private equity firms buy companies by making relatively small investments with no input from the workers or the working management. They saddle the acquisitions with gigantic loan debts, management fees, and contrivances such as "dividend recapitalization." Thousands of employees are laid off to realize immediate profits, workloads are doubled, and research and development are suspended. Profits soar in the first year but the company is deprived of its means of growth, and bankruptcy follows in the second or third year. American Pad and Paper Company, KB Toys, and Beal Brothers retailers experienced just such consequences. It will be interesting to see if Dunkin Donuts and Brusters survive this process they are going through. It is not atypical for private equity firms to invest 10 million of their own capital and walk away in a year or two with 100 million in profits and leave behind a wrecked company in many cases.

Three heads of the Carlyle Group, a private equity fund, made 400 million among themselves in one year. Can any CEO deliver a performance that earns that kind of money? Doesn't such profit come by stealth, deceit, power, intimidation, and virtual robbery? Most of that money belongs to the company and the employees in order to up-date cutting edge technology and plant improvements, ongoing training, and crucial research development, which lead to new products and to improve sales and promotion. The raiding of corporations produces painful displacement of workers, loss of jobs, and a widening of the power/wealth gap with a guarantee of poverty at the bottom. The workers are bought and sold as it were almost like inert drill presses or computers. They have no say, no power, and little dignity in the workplace.

Yet, this travesty is waved before us as success. The mega rich ask us what we have against success? To be sure, success is a central part of our great American culture. Everyone is supposedly able to get ahead. Wealth supremacists invite all people to worship blindly what they have come to call success. Never mind the fact that economic mobility is at one of its lowest points in our national history.

It will take a ground swell of popular protest to move our nation back toward some concern for the commonweal. President Obama's focus on jobs and closing the income gap is encouraging. The un-equivocal voice of Pope Francis against the evils of unregulated cap-italism, and his forceful voice for a preferential treatment of the poor along with his critique of structural violence may change the tone of political rhetoric. Theirs is a clarion call and wonderfully welcome voices. It may eventually be a positive influence in creating a readiness for conversation across the political aisle. Hopefully, it will develop into more that just talk.

The 1% are well entrenched and will not give up power easily. Why the populace allows that entrenchment and entitlement is an-other question. All who stand by and allow the poor to suffer and the middle class to sputter without raising a voice are complicit in the injustice. At least, there is more awareness of the problem as witnessed in the Occupy movement, the verbal commitment of the President to make inequality the defining issue for the rest of his term, and in the fresh breeze coming from Pope Francis. But the entrenchment of massive power in the hands of a few has scarcely been challenged.

Why the entrenchment of the abuse of power?

Why hasn't a popular cry been heard much louder and sooner? One element causing political passivity and silence may very well be that part of the teaching of the Christian church exhorting believers always to be "nice." Part of that teaching is what helps to build and maintain the backbone of America, and another part of that teaching, paradoxically, makes political milk toasts out of Christians. First, look at the positive effect of the teaching. The oft-quoted passage in Galatians asserts that "The fruits of the Spirit are love, joy, peace, pa-tience, kindness, goodness, faithfulness, gentleness, and self control." This list is repeated in Colossians, and the virtue of love in extensively encouraged in I Corinthians, Chapter 13, "The greatest of these is love." Other great religions share some of these virtues.

These positive characteristics are to be lived out by Christians in a strong and virile manner. There are ample guides and metaphors in the New Testament that Christians are to practice similar to long distance runners being cheered on by a great cloud of witnesses. The Christian is not to be a wet noodle and is not to be conformed to every whim of this world and external force. A healthy sense of power is seen in the believer who is in control, not washed about by the latest fad. The Christian believer could embrace a healthy sense of personal power, while recognizing that it comes from a Divine source and is to be lived out with humility and meekness before God and our fellow beings.

Meekness throws a mean curve in this business of being nice. Why is the value of meekness used as a justification for passivity and submitting as doormats for abuse? A respected New Testament scholar, Kenneth Bailey, contends that the Greek and Aramaic meaning of meekness refers to those who are angry at injustice and act halfway between recklessness and cowardice. Partnership, teaching, and admonishing one another are central attitudes that speak of cooperation and humility rather that arrogance, but above all strength. Many early Christians became martyrs dying in flames, on the rack, and on crosses. They were athletes in faith, life and death. Personal power, well qualified, should not be anathema to Christian belief and practice.

Whether one is a believing Christian or a secular person for whom these virtues are important, regardless of how they are attained, these virtues point us in the direction of a stable, caring, giving, and vital society. When there is so much that is mean, ugly, greedy, crass, hedonistic, and violent, virtues may be thought of as the backbone of our society and a correction to the ugly underbelly side of our society. It would be a drastic loss for society to lose its grip or these virtues.

The down side of this list is that it would seem to be the basis of being too nice, too passive, and not balanced with a harder, firmer side. The milk toast image of the Christian has worked its way into the attitude of many. The cheap prints of Jesus hanging on Sunday school rooms convey an effeminate creature with long lustrous hair as though he just came out of a beauty parlor. Instead of wearing a sweaty, stained robe from hard hours in the desert or on a fishing boat, his robes are pristine white. He is indeed "gentle Jesus meek and mild." One seldom sees a classic print of Jesus throwing the moneychangers out of the temple. Or a depiction of Jesus accusing the religious leaders of being a mob of vipers or like manure covered tombstones. Perhaps the Catholic rendering of the crucifix is more helpful than the empty cross in this regard; there is ultimate love and toughness rolled into one. Compassion and toughness, love and judgment are inseparable in the Incarnation and by extension to all Christians.

How else do we get this decorum of silence about speaking about these important religious matters in public and what their application may mean in society and politics. It is, of course, understandable that we want to avoid offending those with whom we live and work. We need to expand our capacity to distinguish between constructive critique and hostile criticism. But the existing taboo against speaking about the malignancy of unfettered power is causing us to shoot ourselves in the foot, as it were.

In the Massachusetts Bay Colony in the 17th century, the Puritans saw material success and wealth as a sign of the favor of God and being among the elect. Successful business people were not uncommonly viewed this way during the years of our industrial revolution. Following the massive railroad strike in Pittsburgh, a Presbyterian seminary professor affirmed the virtue of the powerful and successful railroad executives, but contended that the role of the strikers was "the destruction of that divinely ordained order of society wherein individual men by various personal gifts are made by God superior to others, and invested with power over their fellows." This sentiment was not an exception. (See E.W. McKinney, pages 454 ff.) The divine right of Kings, and a secular vestige of that elevated blessing for Presidents and moguls of business and finance have not entirely vanished. The myth of their goodness entitles them to be above the law, beyond prosecution, indeed still elevated on a kind of subconscious throne. The divine may have been replaced by the secular, but the special elevation to "goodness or privilege" is still there.

We can recognize that there are people of integrity at all levels of society, but what keeps our lips so sealed against exposing the scoundrels, and what keeps us from transforming work back toward a more caring context? There is supposedly something boorish and unrefined about serious political discussion in many settings. The Christian church in America has certainly been silenced. The church is largely irrelevant in the public sphere. The deep voice of a Martin Luther King, Jr., condemning racial injustice but, more sweepingly, calling for fundamental economical reform is seldom heard. Jim Wallis and the Sojourner effort are exceptions. There are others. But so few. The pulpits on main street sell personal salvation and being nice and helping your neighbor. All to the good, but the church is frozen in any effort to bring moral reasoning to the public sphere.

We should be outraged at how far our nation has gotten off track—greedy, stingy, cruel, and callous. The political fundamentalists will not support unemployment compensation when there are no jobs. Saying the poor are lazy and something is wrong with them qualifies as an obscenity. They clutch their fundamentalist "no-new-taxes" dogma while they pay at very low rates and, in many cases, do not pay at all. In the Eisenhower era, top earners paid 90%. Under Reagan, it went from 70% down to 28%. The beast (government) is being starved, which means it is not rebuilding. The rich have theirs and the rest are considered takers and losers. How is it that we have again allowed a super race to emerge within our democracy without a protest? When one person owns more wealth and power than several poor countries together, democracy is threatened. When multinational corporations and the banking industry have more direct influence over Congress and the President than some of our regulatory agencies, the normal citizen is going to be crushed. When CEOs make 400 times more than the average worker, poverty will be the only thing that trickles down. A kind of social rape is occurring before our eyes and we are silent, nice people.

Greed alone should be enough to explain current wealth and power disparity. But a slight modification in the greed explanations lies in the resurgence of wealth and capital gains growing at a much more rapid rate than wages over the last four decades. Inherited wealth is growing faster than the economy. This disparate growth rate, coupled with the excessive benefits paid to the elite and combined with the iron-clad control that the 1% have over any reasonable tax increases, all add up to a great wealth and power disparity. Even worse, these three patterns seem to be progressive in the disease sense; therefore, it is likely that the disparity will get progressively worse. If the 1% owns about a fifth of the national wealth today, it will move to at least a quarter and possibly much higher. The 1% has gained the power to control this disparity. The observations in this paragraph and the paragraph below are based on over a century of hard data from over 20 developed countries.

The wealth-to-wages-disparity curve dipped significantly during our post World War II period of prosperity only to rise again in our current period. It is argued that deliberate political policies, primarily taxes, caused the decline in disparity during that period of prosperity. It is argued that the free market does not inherently have the dynamic to even out disparities over time. See the reference to Thomas Pikkety in the reference section below and the wide attention his book is having.

A significant part of the redress of the wealth gap would be for the super rich to pay more for the infrastructure of the nation that they use to make their wealth. It is silly to allow the rich to say they built it themselves. Tax rates for the rich would have to go back up to the late Eisenhower days and early Reagan days. Current tax rates for the wealthy are an anomaly. Historically, they have been many times higher, as already noted. It should also be make clear that those higher tax days were during times of prosperity. Contrast that to about a 15% rate today and much lower that that when all the loopholes and off shore advantages are used. Short of major social unrest and dramatic and sustained upheaval that might threaten the 1%, they have won. They will continue to reduce their own tax rates, and they will continue to suppress measures to ameliorate the decline of the middle class and the poor. The super rich will continue to devastate business and industry, contrary to their pro-business rhetoric.

Activating people against their own interests

The abuse and maintenance of power is further facilitated by skill-fully constructed propaganda. For example, why do so many people with few resources vote for candidates who will actually make them poorer while the candidate will get richer and more powerful?

Brilliant propaganda is not necessarily constructed of lies. Blatant lies are too easy to detect. Clever propaganda actually champions great truths but omits equally important but inconvenient truths. A massive amount of propaganda promotes the value of freedom but cancels the balancing value of equality. In other words, the current reading of the Gettysburg address as interpreted by Tea Party folks should be limited to "we are conceived in *liberty*." Deleted is "all men are born *equal*." The Preamble to the Constitution clearly couples "general Welfare" with "Liberty"; propaganda would cut out "general Welfare."

In short, the two pillars of democracy are freedom and equality. When one is removed, democracy falters or fails. The ubiquitous chorus that fills the current airwaves proclaims that freedom is the sole pillar by omitting the other pillar. Freedom is the hook that snags us and makes us speak against our own interests without our even knowing it. The freedom hook grabs our psyche on 1) anti health care, 2) anti taxes, 3) anti government, 4) anti deficit/anti investment, and 5) anti gun regulation.

Anti-health care

Think tanks, such as Americans for Prosperity, would have us all believe that our freedoms are at stake as the government encroaches on all five of these issues. They say that if government controls health care, it will essentially control our whole lives. The chant against health care is silly and anachronistic. All seniors who have been cared for by Medicare for years have found their freedom enhanced instead of diminished. And, incidentally, its overhead is around 3%; whereas, the large private health agencies use up as much as 13% on overhead.

Most developed countries have had national health care for many years at half the price of ours and of comparable quality. A friend of the writer visiting relatives in Scotland became ill and was treated immediately and well under the friend's national insurance. It seems fatuous to the Scottish people that some of us think of national medicine as sinking into some kind of downward spiral of socialism. Social Security, Medicare, Medicaid, and Head Start, to name a few, have not threatened anyone's freedom. To the contrary, they create freedom via more equal opportunity. The threat to freedom is an absurd charge, but it works and deceives many Americans. They loathe Affordable Care and vote for candidates and issues that will make them poorer.

Anti-taxes

Many are brainwashed to believe that taxes are a great threat to our freedom. The powerful tell us that taxes have never been higher, contrary to fact. They have never been lower for the super rich and that is the way the rich want to keep it. Political fundamentalists publish and disseminate what they believe as an absolute truth: "Taxes must never increase and should be decreased." Grover Norquist is the front man, undoubtedly, with the muscle of big wealth behind him to intimidate legislators into signing the juvenile no tax pledge. Nearly all Republican in Congress have affixed their signatures, although a few have withdrawn recently.

The greatest deception of all is that the average person is led to believe that think tanks, like the Heritage Foundation, will fight taxes and lower the taxes of the little guy. The regular people who are members of the Tea Party thus have been suckered. Supposedly, a measure of freedom will be restored for all of us by getting the government out of our pockets. Partially correct, mostly wrong. The super rich have the power to make the rules. Those rules maintain their whole gamut of tax protections for themselves. Consequently, 99% or perhaps 90%, will be stuck paying more to keep the nation afloat. Remember, we still have to pay for two dirty, wrong-headed wars that we launched on borrowed money. Anti tax measures will give more freedom to the rich and limit the middle class and the poor more.

Anti-government and anti-regulation

We are inundated with the cry that big government is over regulating and generally stifling our economy and thus taking away our freedoms. The heading of the website home page of Americans for Prosperity declares, "Economic Freedom in Action." The so-called free market has rules made up by the 1% and for the 1%. But we are led to believe that big government robs the little guy and small government will free the little guy. Watch the slight of hand, as it were, "Down with rules, Oh, rich rules." The truth is that small government, with the regulators put to sleep, will free the fraudulent practices of the rich (as happened in the 2009 crash), which will oppress further the middle class and the poor.

Class warfare has been waged and won by the super rich. Class warfare has dramatically redistributed wealth to the top over the last 40 years. Small, cheap government will eviscerate the majority of the people who make up our nation and will increase the power at the top to bully the rest even more. Who will assist and protect the poor children, the child born with a cleft palate, children with cancer, children with an ever-weakening public school system? It is said of the children, the poor, the physically and mentally handicapped, "They do not produce anything; they are just takers." Nothing will ever be more obscene, mean, and depraved. It is time to call it that. And to act differently. Obsessive worship of the golden calf is surely base behavior.

The anti-deficit ideology

The anti-deficit issues are a concern to most of us. However, on balance, the deficit is not that overwhelming. Many of us could pay more, and some of us could obviously pay a lot more without a bit of pain, and if we reinvested in the vital organs of our nation, the deficit could be reduced rather quickly. The deficit scolds create a mythic atmosphere of severe scarcity that is used to justify strangling public programs of human development and business and industrial rebirth. The deficit allows the 1% to craft the rules even more strongly in their favor and for their entitlements. The myth of scarcity is a wall of security for the rich, and a highjacking of renewed opportunity for the rest of us. The deficit is not what is limiting our opportunities.

Anti-gun regulation

The National Rifle Association and its supporters further feed the freedom frenzy. They say that what the gun control advocates are all about is not just taking your guns away but taking your wider freedom in the process. It would seem that two things encapsulate the genuine fears that have been instilled in so many of our citizens. The first dynamic that fuels the exaggerated propaganda of the gun lobbyists and the "over-my-dead-body" celebrity spokespersons is a very large industry representing a lot of money. The second dynamic is that the gun scare is yet another way to starve the beast of government. The message is, "Government is bad; they are taking your guns and your very freedom; therefore, speak for and vote for those who protect your freedom." It is silly but it works. The government has no interest in taking away our sporting arms or self-defense weapons.

The rich and powerful make us feel like they are protecting our freedoms when, in fact, by and large, they are defunding and deregulating, which benefits them handsomely and further impoverishes the rest of us. But we get sold. Of course, we vote for freedom.

For conflicting groups who realize that something has to change, the model of conflict reduction in this book, I believe, has much to promise. Timing obviously is part of what makes for readiness to change. For the time to be right, it took Mandela 27 years in prison and several years after his release, and it took de Klerk and the standing government all that time while sanctions and pressure of most of the free world were brought to bear on the shameful practice of Apartheid. It would be mindless and untimely to suppose that two enemies blasting away at each other in the heat of battle with their proverbial 16-inch guns would be ready for talks. Conversely, we may have to work to make the time right. True freedom for all needs to be cheered on, and equality must run in tandem with freedom.

★★

Goodman, Amy, and Moynihan, Denis. 2012. *The Silenced Majority.* Chicago, Illinois: Haymarket Books. A collection of the brave but reasoned critiques of Amy Goodman, an independent voice, on a host of major current issues.

Greenwald, Glenn. 2011. *With Liberty and Justice for Some, How the Law is Used To Destroy Equality and Protect the Powerful.* New York: Henry Holt and Company, LLC. This book is a brutal facing of the fact that reconciliation and especially clemency for powerful figures, rather than judgment and punishment, creates two tiers of justice, in effect putting the powerful above the law. A key writer in the dissemination of the Edwin Snowden papers.

Holy Bible, New International Version. 1984. Grand Rapids, Michigan: Zondervan. It speaks for itself and of course results in many interpretations.

McKinney, William W. 1958. *The Presbyterian Valley.* Pitt: Davis and Warde Inc. An old source but revealing both the ups and downs of a denominational history, and specifically the all too frequent religious blessing of the rich and denunciation of the poor.

Nickel, Kate. 2000. Changing Attitudes Toward the Widening Income Gap Using the Elaboration Likelihood Model. Undergraduate Senior Research. Westminster College, New Wilmington, Pennsylvania.

Pikkety, Thomas. 2014. *Capital in the Twenty-First Century.* Cambridge, Massachusetts: President and Fellows of Harvard College. Documentation of the capital vs. wage disparity over time in many countries. This analysis suggests that the income gap will get worse in the future.

Pope Francis. 2013. *The Joy of the Gospel, Evangelii, Gaudium.* Frederick, Maryland: The Word Among Us Press. A 212 page apostolic exhortation which critiques structural and societal causes of poverty, as well as a Christian plea for personal piety and compassionate living.

Stassen, Glen Harold. 2012. *A Thicker Jesus, Incarnational Discipleship in a Secular Age.* Louisville: Westminster John Knox Press. Son of Harold Stassen, Professor of ethics at Fuller Theological Seminary, Glen argues that the church should influence the moral compass in public affairs while keeping church and state separate organically.

Wallis, Jim. 2005. *God's Politics, Why the Right Gets it Wrong and the Left Doesn't Get it.* New York; HarperCollins. Chapters 15 and 16 on the societal visions of Amos and Isaiah are reinforced by the perspectives of Breuggemann.

Chapter 13: Sharing Power

A NORMAL AND healthy sense of having reasonable control over one's life is essential in the pursuit of happiness and mental health. Powerlessness, on the other hand, tends to extinguish hope and fosters apathy and despair. The positive nature of personal power and self-control takes on bold relief when we look at it's exact opposite—powerlessness. Shared power in various sized groups will also be examined.

If government is ever again to be of the people, by the people, and for the people, and if business ever re-captures a sense of caring, then power must be addressed. It may be a dirtier word than politics in general. It is not only a pivotal word for every person; it is what makes the world go round along with its correlate of wealth.

Loss of personal power and control

When one steps on the brake pedal in the car and there is an immediate response, it is very reassuring. On the contrary, it is a helpless feeling when the brakes fail as one approaches a dangerous intersection or descends a steep hill. Once, while waiting to go into surgery, I sat with an executive. He was used to being in control and, thus, felt especially anxious as he was turning complete control over to the surgeon. This fear is common whether riding on a run-away horse, slipping out of control on the ski slope, and fearing that one's parachute is not opening on time.

Many millions of our poor struggle daily waiting for public transportation, unable to provide for their kids, living with unemployment or on the edge of unemployment, a hair's breath away from eviction in the middle of winter, lacking helpful family connections, and not knowing if their children are going to be caught up in the drug culture or in the cross fire of a street shooting. Being randomly mugged, beaten, robbed, stabbed or shot fits the definition of terrorism. The horrors of 9/11 were touted as totally new and changing everything; it changed things for the rich and powerful, but it was nothing new to the poor and minorities. Our poor and minorities have lived with terrorism throughout the long dark side of our national history.

Clinical forms of powerlessness appear in the ancient belief in demon possession and in the modern rubrics of clinical depression, schizophrenia, and a catalogue of other debilitating disorders, including drug and alcohol addiction. Here people have no ability to change. They have no control. One of our barbaric policies is to incarcerate these people, and at staggering rates.

Most of us average people spend most of our waking hours at home or at work. In the family and, at least in modern marriages, health and well-being depends on equal sharing of power between spouses. Historically, the position of the wife in the marriage relationship has been one of subordination to the husband. Father knows best both for the children and the wife. This lopsided view of marriage has been mostly discarded today because it squelched the vitality and dignity of the wife and artificially bloated the ego of the husband. The consequences have been detrimental to the wife and, actually, to the husband as well. The same, of course, goes for the live-in boyfriend or girlfriend. Psychological and physical domestic abuse endures because of the imbalance of power. The wife or girlfriend often has no place to go, and the sole power of the husband or boyfriend ensures abuse will continue. If the wife has some independent resources and a safe way out of the home and the marriage, the cycle is much more likely to be broken because the power of the wife is increased and the power of the husband decreased. Women's shelters of various kinds have ameliorated the problem somewhat, but many women remain haunted by the threat of the husband or ex to harass, beat, and even kill.

We are all aware that less than a hundred years ago, women were considered emotionally and intellectually incapable of understanding public and political affairs. It was not uncommon for medical experts to advise that women would encounter greater illnesses if they were exposed to the stress of political discussion. Only after strong, well-organized women confronted the Goliath of male dominance with persistence did women finally gain the vote as full human beings (the 19th Amendment, ratified on August 18, 1920).

Egregiously lopsided power is destructive in marriages as well as in many other human relationships. There is strong evidence for this contention in the research of organizational and social psychology and other branches of the behavioral sciences. Sadly, lopsided hierarchical power has become so common in the workplace that it receives scant attention. Things like leveraged buyouts, corporate raiding, cheating, and fraud in high finance are enabled by marked concentration of power in the hands of one person or a powerful few.

The gains made in participative management and democracy in the workplace made in the seventies have been nearly eclipsed as corporate America has swung toward extreme hierarchical power structures. The avalanche of wealth surging toward the 1% means power is *ipso facto* in the 1%. The mass firing of the air traffic controllers by Ronald Regan remains as a salient benchmark of the decline of the worker. Unions, in spite of having their fair share of corruption and ineptitude, are one of the few ways in which the worker can even the playing field with the great power of the corporations. At any rate, the worker has very little say today in the workplace. Recent passage of so-called "right-to-work" legislation in nearly 30 states further weakens the worker. Layoffs mean that remaining workers are often expected to carry a double workload. Cutbacks often mean that health support is diminished and pensions threatened or obliterated. Plants are moved, sold, or closed without any voice from the employees. The virtual selling of humans in the company is not new and hardly pretty.

Shouldn't this pervasive devaluation of the worker and the ultimate elevation of the wealthy to maximize profits be seen as a systematic de-humanization of the human being? Historically humans have been sacrificed to the gods, to the Reich, or to the good of the

Soviet state. Is it time to recognize that humans are now sacrificed to the multinational corporations? Are workers being re-categorized as *untermensch*? Less that human? Below consideration? And could the culprits be dressed in the finest designer suits? Arms displays and massacres by military dictators are not necessary to centralize and monopolize power and abuse.

The excuse for cutbacks, buyouts, and moving overseas is always competition and survival via globalization and technological change. Granted, sometimes bone fide survival is at stake, but all too often, cutbacks are not to survive or to increase market share reasonably, but to maximize profits. The 1% demand millions and billions. When profits are maximized, all else is minimized. I am tempted to suggest that this is a new more savage capitalistic formula than ever before, but that apparently would not be accurate. It would seem that maximizing was the formula of the early industrialists like the Fricks and the Carnegies. Whether overt or covert, maximizing profits minimize the worker. It is now the avowed, explicit, and celebrated ethic of the 1%. The commonweal has dropped out of the equation entirely. This seems to be the critique of our current Pope Francis.

It may very well be that this shift in power is a crucial influence in the unraveling of our society. The current extreme form of free enterprise, coupled with the suppressed economy, has put the worker in a powerless position. The worker has no control within his or her own company and has few options to go elsewhere. Maximizing profits leaves no room for respecting workers' dignity. It leaves no room for mutual long-term commitment between workers and companies, no room for pride in the quality and durability of the product. The worker is a commodity to be used like a pile of coal or a barrel of oil, nothing more. The worker is eviscerated, and, then, it is no surprise that he or she feels compelled to get back at the company in a variety of creative ways. Mutual loyalty is stricken from the business dictionary. Mutual respect is shattered. The fabric of the workplace is torn and unraveled.

Powerlessness morphs into an array of possible responses as we have noted previously. Perhaps, the most common response is apathy and disengagement. When apathy fails, anger builds up in response to mistreatment and manifests itself in aggression and violence. Do these responses to powerlessness in the workplace reflect behaviors in our workforce today? It is amazing that so many workers remain industrious and positive in spite of their limited powers.

A common finding in social psychological research is called learned helplessness. When one's freedom and options have been markedly limited for a long period of time, even after the restrictions are lifted, a person may continue to feel the bonds and act as though still fenced in. Farmers often use electric fences keep cattle on meadows for temporary pasture. One strand of smooth wire with strong, but non-destructive, alternating current will condition the cattle to stay away from the fence line. Surprisingly, even after the fence is taken down, it may take several days before the cows overcome fear of the fence and finally cross the line. After the Iron Curtain came down, low worker motivation was a problem in the old Soviet countries because the workers had learned that there was nothing they cold do to change their lot; incentives had been absent for 70 years.

The negative effect of scarcity has received book-length treatment. Scarcity for victims held in the death camps by the Nazis, scarcity for the homeless, scarcity for a single mother with children and a low level job, all affect behavior powerfully. The persons experiencing scarcity know its reality all too well; they are shackled by the boundaries each minute of day in contrast to people who just talk about it. Whether the boundaries are real or imagined, they add to powerlessness.

All this destruction could be avoided if the balance of power were corrected and equality of opportunity were re-introduced into the political and corporate vocabulary. The word "freedom" is ubiquitous in current business vocabulary. Where has the word "equality" gone? Democracy fails when it stands only on the freedom pillar of democracy without the support of the equality pillar. When the CEO and the upper level management have all the power and the worker has none, little equality of opportunity exists. The people at the top have all the opportunity. Democracy has been squelched. Poverty is incubated and multiplied. Sharing of power and opportunity is anathema to the 1%.

If the middle class and the working poor no longer have a strong identity with the establishment and the corporate structures, how much less are the unemployed, poor youth, and underclass? Our laws, mores, and norms mean nothing to them. They are economic losers in an unregulated capitalism; they know it. They stand and act outside the markers that guide the rest of us. Their markers are the gang, the gun, the needle, and a different language. They know they have nothing, so they know they have nothing to lose. They don't live among us in the biblical sense; they are not participants.

Understanding something of the alienation of our own underclass, we should have some empathy for the many underdeveloped countries we invade and occupy. Much of the life and culture of Afghanistan is outside the realm of Western thought. Tribal life has been shaken and shredded by three empires over a number of decades: the British Empire, the U.S.S.R., and now the American empire. We would not be too happy about giant foreign powers occupying our land three times in less than one century. We indulge in the arrogance of exceptionalism and are blind to our own ignorance and arrogance. We declare Shock and Awe, show off our high tech weapons of mass destruction, wreck a country, and expect to win. The last time I checked, if one thrusts a stick into a hornets nest the outcome is painful.

Isolationism is not the way to go, and Afghanistan may need help from the outside world when the time is right. There must be alternatives to isolationism on the one hand and maintaining over 160 military colonies around the world on the other. These colonies drain our resources and often do more harm than good. To think our bases in foreign countries are serving our national interest and national security does not adequately disguise our total motivation, which includes the securing of our multinational corporations to make money. Too much of our war on terrorism is economic opportunism. The goal of killing all terrorists is wrongheaded because their fighting back gives them a cause. We invade countries where unemployment is 60%, and where the "enemy," in turn, offers the kids a loaf of bread and an AK-47 to go to war and fight the infidels. It is a guarantee for multiplying terrorism.

We need mechanisms to detect real plots to attack us or our allies and the capability to crush those plots, but that is radically different from what we are doing. The expense of overextending our empire-like presence around the world is draining our resources away from fixing our problems at home. We can see the human rights abuses abroad but are blind to our flagrant and massive abuse of our youth in our prison system at home to cite just one example.

It might sound funny to say that mixed with old tribal rivalries and age-old tribal warfare there was an iron clad norm of hospitality in the Hindu Kush and the Peshawar region and many of the eastern lands (See *Khyber Knights*). In our arrogance and ignorance, we miss elements of humanity and wisdom in ancient cultures repeatedly (See Jared Diamond).

Sharing power

For workers to identify with their company, they need to be paid and compensated well, have humane work places and conditions, and sense that the company respects them. Sharing power conveys respect because workers have a real opportunity to buy in and have a sense of ownership. In the other chapters on equality, and especially functional equality, there is the realization that lower level workers often have knowledge, experience, and information that management may not have; thus, workers are included in decision making and problem solving regarding issues that are closely relevant to their scope of activity. When management is willing to take some risk in including workers in decision making, the workers get the sense that they are valued, their knowledge is valued, and they are, in fact, an integral functioning part of the company.

The opportunity to invest and influence the direction of one's work creates care and commitment. One does not neglect what one has invested in. When a mother carries a baby for nine months followed by years of intimate nurturing, she makes an ultimate investment, just short of literally giving her life. When you have money in a bank, you desire that that bank remains sound and solvent. Investment creates care, commitment, and loyalty, all ingredients that have been lost in our current version of the American way and needs to be restored if we are to move toward a more equitable society. Wealth and power have been redistributed upward into the hands of a very small percentage of our population. It is time for wealth and power to shift to provide more equitable opportunities. Reasonable redistribution downward would correct the massive redistribution upward that has occurred over the last four decades.

Organizational behavior researchers would have us look at many qualifications and detailed guidelines as to when and how many democratic policies should be incorporated into the workplace. Here are a few highlights. Just as the individual developmental level of the child or teenager should determine the degree of self-governance given the youth, so the skill and experience level of a work group will obviously determine how closely they should be supervised versus given latitude, autonomy, and inclusion in decision making. However, even with inexperienced groups, they have knowledge the boss does not have, like what are they experiencing as newcomers and how they perceive their workplace. That says nothing about what hidden transferable skills they may possess.

For the moderately skillful and, certainly, highly skilled groups, it will be especially insulting not to include them in the circle of power. Rule by fiat and exclusion for these employees will also be wasteful and expensive. Their contribution of talent will be thrown away. The obsession of managers to control and show who is boss is very poor management of resources. The soft side of any business is half the show; this side is grossly neglected and overshadowed by the short sightedness of seeing only the end-of-the-month numbers. If a manager fails to account for or a tanker of oil, a barge of coal, or thousands of dollars of inventory, that manager will be in big trouble. But wasting human intelligence and abilities goes by without note. It is bad business but only a too common practice.

The type of task should affect management style. If work is highly programmed and the production procedure is highly refined and possibly automated like continuous-process manufacturing in a chemical refinery, then, the amount of collaboration of management and labor will be less necessary. Nevertheless, even under these conditions, all issues directly affecting the worker, such as threats to health, compensation and benefits, and even critiquing the efficiency of the production, should be under open and favorable periodic review, with each worker being a functional equal in the discussion. The boss will still always be the formal superior and that should be no problem in a group where the norms of functional equality and mutual respect have been established. Incidentally, unions would be less necessary if the management treated the worker like something more than a commodity.

Labor in a modern auto assembly plant is highly programmed and, to a great extent, automated and robotized. Input from the worker is understandably limited, but not out of the question. There are still routine and repetitive stations on the assembly line. Monitoring the computers that control the robots may be a higher level of work, but even those types of tasks produce mental fatigue that reduces vigilance, i.e., the human factor is still there. In the 1970s, there was much labor unrest at the GM Lordstown plant, near Youngstown, Ohio. Work on the line was very repetitive, limited in scope, rushed, and all in all numbing. This work climate cannot be totally offset by good compensation alone. Worker violence, drugs, and acrimonious conflict there were documented widely in the newspapers and in documentary films. GM learned from that era and instituted more meaningful assignments of greater breadth and depth via meaningful negotiations.

Public education is a prime example of how the arrogance of the hierarchical model condescends to the professionals in the trenches, the teachers. Educational reform is nearly always generated from the very top, regardless of the party in office, with little regard for the intelligence and collective experience of both veteran and newly trained teachers. People in the trenches have information and wisdom that the people at the top do not have. It seems to be asking too much for the perspectives of the two sides to be shared, resulting in better information. National leaders and the populace in general seem to think that the problems of poverty and social decay in our society can be fixed in the schools. Some of it might be fixed in the schools if all the constituents would work together. There is quite a bit of sentiment that teachers are lacking in motivation and fail to take initiatives that would help to improve education. If some teachers lack motivation, I wonder how they got that way? "No child left behind" was apparently well meaning to raise educational standards. But I do not think most teachers would vote to suffocate the spirit of learning with excessive testing, competition between schools instead of cooperation between good and bad schools, and punishment for poorly performing schools. Taking power and control away from teachers reduces motivation and initiative.

Centralized planning was one of the showpieces of communist organization. I do not think it is a foregone conclusion that centralization is always destructive or that decentralized approaches are always good. Privatization or nationalizing is not always intrinsically good or bad. It may be easy to determine how democracy should be applied to some situations but very difficult to make that determination in other cases. Centralized one-payer national health care has been demonstrated to be superior in many developed countries to our current system with a track record of several decades of success. Management of prisons is just the opposite. Privatization of prisons has the goal of getting more customers and keeping them as long as possible. This is the terrible opposite of what is called for in our excessive use of incarceration. Competitive private delivery companies such as FedEx and UPS seem to be far more efficient all around than the national postal system. The simple question of which is best in all situations is a dumb question. A smart question is what will increase worker motivation and initiative to be more productive, creative, and to do so for the commonweal.

Centralization in the Soviet Union simply spelled destruction. Members of the Politburo made decisions about what farmers could plant on farms that were several thousand miles away. Some of the members had no agricultural knowledge. The collective farms were not productive because they killed initiative. I was in Warsaw in 1990 when the iron curtain was coming down and observed two construction sites. One hotel was covered with rusting scaffolding while being refaced. The scaffolding apparently had been in place for years. Some workers moved around at a sluggish pace and seemed to care very little and did little. The same was witnessed at a subway construction site. Steel braces holding up the excavation banks appeared to have been there a long time and industrious activity was absent. As the good comrades said, "We pretend to work and we pretend to get paid." There was no incentive to work and no chance of getting ahead.

Small group communication structures in laboratory settings have been revealing. Two basically different communication structures have been examined: open and closed. Open structures can be pictured as a circle of six to ten people where the rule is that anybody can speak to anybody else at any time. Closed structures may be pictured as a Y with individuals out in each leg and one person at the confluence. All messages must come through the person at the confluence, as the illustration would suggest. This person becomes a *de facto* authority and valuable controller of a body of information. The authority figure can censor the passing communication from the extremities if he or she so wished. What are the behavior and attitudinal results of being placed in either of these structures? Striking.

Persons placed in open structures were, in fact, handed roles that were active and of equal status with all the other participants. These structures produced feelings of commitment and self-worth, as well as behaviors of creative and quality production. Persons placed in closed structures were essentially given passive and low-status roles with the exception of the center person. These closed structures produced attitudes of apathy and separation, leading to poor production, withdrawal, and even acting out. Once again, we see the power of structures on the individual.

I would speculate that some leaders who rely strongly on top-heavy hierarchy and command and obey structures do so out of fear, incompetence, and weakness. Hitler seemed in his early years to be a weak person who wandered around Vienna, failing in his attempts to enter art school, a lost soul eking out an existence. A person like that may never be strong enough to be a democratic leader with all the ambiguity and political conflict that entails. Surely, many leaders who bend over backwards to create a macho image are the very opposite of strong. Weak leaders have to rely on engendering fear in their subordinates via coercion and demanding absolute obedience.

Really strong leaders earn the respect of their work teams by their competence and understanding. Competence may take the form of inspiring confidence in workers by demonstrating skillful planning and execution or demonstrating thorough knowledge of a particular business or product. Jurgen E. Schrempp, at one time head of Daimler-Chrysler (often compared to Jack Welch formerly of General Electric), may have been overly heavy handed, but he commanded respect partly because he spent years as an apprentice mechanic gaining a thorough understanding of the business from the ground up. German architects must serve a full apprenticeship in one of the building trades before they begin architectural training. When a leader possesses competence in his profession and workplace, he can be less worried about his workers pushing him around and less concerned about loosing control.

While discussing Germany, it may be informative to note some of the cultural differences to the States in business. It is ironic that the German manager tends to remain more formal in dress and addresses peers as Mr., Mrs., Ms., and Dr.; whereas, first names are more common here in the States. But behind the formality there is a more thorough and shared examination of the evidence supporting decisions. There is more approval for hard-nosed critiques of proposed projects without taking the form of personal attack. This is what good democratic problem solving demands. Cooperation does not mean glossing over conflict and alternate solutions. In fact, part of the mature democratic leader's task is to encourage, support, and make sure alternative solutions are fairly aired and fully examined.

German business culture seems to place a positive connotation to the word "problem," and, thus, problem solving; whereas, we tend to connect the connotation of trouble to the word "problem." The tendency of German companies to make fairly major decisions at a lower departmental level, rather than at the top, indicates a sharing of power. The decision to purchase a major piece of heavy expensive equipment is more likely to be made at the departmental level, assuming the departmental budget and guidelines accommodate the decision. In the States, this type of decision would be made at a higher level.

These insights into shared power may help to explain Germany's relative prosperity even during downturns in the economy. We can mention one more thing here, the German practice of codetermination. By law, workers must be included in a council that helps to oversee company activities. Instead of letting the workers build up resentment and hostility because of being kept on the outside and powerless, they are given a continuous ongoing voice. More than that, many of the council members have full voting rights and work in concert with the standing labor unions. Rank and file elects council members. It all seems to be far better than the acrimonious history of labor and management in the United States. Our history of violent riots, mass destruction of property, and lockouts, I believe, are all an outcome of failing to share power.

Meaningful power is shared when all the players can participate as functional equals. For everyone to win, there must be hardheaded analysis where everyone's position gets full attention and all players have the security of being respected and not attacked. The alternative dictatorial style tends to lead to groupthink, muddle headedness, and incomplete analysis, all adding up to poor decisions.

★★★

Diamond, Jared. 2012. *The World Until Yesterday, What Can We Learn from Traditional Societies?* New York: Penguin. Comparing many instances of the wisdom and keen knowledge of very early peoples to many modern patterns that are very wanting.

Greenberg, Jerald, and Baron, Robert. 2003. *Behavior in Organizations,* 8th *ed.* Upper Saddle River, New Jersey: Prentice Hall. Pages 436-437. A typical textbook on organizational behavior documenting many of the topics in this chapter and others.

Johnson, David W., and Johnson, Frank P. 2014. *Joining Together: Group Theory and Group Skills,* 11th edition. Essex, England: Pearson Education Limited. Helpful research based work on group dynamics.

Mullainathan, Sendhil, and Shafir, Eldar. 2013. *Scarcity: Why Having so Little Means so Much.* 2013. New York: Henry Holt and Company LLC. Very creative treatise on how limited resources shape our thinking and behavior.

O'Reilly, CuChullaine. Not dated, about 2005. *Khyber Knights, An Account of perilous Adventure and Forbidden Romance in the Depths of Mystic Asia.* Writer's Guild of America. ISBN 1-59048-000-7. One of many accounts of marathon horseback rides; relevant here for the culture of hospitality in what has become an inhospitable land.

Ravitch, Diane. 2010. *The Death and Life of the Great American School System.* New York: Basic Books. Former assistant secretary of education under George W. Bush and former supporter of no child left behind and now opposing the same.

David Gray

Shaw, M. E. 1978. Communication Networks Fourteen Years Later. In M.L. Berkowitz (Editor), *Group Processes*. New York: Academic Press. Great insight into the principles and consequences of open participative communication networks contrasted to closed authoritarian ones.

Chapter 14: The Place of Friendship in the Model

As we have already noted in Chapter 1, friendship can play a significant facilitating role in problem solving and conflict reduction. Before we consider friendship as a separate entity, we are reminded that the experience itself of working with someone toward a superordinate goal should produce more positive feelings between the participants, provided other critical conditions of the model have been met. *Esprit de corps* can be developed on the job or in the combat trenches when there is much at stake. In Outward Bound, the superordinate goal of rappelling up a cliff is a means of bringing antagonists together. This happens because members are dependent on each other for their very lives. So the task itself, theoretically, has the potential to create mutually good feelings. All the inequalities, status differences, and social distance that may have existed before the climb are meaningless and suppressed while on the cliff and should make it more possible for bonding and solidarity to occur.

The friendship topic here is separate and different from the task per se, but becomes a by-product of rappelling. The focus of friendship occurs after the cliff has been conquered. Typically, Outward Bound provides a food drop on top of the cliff for the evening meal. Everyone cooperates in preparing the meal. Conversation is the only form of entertainment after the meal. All radios and electronic devices are forbidden except for emergency phones. Conversations, of course, roam over topics like where each person comes from, what they do, what the families are like. Good times, bad times, likes and dislikes, and beliefs all unfold. Sports, sex, disappointments, joys, all come out. They get to know each other. On the cliff, people started to trust each other, but around the campfire, personal knowledge of each other is shared. At least, the rudiments of friendship are being formed.

In a study by Cook (1967), black and white women ran a simulated railroad in a study at a southern university back in the 1960s when color lines were deeply etched. A lunch was provided by the study, which ran for several days. Conversation opened up astonishing insights and intimacies never shared before between these women. Near the last day, a white woman said to a black woman, "Would you mind terribly if I finished that blueberry pie you just pushed aside?" Unheard of at that time. In the Robber's cave study in the first chapter, the boys who had been hostile became very good friends, evidenced by exchange of letters months after the camp was over. Moreover, by making genuine friends from the former enemy camp, a whole series of psychological changes took place.

Expanding our views of others

Participants in activities like those above start to see each other as multifaceted instead of just the one narrow picture of a cranky boss or a lackadaisical worker. They see each other as playing a number of roles, and each of the roles reveals a great deal of information about a person. The cranky boss may also be the husband of a very easy going wife whom he seems to adore and the father of a 14-year-old Downs son who gets a lot of good attention from his father. The cranky boss is also the son of an elderly father in a nursing home who does not even recognize his son any more. And so it goes. It is surprising that another very quiet unassuming participant is an outdoor enthusiast seriously into backpacking, kayaking, and biking. The lackadaisical worker occupies the second violin chair in the metropolitan symphony by night. People are transformed from flat creatures to multidimensional beings revealing a richness of personal characteristics.

Our dislikes and stereotypes about people are often based on incomplete information and gross overgeneralization. Seeing the multiple roles that all people occupy is like opening a row of fire hydrants. Each role releases a full stream of new information about a person. It can be further noted that this expanded view of people may enrich and open up new approaches in trying to work out future problems.

Discovering common and universal needs

Beneath the outer layer of cultural differences lie universal needs and desires which provide another chance of finding common ground with prior antagonists. For example, everyone wants to be respected rather than disparaged or insulted. Feeling valuable instead of being put down as worthless or totally insignificant would seem to be a widespread need. Psychopaths, masochists, and a few other cases are exceptions.

However, the manner in which we get or give respect is more cultural than personal. An urban gang member may gain respect by "taking out" a rival, making a drug haul, fitting into the rules of the gang, and sporting the right clothes, the right gun, and the right kind of car. The middle class youth might gain respect differently through sports and school achievements, but may gain respect in a similar way to the gang member through clothes and a car. But even with the similarity, the type of clothes and car would likely be different. In other words, we all gain some respect by looking good, but how to look good is entirely cultural. A Muslim bride from Pakistan may appear with several different changes in dress during the wedding reception. Each dress is an exotic, colorful, beautiful silk sari; whereas, an American bride will remain in her white wedding gown throughout the reception. The common need is to be respected by looking good. What we are not talking about here is an obsession that leads to endless vanity and narcissism.

The master need for stimulation is one that is wrongfully minimized or overlooked entirely. It may seem like a luxury, but it is a necessity for anything like a fully functioning person. Wanting stimulation is akin to wanting to be bigger rather than smaller, wanting the see more things, feel more things, hear more, do more. There seems to be a rather widespread need to grow rather than to shrink and atrophy because growth is stimulating.

Unfortunately many of our jobs are inherently boring and mind numbing. Inserting a bolt into the same hole in the assembly plant day after day and year after year, or keyboarding the same type of information day after day, is destructive not only to the wrist, but to the mind as well. That kind of work is meaningless because no resulting product in which she can be proud results from the effort. Home life for millions is restricted to small spaces, few resources, lots of noise and stress, and the same humdrum life day upon day is never punctuated by a vacation or something new. Many work the two meaningless jobs and muddle through. Is it any wonder that television is a high priority; it offers at least some low level of variety and stimulation. One may have no illusions about aspiring to become the rich and the famous on the screen, but one can get a lift by vicariously watching the Rich and the Famous or the most recent pop star.

Breaking stereotypes

If your antagonist is an Arab, and you have somehow picked up the stereotype that all Arabs are "slippery and will steal the shirt off you back with your scarcely noticing it," that stereotype will be challenged by a friendly Arab with whom you are forming a friendship. Friendship formation with a person conflicts with the negative group stereotype associated with that person's group. The dissonance created by the negatively signed group and the positively signed friend will be resolved by signing the group more positively. Part of the reason why a friend will win out is that the friend is real, living, and has existential value; whereas, the group is more likely to be abstract and distant.

Furthermore, for the dissonance reduction just described in the above paragraph to be effective in reducing the negative stereotype of the total group, a new friend, Arab, or whomever, must maintain a clear identity. That does not mean that an Arab must wear a head cloth and a floor length garment. He may wear a business suit, but he must care for his history, his part of the Arab world, and show concern for its future. He must remain an Arab in identity. There was much condemnation of upper-class blacks in the civil rights era who became materially successful but wanted nothing to do with the black community and distanced themselves as far as possible. If the black had no black symbolism or cue value, in short, he had become white as it were and was referred to as an Oreo, black on the outside but white at heart. The American Indian who divorced himself from his people was like an apple, red on the outside but white on the inside. In these instances, one's feelings about a friend will not carry good feelings over to his group.

Creating friendships though shared coping

Esther Olavarria and Rebecca Tallent, from radically different groups, became friends while working on immigration reform proposals. Esther Olavarria is a Latino and a Democrat. She worked as Senator Edward M. Kennedy's top immigration lawyer. She currently holds a post in the Obama White House. On the other side of the political fence, Rebecca Tallent is a fair-haired Republican from Arizona. She was Senator McCain's head of staff for a time and briefly advised Sara Palin's campaign. Rebecca Tallent is now a top policy aide to Speaker John A. Boehner. Their entrenchment in two separate political camps could hardly have been more dramatic.

In 2003 they were commissioned separately by their two respective parties to draft working immigration papers to secure the border better and increase the flow of legal workers. This effort was spearheaded by the bi-partisan vision of Senators Edward Kennedy and John McCain. Based on the laborious and thorough joint efforts of Olavarria and Tallent, Kennedy and McCain were able to announce major immigration reform that seemed to be constructive for the immigrants and the nation. It was a great accomplishment and gained political support, but not enough. The case could certainly be made that the efforts of that team were successful, as far as they could make it be so. At any rate, Olavarria's and Tallent's friendship was established and has been maintained throughout the subsequent years.

The two women have been back at the task for some time trying again to draft immigration reform that has a chance of passing.

Olavarria is working for Obama, and Tallent is working for Boehner. Unfortunately, the outcome will be based substantially on election projections and not on the merits of the proposal. The outcome aside, this is an inspiring story of friendship formed via work on a nearly insurmountable task. The two still socialize outside the bounds of their jobs (*New York Times*, Feb 22, 2014).

It is not nearly as clear concerning the greater friendship of Kennedy and McCain as a result of the early 2000 work on immigration. At least, it did not seem to lessen their cordiality. We are told that Senators socialize far less today than previously. It is understandable, but opportunities for friendship are being lost.

Missed opportunities to foster friendship

President Barak Obama and Speaker of the House John Boehner had worked together, apparently seriously, several years ago on some major budget strategies entailing compromises. They demonstrated some flexibility and problem solving across party lines in regard to the conflict of deficit issues versus investment. Some legislators on Boehner's side wanted the whole loaf so the cooperative work was in vain. From the distance of a regular citizen, it appeared that Obama could have done much more in pursuing a personal relationship with Boehner. It is reported that they golfed only once together. A more personal relationship with Boehner may have led to better connections with other Republicans as well. It probably would not change the current stalemate, but any investment in reconciliation can have unexpected results and an investment in the bank of good will. It does not seem that these two men despised each other, which further suggests more could have happened in the way of friendship. President Obama seems to count on rational, heady analyses and forgets that emotions as well propel many decisions.

It would be easier to understand the distance and icy feelings between President Obama and someone like Ted Cruz or Paul Ryan. Some distances are too far and too hard to cross. Political fundamentalists are sure that they have the absolute truth and, by definition, are psychologically shut off from any new information. To be resolute in one's ethical principles and solidly grounded in a worldview is commendable. But to be shut off from any growth, any new information, any fundamental change in circumstances is to be incorrigible. Pragmatism and experimentation must play a role in large societal affairs if a society is to thrive.

Mitch McConnell's avowed overarching single mission was to get Obama out of the White House in in the 2012 election. That does not leave much room to do anything to serve the needs of the nation. It would not change Washington, but it would be a step in the right direction, if Harry Reid and Mitch McConnell could do a bit of socializing. Very few leaders are big enough and secure enough to jump that social divide when it is as vast as it is today. Each little step of non-political human interaction between these disparate leaders would contribute to detoxifying the Beltway atmosphere.

Realistically, the expectation that friendship will expedite better working relations, or just pursuing social exchange per se, may often be untimely at best and maybe impossible. When the zeitgeist is intensely unfavorable, any rapprochement may be better left until later. Waiting for a favorable time is often an excuse for doing nothing, but moving boldly when the atmosphere clears can maximize success. In Syria, the long years of drought have displaced over a million farmers, so the topic of climate change is in their conversations now even though a civil war is raging. In the States, the zeitgeist has shifted enough that poverty and the wealth/power gap is at least emerging on the national agenda. It is amazing that Vietnamese and Americans can do business today easily and form human bonds as well.

The main thrust of this chapter is that friendship is likely to emerge for former antagonists as a result of successfully completing a cooperative task. Friendship is a natural by-product of working together successfully under the conditions set forth in the shared-coping model.

★★

Ashmore, R. D., and Collins, B. E. 1970. *Social Psychology, Social Influence, Attitude Change, Group Processes, and Prejudice.* Reading, Massachusetts: Addison-Wesley.

Cook, S. W. 1978. Interpersonal and attitudinal outcomes in cooperating interracial groups. *Journal of Research and Development in Education, 12, 97-113.*

Shear, Michael D. 2014, February 22. Two Friends Reach Across the Isle on Immigration. *New York Times.*

CONCLUSION

Practicing When Everyone Wins

WE CANNOT DENY that there are problems and tasks by their very nature where one side has to lose and one win. Most distressing is the fact that some groups are so dysfunctional and conflicted that lose/lose is the most likely outcome. There are many more tasks where the outcome could be win/win. This is certainly not a unique claim, and hopefully, a serious read of these chapters will encourage and enable more people, especially leaders, to work harder at the approach where everyone wins.

A problem-solving checklist

Let me emphasize again that the application of the direct-contact model is appropriate for groups of all sizes and types. The successful Oslo Accords were informed by this approach; unfortunately, the two sides were not willing to follow through at that time. For leaders in any business who are equally concerned about the dignity of the workers and the quality and success of the product, the following ten-point checklist may be helpful. This list assumes that if we want to solve a fairly complex problem without a clear company precedent, it will be resolved best by full participation of the whole work group's participation leading to a consensus. When all parties of the work group are deeply and directly affected by a decision, their full participation is indicated. The following "ten commandments" may help to carry out the model of cooperation.

One: Is there a genuine problem?

Mutually determine if there really is a problem. The leader might say, "I think there is a problem here and, in brief, here is my reasoning. Does this need our attention?" Over-reacting is just as counter-productive as sweeping a problem under the rug. Quality control, as worked out by the Japanese, established something akin to a standard deviation and band of normality around a mean (average) production standard for a given company. If a company's performance drops, but not beyond the lower limits of the band, the interpretation is a wobble in the curve and doesn't warrant any immediate alarm. In other words, there is no problem. If the performance exceeds the upper limits of the band, it is probably no reason to celebrate or to accept complacency. It is just a positive variation to be watched. Quality control is in no way excuse-making. It is just the opposite. Modern Japanese manufacturing has been known for its striving for perfection. Furthermore, every employee is empowered to be responsible for high quality, not just one designated official.

Two: Defining the problem requires input from all participants.

Mutually define the problem. The definition itself will set the tone for the whole problem solving process and will probably imply a given solution, which may turn out to be very wrong. When 9/11 was defined as a war, the solution was forgone—military action. If it had been defined as a criminal act, apprehension and prosecutions of the guilty would have been suggested. We own what we invest in. If a boss defines the problem, it is his or hers, but worker commitment may be lacking. If the group invests in the definition, it is theirs and effective follow through is much more likely.

Three: Construct a clear and specific goal.

Agree on the goal. The goal will be largely determined by the definition of the problem. Is it a war or a crime in the example given above? So is the goal to kill all terrorists? Kill them over there before they kill us over here was a slogan. Or is the goal to punish those responsible for the tragedy and quash other detected plots? Is the goal to boost the rate of production in a manufacturing setting or is the goal to reduce rejects? Actually, by reducing the rate of production but strengthening quality control and, in turn, reducing the number of rejects, the end result may be to increase profits because there will be a savings in labor, raw materials, and energy use. Therefore, for the boss unilaterally to force a goal of increased production may be costly. This is an old example from a worldwide assessment center, Development Dimensions International, in Pittsburgh, Pennsylvania.

The magnetic-like nature of goals has a powerful influence on directing behavior. In instinctual and low-tech hunting archery one must never slip into the lazy habit of just shooting at a deer. An imaginary pinpoint spot must be visualized at the center of the vital organs of heart and lungs. All else is blotted out of the visual field. This visual concentration apparently helps to call upon one's best eye-to-hand co-ordination and muscle memory from past training. In target shooting, intense focus is channeled and riveted upon a pinpoint in the center of the bulls-eye. The rest of the target rings do not exist, as it were.

Four: Assume that there will be serious obstructions.

Clarify the barriers. What is blocking goal-driven behavior? Is it capital, inferior technology, untrained personnel, outside competition, or blind tradition? What are the costs and time frames for surmounting the critical barriers? If there are large risks involved, all players must be fully aware of some of the possible negative consequences. If the workgroup has developed a climate of trust, unanticipated barriers are more likely to be revealed and dealt with productively.

Five: Develop a list of solution options.

Generate a set of alternative realistic solutions. If a work group has been nurtured to be open, rational, and analytic, not bound by the habitual use of constricting categories, there will most likely be different ideas about how to solve the problem. This is not the place to evaluate different possibilities, but to generate a list of realistic alternatives.

Six: Challenge each alternative solution.

Test the alternatives thoroughly. What are the likely consequences of each alternative? Each alternative should have as fair a hearing as possible. Ironically, differences are the very things that threaten the traditional leader. Diversity of ideas is the stuff of vitality and great decisions. They should all be tested in the fire of careful thought and analysis. A by-product of this dynamic is that each contributor knows that he or she is respected because ideas are carefully honored even though they may not be used in the end. A particular proposal or alternative solution is usually the product of one or a very few people. Conversely, the total group excels at evaluation because of bringing multiple perspectives to the evaluation process. Entirely new superior and synergistic solutions may emerge from this crucible of creative thought and thorough examination of the available data and perspectives.

Seven: Select among the alternative solutions.

Decide on a best solution. Remember that this solution may not be what anyone anticipated at the start. It may not fit old comfortable biases and ways of doing business. The solution is directly connected to a newly formulated goal or goals. The ideal is not to compromise or even vote. Persist until consensus emerges. In large heterogeneous political settings compromise may be the only realistic outcome.

Eight: Activate the solution.

Start executing. Sometimes small test runs are possible in the nature of an experiment. Review and clarify the goal and the solution at pre-set time points. Coordinate work assignments and the various arms of the project. Set timetables including ways and times to evaluate long-range progress.

Nine: Monitor vigilantly.

Coordinate all parts of the project to keep it on course. Determine what is needed to strengthen weak spots? Are the needed supplies adequate and are the personnel adequately encouraged and supported? Use the Japanese ideas of quality control. Do not over-react or under-react to apparent production fluctuations. Is everyone on board as a quality control participant?

Ten: Have a plan for long-term evaluation.

Are short and long-term goals being realized? What long-term corrections or changes are needed? How are the strengths to be reinforced and maintained? How is group "intelligence" being used to determine how your performance is doing compared to relevant competition in your field? Are there appropriate incentives to keep the workgroup committed to the goal? Does the top leadership keep the goal visible and celebrated?

This decalogue for group problem solving is part common sense with doses of organizational psychology. The list may come across as pat and wooden, but there are liberal insights from group dynamics research folded into it. The list, in the context of the larger direct contact model, can make a noticeable difference.

Selection, training, and development

If a leader has the chance to start a new work group, recruiting the new members cannot be taken too seriously. Personnel decisions are cluttered with more mistakes than any other endeavor, and the consequences are usually long-term. If the basic philosophies of the new members are radically different, the direct contact method is seriously challenged. Rather, recruiting for homogeneity on the very basics of the mission, and beyond that, diversity on all other issues will actually be enriching.

Personnel consulting firms like Development Dimensions International expose a potential candidate to a series of behavioral tasks simulating the actual workplace, tasks like working through a backlog of business e-mails, prioritizing a calendar and agendas, meeting with workers in conflict, and working with a small group on budget building. The assessment may take a few days. It is all video recorded and coded on a series of dimensions. It is an effective way to reduce hiring and promotion errors. Success depends on not what a person says as much as what a person does. The materials are in multiple languages since they have offices around the world. Every year while I taught, I would take my organizational class to their corporate offices in Pittsburgh to get first hand exposure. This firm has been in existence for several decades, and I encourage people to use them because I am confident about the validity of their assessments. One has to be careful because many consultants have slick fronts, appeal to the latest fades, and are swimming in buzz words, but are woefully lacking in evidence of validity.

The electronic and gaming age introduces even more choices and whole new horizons. A firm in Silicon Valley claims their human resources video games have the power to assess professional skills, such as speed of decisions, sequences of action, checking divergent actions quickly, and style of problem solving. The games are serious attempts to quantify these types of dimensions very quickly. The designers are highly qualified neuroscientists, psychologists, and information scientists. It will take some years to determine the predictive validity of these games. There are many questions to be answered. Do the games have the potential to damage lives and careers via flaws in the conception of the measurements, and will they fall short in measuring the more intangible dimensions, like honesty and sensitivity? They may come to have a supplemental role in assessment.

Something called "people analytics" is coming on strong and is probably here to stay. It seems to me that people analytics are a sophisticated extension of widely used yearly job appraisals. This approach tries to avoid purely subjective evaluations and tries to rely on behavioral dimensions. It appears to me that they appear to have modest face validity, but the ratings are still subjective. But much more importantly, the quantified dimensions are weighted in multivariate analyses and used to predict performances like production levels, reject levels, conservation of energy and materials, new sales, and so forth. These techniques are being seriously implemented by major firms like Google, HP, Intel, General Motors, and Proctor and Gamble, as well as among small companies. Google seems to be using these techniques not so much to select or weed people out, but as a supportive career advancement tool.

Small but meaningful beginnings

If you are a leader or manager of a department and the larger firm allows varied styles of leadership, that permission should be an invitation to gradually start to implement some of the principles of the direct contact model. Start to get the workers input on problems and issues. Begin supporting minority voices and show that they may turn out to have value. Showing respect by having new ideas and worker suggestions fairly evaluated without slipping into phony niceness is a beginning. If you have no formal leadership role and you would like to see your division be a bit more democratic, start to monitor your own behavior more astutely. Do you ever offer assistance to someone you disagree with in order to help them make their point clear? Do you ever cover for someone you do not particularly like? Do you ever say a nice word when your antagonist does something good? Do you ever include an outsider in your group for lunch? Do you need to distinguish more clearly between being assertive and being aggressive?

Much of our social and business culture will tell you to stay out of trouble, mind your own business, act like you are working while doing as little as possible and just get by. I expect you to insist on your own way without expecting much from the others. That mentality does not make one want to go to work on Monday morning. Everyone has some leeway to change the negative workplace or home life. What part of the ten commandments of problem solving can you start to implement independently? There is always some degree of opportunity to begin to move toward experiences where everyone wins.

If you supervise a small group of workers and have a yearly or twice-yearly evaluation instruments, you might start by being less dictatorial and declarative. First of all, make sure a worker has a protected time to review his or her record with you. If the record has many negative evaluations, such as excessive tardiness, aggravating other workers, customer complaints about service, broken equipment not reported, the leader has two basic choices—either to attack or to promote understanding.

A supervisor can begin by showing anger and disappointment and an immanent threat of firing or can be firm without being in the attack mode. She might say that she would like to understand better what is going on. She can state that her perception is that there seem to be some serious issues. She can review the list of infractions with the full record clearly visible to both persons and then ask the worker what his or her perceptions are? If the Super is serious about functional equality and shared power and respect, this is worth doing. By asking for the worker's perception, she is giving some space instead of cornering him. She is asking him to participate as a functional equal in the evaluation, even though the Super has the formal authority. The employee's behavior in a less threatening, but firm, environment will be a better gauge about whether he is worth working with or not and how you might encourage him.

Dictating and declaring are quite different from saying, "Let's look at this." When I had students coming in fearing they were failing a course and arguing that the grade was unfair, it would have been easy me as the authority figure to be irritated because of being questioned. This would not be a helpful way to start the review. I would usually say, "Let's look at all the marks for the course. I'd give the student a copy and give him time to digest it. He may not have kept a running record and may forget some of the test scores or projects' evaluations. I, then, would say that my perception is that according to the scale in the syllabus the performance has earned a D or F, or whatever the case was. And then I'd ask for the student's perception. The word "perception" is key because it keeps the exchange open and respectful. Of course, sometimes the student response will be unbroken hostility. The professor can only reassure that it is his responsibility to assign all the credit that the student has earned, and, furthermore, there is a board of appeal. But the more frequent student response in my experience has been that the student now sees the pattern and how it adds up, and there is acceptance. The air is cleared to go on and do something better. Or if I've made an error, I can correct it. Intimate extenuating circumstances also have come out of these conferences. One student learned during the semester that he had a brain tumor and wanted to keep it quiet. I checked it out and it was genuine.

The effectiveness of models

If you want your division or department to become more democratic or accept a new procedure or produce a new product, there is often resistance. There is fear of losing more than will be gained. Will it entail more unnecessary work and reduce job security? One of the best ways to let people quiet their own fears is to see the proposed innovation working well somewhere else. At a meeting, you might review the website of a successful model company using this new approach. You provide ample information about the model rather than just depending on your own testimony, as it were. Best of all, if you can find a model within an easy drive, you can visit, meet the people, and see the model first hand. It is a simple but a powerful way to get people to open up and lower their defenses. Seeing real people apparently enjoying the new approach will go a long way to make a change more likely. If logistics prohibit taking your people to another site, then an alternative is to try to arrange for the model company to send one or two people to tell its story first hand.

Sharing power and participation comes in many degrees. If a manager wants to introduce participation in small increments, then, models that do this very incremental approach is where she wants to start. NuCor Steel has become the largest and most progressive steel producer in the country and is a great example of having a history of innovative steel production techniques, but it has a traditionally hierarchical structure. Nevertheless, it seems to remunerate its employees well and welcomes serious input from them. NuCor employees do not have structures for extended open discussion with management or give-and-take exchanges. So if I read their literature correctly, they share power with their employees in a real but minimal manner.

Namaste' Solar would be another example of minimal, but helpful, empowerment, probably a step up from NuCor. A wide sharing of company information with all co-owners seems to be their approach to sharing power. Traditional fiscal secrets are fully shared and the company trains the co-owners in financial literacy. The fact that some of the employees become co-owners is another benefit to empowerment.

Team-based financial rewards as well as individual rewards indicate strong support for cooperative teamwork at WD-40, a lubrication manufacturing company. Top leadership sets the example of teamwork by frequently suppressing top salaries in order to reimburse all levels of the workforce better. Probably at a similar level of empowerment is Davita, a large healthcare company. The company determines select issues to be decided by company-wide voting of the employees, and the results are final. The workers do not select the issues nor do they construct proposals.

Two companies that extend the empowerment to widespread co-ownership and substantial employee management and decision-making are the South Mountain Company and the New Belgium Brewing Company. South Mountain, a design and construction company, is in Martha's Vineyard. Belgium Brewery is the third largest brewery in the US.

A very interesting story of intense employee empowerment is that of Johnsonville Sausage in Wisconsin. The CEO, Ralph Strayer, realized that the workers knew more than he did about their specific activity on the floor, and he wanted them to be able to act on that information. He struggled for several years, not wanting to give up total control and yet wanting to pass large chunks of it over to the workers.

The story is entitled "How I Learned to Let My Workers Lead." The story is dated 1990. Today the firm has grown into a successful giant in the industry and has been able to maintain some of the same worker participation as when the company was much smaller.

The point is that there are many ways and degrees to which a leader can introduce democracy into the workplace. Any given manager has to determine how to get started and how to progress based on his or her specific circumstances.

If the leader deeply believes that abilities and potential reside in his workforce, although it may not always appear that way, the leader will move toward more participation. And if the leader is absolutely convinced that functional equality and shared power can be transformational, that leader will work toward more cooperative work arrangements and will be rewarded.

★★★

Garvin, David A. 2013, December. How Google Sold Its Engineers on Management. *Harvard Business Review.* Fairly detailed account of people analytics at Google. Most of the issue is dedicated to the phenomenon of big data.

Nader, Ralph. 2012. *The Seventeen Solutions.* New York; Harper. Mr. Nader's solutions are all his own and do not necessarily track the model in this book. The spirit, imagination, and structural depth of his solutions are, however, in sync with this book and are highly recommended. Mr. Nader made our autos safer; here he could make our nation more humane and productive.

Peck, Don. 2013, December. They're Watching You At Work. *The Atlantic.* A good introduction to the idea and practice of people analytics.

Strayer, Ralph. 1990, November-December. How I Learned to Let My Workers Lead. *Harvard Business Review.*

Endorsement of *When Everyone Wins: From Inequality to Cooperation*

This is a wide-ranging, scientifically sound, and timely volume. Professor Gray addresses conflicts at all levels of human society – between husbands and wives, between workers and employers, between groups within a specific country and between nations. A special conception of cooperation is presented to alleviate these diverse conflicts. The author is not naïve. The many caveats of the model and the difficulties of implanting it on a wide scale are acknowledged and addressed. My hope is that the caveats and difficulties of implementation will not deter the reader from learning that there is a way out of the many "shared threats" confronting the modern world (poverty, environmental degradation, and terrorism to name just a few). This volume gives us not only optimism that we can do something about them, but also a blueprint for how to proceed in this important task. If we can follow this blueprint we will all win.

Richard D. Ashmore,
Professor of Psychology Emeritus,
Rutgers University

ABOUT THE AUTHOR

DAVID GRAY, A Professor of Psychology for many years, specialized in his later years on the effect of the belief in equality on democratic leadership in the United States, Germany, Poland, and Russia. He advocates strongly for international educational experiences. David lives with his wife Phyllis in New Wilmington, Pennsylvania.